JANE AUSTEN
THE WORLD OF HER NOVELS

JANE AUSTEN
The World of Her Novels

Deirdre Le Faye

BBC
LARGE
PRINT

First published 2002
by Frances Lincoln
This Large Print edition published 2009
by BBC Audiobooks Ltd
by arrangement with
Frances Lincoln Limited

Hardcover ISBN: 978 1 408 43099 6
Softcover   ISBN: 978 1 408 43100 9

British Library Cataloguing in Publication Data available

Printed and bound in Great Britain by
CPI Antony Rowe, Chippenham and Eastbourne

CONTENTS

INTRODUCTION

In 1816, when Jane Austen had finished revising her early manuscript of *Susan* (now known to us as *Northanger Abbey*) and was intending to try for a second time to get it published, she felt it necessary to add a foreword, or 'Advertisement' to her text:

> This little work was finished in the year 1803, and intended for immediate publication. It was disposed of to a bookseller, it was even advertised, and why the business proceeded no farther, the author has never been able to learn. That any bookseller should think it worth while to purchase what he did not think it worth while to publish seems extraordinary. But with this, neither the author nor the public have any other concern than as some observation is necessary upon those parts of the work which thirteen years have made comparatively obsolete. The public are entreated to bear in mind that thirteen years have passed since it was finished, many more since it was begun, and that during that period, places, manners, books, and opinions have undergone considerable changes.

If Jane Austen was afraid that her book might seem outdated after a lapse of thirteen years since its completion, she would be utterly amazed to learn that her works are still enjoyed two hundred years after she first wrote them. This enduring popularity is a tribute not only to her skill as an author, but also to the accuracy of her plots in identifying the basic and unchanging truths of human nature. To meet one's ideal marriage partner is still the hope of every young man and woman, even in the twenty-first century, and family background and economic factors still help or hinder the achievement of this hope. But the places, manners, books and opinions with which she was familiar have changed not merely considerably, but beyond the scope of her wildest imaginings. Society is always changing, but as the river of time flows inexorably onwards the changes happen so gradually and silently that we do not take note of them. It is only when we look at old photographs, or when television programmes re-run newsreels of fifty years ago, that we realize just how much our lifestyle has changed even within living memory; and once memory is no longer alive, we have to turn to history books to read about that familiar and yet strangely different country which is the past.

The object of this book, then, is to provide for the modern reader an outline of Jane Austen's own world—her biography and background—and to fit into this historical framework specific and often long-forgotten details of the late Georgian and Regency social scene. Because all her novels were published close together, between 1811 and 1818, and because modern film and television productions usually portray the characters as dressed in the fashions of those few years, it is easy to think of Jane herself as being a product purely of the Regency. In fact her all-too-short life spanned the change from one century to another, and she grew to womanhood and formed her opinions in the context of Georgian society. Her first three novels were all composed in the 1790s, and it is only the later three which can be considered to be truly of the Regency period. As it happens, the reign of George III, from 1760 to 1820, including the years of the Regency, encompasses the whole length of time from the marriage of Jane's parents in 1764 to the posthumous publication of *Northanger Abbey* and *Persuasion* in 1818. That reign, therefore, is taken here as setting the boundaries of her life and times.

It is intended that these details of social history, together with the illustrations that accompany them, will serve to throw light on Jane Austen's second world, that of the novels she wrote and the lives of the characters she created, and so make for deeper understanding and even greater enjoyment of her works. One of Jane Austen's very earliest readers wrote of *Emma*: 'I like it better than any. Every character is thoroughly kept up. Miss Bates is incomparable, but I was nearly killed with those precious treasures! They are unique, & really with more fun than I can express. I am at Highbury all day, & I can't help feeling I have just got into a new set of acquaintance.'

It is hoped that the following chapters will help present-day readers to feel that, like Alice, they can step through the looking glass and on the other side find themselves in the England of two centuries ago, ready to become personally acquainted with the Bennets, Bertrams, Knightleys and Elliots.

PART 1

THE WORLD OF JANE AUSTEN

JANE AUSTEN AND
HER FAMILY

Jane was born on the cold frosty night of Saturday 16 December 1775, in Steventon, Hampshire; and the next morning, while Mr Austen was in his study writing to his sister-in-law Mrs Walter in Kent with the news of this latest addition to his family—'We have now another girl, a present plaything for her sister Cassy and a future companion. She is to be Jenny, and seems to me as if she would be as like Henry, as Cassy is to Neddy'—the other children were no doubt brought to their mother's bedside for a first sight of their new sister. James was ten, grey-eyed like his mother, dreamy and bookish; Edward eight, fair-haired and small for his age, but giving promise of all the practical abilities which James lacked; Henry only four, with his father's bright hazel eyes and long legs and already nearly as tall as Edward; Cassandra just three, with dark eyes and a pale face; Francis, a small but very active toddler of some twenty months. The only one missing from the family group was the second son, George, now aged nine. From early in his infancy he had suffered from epileptic fits, and his parents were compelled to acknowledge that there was something congenitally wrong with him—it seems probable that he was deaf and dumb. Mrs Austen had tried to rear him at home, but her other domestic cares and duties made it an impossible task; and so, in accordance with the custom of the time, George was boarded out with a respectable cottager family in the nearby village of Monk Sherborne. His parents, and later his brothers, kept in touch with him and paid for his upkeep, and he was evidently well cared for, as he lived many years into the nineteenth century and died at the respectable age of seventy-two. After Jane the Austens had one more son, Charles, born in 1779, and he grew up to be very much like Henry—tall, thin and handsome. Cassandra and Jane used to refer to him as 'our own particular little brother'.

A few days after Jane's birth a blizzard struck and paralysed all the south of England, making travel almost impossible as snow drifted deeply and blotted out all signs of roads and tracks. On four nights in January the temperature sank so low that even urine in chamber pots underneath beds became frozen. It was weeks before a thaw occurred, and even then the spring was very cold, so Jane was not taken out to Steventon church for her christening until early April 1776. No doubt the Austen boys were delighted to run snowballing in Home Meadow while little Cassy perhaps hung over the cradle and helped her mother to make sure that the baby kept warm; but not much is known about the earliest years of Jane's life. It is time to consider instead the world and the family which she had entered.

Jane's father, the Reverend George Austen (1731–1805), who was rector of Steventon from

1761 until his death, was not Hampshire born and bred, but came from a Kentish family whose branches had spread out for many generations in the villages around Horsmonden, Sevenoaks and Tonbridge, gaining their prosperity from sheep-farming and the woollen trade. George was orphaned young, but luckily had Austen uncles and aunts who brought him up and saw him through Tonbridge School and on to St John's College, Oxford, after which he took Holy Orders and for a few years was a don at his old college. He was tall, thin, scholarly and good-looking, with chestnut-brown hair that turned silvery white in later life, and peculiarly bright hazel eyes. A distant cousin of George's, Mr Thomas Brodnax May Knight of Godmersham Park in Kent, also owned two estates in Hampshire, Chawton and Steventon, and so was able to present his young kinsman to the living of this latter small rural parish, which would provide an income just about sufficient to support a family. George then chose as his wife Miss Cassandra Leigh (1739–1827), the younger daughter of the rector of Harpsden, near Henley-on-Thames in Oxfordshire. The Leighs were another large family, widespread throughout Gloucestershire, but of higher social standing than the Austens, landed gentry rather than farmers. Cassandra was small and slender, with a clear pale complexion, grey eyes and dark hair, sprightly and quick-witted and with a good sense of humour. The young couple were married on 26 April 1764 in Bath, where Cassandra had been living with her widowed mother, and set off straightaway for Hampshire.

However, Steventon rectory was already old and dilapidated in 1764, and George could not take his

3

bride there until he had repaired and enlarged it. So for the first few years of their married life the Austens rented the parsonage in the neighbouring parish of Deane, and it was here that their first three children were born—James (1765), George (1766) and Edward (1767). In the summer of 1768 the family moved down the lane to Steventon, where the house was now fit for habitation, and here the rest of their children were born—Henry (1771), Cassandra (1773), Francis (1774), Jane (1775) and finally Charles (1779).

The repaired rectory was a reasonably comfortable, if rather old-fashioned, family home, constructed mostly of whitewashed brick, with small casement windows and a red tiled roof. On the ground floor were the best parlour, the common parlour and Mr Austen's study, as well as the kitchen and the back kitchen. Upstairs there were seven small bedrooms with three garrets under the eaves. The ceilings were low and the interiors of the rooms very plainly finished, but on the whole the house was considered to be better than the average country rectory of the time. Mr Austen's study was at the back of the house, on the warm southern side, overlooking the walled garden with its sundial, espaliered fruit trees, vegetable and flower beds and grassy walks; Mrs Austen used the best parlour, with its clear north light, for her sewing room, where she was always busy making and mending the family's clothes. This was Jane's home for the first twenty-five years of her life, and where her three early novels were composed.

In the eighteenth century Hampshire was renowned as being one of the most fertile counties in England. Its landscape was very varied, from the

4

range of chalk downs across the northern part of the county, through well-watered rich meadows and fields in the centre, on to the woodlands and sandy commons of the New Forest on the western side, and the seacoast and Isle of Wight in the south. It could therefore produce fine corn and hops, very large flocks of cattle, sheep with excellent wool, bacon from its own particular breed of Hampshire hogs, honey and timber. The buying and selling of these agricultural products kept the market towns thriving. On the coast, at the head of a wide tidal inlet, stood the town of Southampton, which carried on a considerable maritime trade; and not far away to the east was the great naval dockyard town and garrison of Portsmouth, guarding Portsmouth Harbour where the English fleet could lie at anchor. The city of Winchester, in the centre of the county, had once been the capital of the Anglo-Saxon kingdom of Wessex, but now lay quietly asleep around its vast and ancient cathedral in the river valley, while the two newer coastal towns gradually outstripped it in size and wealth.

The little village of Steventon is tucked in a fold of the chalk downs, in the north-east corner of Hampshire, and in Jane's day more than a thousand sheep roamed free on the rough hillsides. Below, surrounding the manor house, church, rectory and thatched cottages, were the planted copses and enclosed fields with their arable crops, and here and there elms and oaks stood out above the hedgerows that flanked the narrow lanes. The old manor house was so thickly hemmed in by trees that from the Austens' house only its topmost chimneys could be seen. At the manor house lived

5

Mr and Mrs Hugh Digweed with their four sons John, Harry, James and William, nearest neighbours to the Austen family. The Digweeds had occupied the house and its 900-acre farm for several decades, renting it from Mr Austen's cousins, the Knights of Godmersham in Kent.

In the adjoining parish of Deane (of which Mr Austen had also become the rector, in 1773), there were two families of landed gentry: the Harwoods, who had lived for generations in Deane House next to the little church of All Saints; and the Bramstons in modern Oakley Hall, which young Mr Wither Bramston had recently rebuilt following his marriage to Miss Mary Chute, one of the daughters of the Chute family from the Vyne estate at Sherborne St John near Basingstoke. The Bramstons never had any children, but the Harwoods had three sons, John, Earle and Charles, and they, together with the Digweed boys, must have been some of the earliest playmates of the Austen children.

Beyond Deane was the parish of Ashe, where the wealthy Revd Mr George Lefroy was the rector. Mr Lefroy had several young children, and an elegant and intellectual wife, known to the neighbourhood as Madam Lefroy; they had arrived in Hampshire only in 1783, but had soon become very friendly with the Austens. The manor house of Ashe Park was tenanted by a rich but dull middle-aged bachelor, Mr James Holder, whose money came from property in Barbados. These few gentry families constituted the very limited society in the district with whom the Austens were on equal standing, for the remaining inhabitants of the parishes of Steventon and Deane—a combined

6

total of perhaps three hundred souls—were mostly agricultural labourers.

STEVENTON TODAY

Anyone who visits Hampshire today in search of Jane Austen's birthplace should avoid the M3 motorway and the tangled knots of roundabouts that surround the modern sprawl of Basingstoke, and aim instead for Overton and Andover, down what was once the Great Western Turnpike Road—now demoted to the B3400—which in Jane's lifetime was the main coaching route from London to the west of England. About six miles beyond Basingstoke the long, low, white-painted Deane Gate Inn, originally the tollhouse for this stretch of turnpike, lies by the roadside at a T-junction where a lane is signposted as 1¼ miles to Steventon. If you turn down here and squeeze under a high narrow railway viaduct arch a mile further on, you will find a few early Victorian cottages on each side of the lane and then, at another small T-junction, a cottage, a little modern village hall and a bus shelter. This was the centre of the Steventon that Jane Austen knew, where a large maple tree once shaded the villagers who gathered there to chat on Sunday afternoons.

Turning left at this junction takes you between thick-hedged meadows until a wooden fingerpost points up an even narrower lane, 'To Steventon Church'. Here, on this corner, is Home Meadow, sloping and uneven, and grazed by a herd of plump and glossy Friesian dairy cows, who sometimes stand in the shade of a few ancient trees—an enormous lime and some horse chestnuts nearly as tall—and sometimes wander past a small rough patch separately fenced off at one end of the field. The uneven surface of Home Meadow, and the separate overgrown patch, which contains the last remains of a well and old iron pump, are the only visible clues to the fact that Steventon Rectory once stood at the bottom of the slope; the pump served its garden and wash house.

Jane's birthplace survived until the 1820s, when her nephew William Knight, taking over the family living, built himself a new rectory—the large white house on the other side of the road. For the sake of an uninterrupted view he cleared away both the old rectory where his grandparents had lived and the nearby handful of untidy thatched cottages with their garden plots, which straggled along the roadside edge of Home Meadow and the field opposite, and made up most of the village of Steventon. His parishioners were re-housed in newly built cottages, those now lying in the shadow of the railway viaduct. The little stone-built medieval church of St Nicholas is half a mile away up the tiny dead-end lane, and stands opposite a modern red-brick version of the flint and stone Tudor manor house that once occupied part of the same site and which, after many vicissitudes and rebuildings, was finally demolished in the 1970s. The church, and Bassetts Farm at the other end of the village, are probably the only buildings now surviving that Jane would have known. Even the elm trees that she mentions in her letters, and their descendants, have gone, all wiped out by disease.

CONNECTIONS TO THE OUTSIDE WORLD
An unusual link to the wide world outside Hampshire was provided by Mr Austen's elder

sister Philadelphia (1730–92). Left a penniless orphan like her brother, she had sailed out to India in 1752 in the hope of finding among the English employees of the East India Company some man who would be sufficiently lonely not to object to taking a wife who could bring no dowry to the marriage settlement—such financial planning for matrimony was an important consideration in the Georgian era. Within six months of her arrival she had indeed married: her husband was Tysoe Saul Hancock (1723–75), a surgeon in the East India Company's trading settlement at Calcutta. Hancock turned out to be a melancholy man, prematurely aged by illness, who had discovered too late that he hated his medical profession. He was an old friend of Warren Hastings—the future Governor General of India who was at that time employed by the East India Company in a less exalted position. Hancock and Hastings undertook various business ventures together which initially proved profitable. The Hancocks had one daughter, Elizabeth ('Betsy' or 'Bessy'), born in 1761, to whom Warren Hastings was godfather, giving her the name of his own daughter who had died in infancy.

In 1765 the Hancocks returned to England, with the intention of investing their Indian fortune and living off the interest. For some three years they lived in London, renewing acquaintance with their Kentish and Hampshire families, but then gradually realized that they were spending at the rate of £1500 a year, nearly twice their actual income. There was nothing for it but that Hancock should return to India and try to amass further capital to keep his wife and child in the style to which they had grown accustomed in Calcutta. He set out again in 1768, in the hope that another three years' trading would enable him to acquire the funds he needed, but his plans failed and he died in India, a disappointed and worn-out man, in November 1775.

In Hancock's absence Philadelphia and her daughter lived in rented houses in the newly developing smart district of Marylebone on the northern side of London, so that Betsy could have tuition in music, dancing, French, arithmetic and writing—all very necessary accomplishments for young ladies. They occasionally ventured away from town life to spend summers in country cottages, as well as paying long visits to their Walter cousins in Kent and the Austens in Hampshire. Hancock conscientiously sent back to his wife fine Indian fabrics for both clothes and soft furnishings—silks, chintzes, heavyweight and lightweight cottons and muslins—and every so often asked her to pass some of these on to the Austens; perhaps baby Jane's eyes looked admiringly at the colours of a flowered shawl, or at a silk Pullicat handkerchief knotted around her mother's neck.

The news of her husband's death reached Philadelphia Hancock in the summer of 1776, but his affairs were in such confusion that it was another year before she discovered that her income as a widow would be only about £600 a year. Of this, indeed, some £400 was the interest from a trust fund which the generous Warren Hastings—whose lucky star had risen as fast as that of Hancock had declined—had set up for his god-daughter some years previously. Philadelphia

10

therefore decided to take her daughter—to be known henceforward by the far more elegant diminutive of 'Eliza'—to Europe, where the cost of living was much lower than in England. They left for the Continent in 1777, and travelled through Germany and Belgium before settling in Paris in the autumn of 1779.

Eliza was now a very pretty and vivacious teenager, and entered whole-heartedly into the life of French high society. She wrote to her country-mouse cousin Phylly (Philadelphia) Walter, lonely at home with her ageing parents in a little Kentish village, with tantalizing descriptions of dances, parties, plays and trips to the French court at Versailles and details of the extravagant dresses worn by Queen Marie-Antoinette. Soon Eliza met a handsome young French army officer, Jean-François Capot de Feuillide, a captain in the Queen's Regiment of Dragoons, and they were married in 1781. In 1784 they left Paris and went to the south of France, where the Comte de Feuillide (as he liked to be known) had a small estate at his home at Nérac in Guienne. During his time in Paris the Comte had achieved a royal grant of an area of marshland not far from Nérac, which would be tax-free if he could drain and cultivate it, and he set to work enthusiastically on this land reclamation project. In 1786 Eliza gave birth to a son, whom she called Hastings, after her godfather. In these pre-Revolutionary years Eliza and her mother were able to make occasional trips to England, and in the winter of 1786 they visited Steventon parsonage for the first time since Jane's birth.

THE AUSTEN CHILDREN

During these past eleven years, the Steventon household had been very busy. Ever since 1773, Mr Austen had been in the habit of taking pupils into his home, partly to give his sons companionship in their studies, and partly to improve the family finances with the aid of the pupils' fees. It was only at Christmas and midsummer, when these boys went home for the holidays, that the Austens had room enough to be able to invite their own relations to come and stay. Although Mr Austen and his sister would have maintained contact by letter, when Philadelphia, Eliza and baby Hastings—now a fat, fair, pretty little boy six months old—arrived at the rectory a few days before Christmas in 1786, they must have needed hours of conversation to bring the families up to date with each other's news.

None of Mr Austen's children could yet compete with their cousin Eliza so far as life in high society and rich marriages were concerned, but they were nevertheless looking likely to be successful in their chosen careers. James, the studious son, had been coached so well in the classics by his father that he was able to matriculate at St John's College, Oxford, in the summer of 1779, at the remarkably early age of fourteen, and had already gained his Bachelor of Arts degree in 1783. He now had a Fellowship at St John's, and would stay on to become a Master of Arts in 1788, and it was accepted that he would in due course take Holy Orders like his father. He was not at home when Philadelphia and her family visited, having taken a year off to broaden his horizons by an inexpensive round trip to France, Spain and Holland.

12

Edward, the practical boy, had been particularly noticed by Mr Austen's rich cousin Mr Thomas Knight II of Godmersham, when the latter had visited Steventon in 1779 on his wedding tour, making the customary introduction of his bride to her new relations-in-law. Quite soon afterwards it had become clear that the Knights were fated to remain childless, and they then decided to adopt Edward as their heir. He was invited to spend more and more of his time with them at Godmersham, the adoption was agreed with the Austens in 1783, and eventually in 1812 he formally changed his surname to Knight. He did not go to university like his elder brother, but was sent abroad by the Knights on a long and lavish Grand Tour, during which he spent a year studying in Dresden. At Christmas 1786 he was in Switzerland; in 1789 he was in Rome and having his portrait painted as a permanent souvenir; and he did not return to England until the end of 1790. The Grand Tour had become an established custom for those rich young Englishmen who wanted to see more of the world before settling down on their country estates. It was usual to visit at least Paris, Florence, Venice, Rome and Naples in order to learn something of modern European culture and also to acquire personal worldly polish, as well as works of art to adorn the country mansion at home.

Henry, tall and impetuous, was still at home being tutored by his father, and was due to go to St John's, like his brother, in 1788, and to enter the Church thereafter. Francis (Frank), small, active and determined, knew that he enjoyed mathematics but not classical studies, and had decided of his own accord that he wished to become a sailor. Mr Austen had therefore entered him at the Royal Naval Academy in Portsmouth in the summer of 1786, and Frank was just briefly at home over Christmas before his term started again. Little Charles, aged only seven, in due course followed Frank to the Naval Academy in 1791.

As for Cassandra and Jane, they had both spent some months away from home recently—first of all, in 1783, in Oxford and Southampton under the care of a kinswoman, Mrs Cawley, while the Austen parents paid a visit to Kent—and, secondly, from 1785 to 1786, when they were pupils at Mrs La Tournelle's Ladies' Boarding School, whose premises were at the Abbey House in Reading, Berkshire. Mrs Cawley's move to Southampton had nearly ended in disaster for the Austens, as the little girls had fallen seriously ill with typhus fever and had to be rescued by their mother. In Reading the school provided a comfortable and well-managed boarding home, and the lessons and hours of study were not exacting; but Mr Austen evidently found he could not afford to keep both his daughters at school indefinitely—Mrs La Tournelle charged about £35 a year for each pupil—and at Christmas 1786 Mrs Austen was able to say firmly that both her girls had now quite left school. These two brief excursions were the only occasions Jane ever moved outside her family circle for any length of time; and she put her experience of the Abbey House school to good use when she came to write *Emma* thirty years later.

Also in the 1780s, James, with his literary interests, organized his brothers and sisters, together with any visiting friends and cousins, into amateur theatrical performances at home—presented in either the rectory dining room or in the barn across the lane—for which he himself wrote versified prologues and epilogues and supervised the painting of a set of theatrical scenes. Here again, Jane called upon her memories of these busy days in the summer and winter holidays of childhood when she made the amateur theatricals at Mansfield Park the turning point for the Bertram family's breakdown. However, this winter of 1786–7, with both James and Edward away, there was no one to plan for theatricals, and instead it was Cousin Eliza who entertained the family by playing on a hired piano so that there could be dancing in the parlour as part of the New Year domestic festivities.

JANE'S EARLY WRITINGS

It was following her return from school that Jane Austen first started literary composition. For the next six years she wrote a number of comic essays, skits and short stories, some of them no more than a page in length and some left unfinished, which she dedicated jokingly to the various members of her family. She later copied out these short pieces into three manuscript books which she called simply Volumes the First, Second and Third. The collection as a whole is referred to as her *Juvenilia*; nothing of it appeared in print in her lifetime, but nowadays it can be found published separately from her adult novels.

In this period, also, comes the first recorded comment on Jane as a child; in the summer of 1788, Mr and Mrs Austen took their two daughters to Kent to introduce them to their Kentish cousins, and one of these, the Phylly Walter with whom Eliza de Feuillide corresponded, took an instant dislike to little Jane, saying she was 'very like her brother Henry, not at all pretty and very prim, unlike a girl of twelve . . . whimsical and affected'. However, by the time she reached the age of seventeen, in 1792, and made her debut into Hampshire society, she had grown tall and slender, and had her father's colouring of chestnut-brown hair and bright hazel eyes, with a clear complexion and pink cheeks; the neighbourhood considered that, though not a regular beauty, she was nevertheless a very pretty girl. One jealous older lady, plain herself and the mother of a fat, plain little girl, saw Jane dancing at a ball in Basingstoke and thought her 'the silliest, most affected, husband-hunting butterfly she ever remembered'. Perhaps the 'affectation' of which these older ladies complained was in fact an early manifestation of Jane's wit and ironical sense of humour, springing from an intelligence in advance of her years.

While Jane was spreading her wings and flitting lightly from partner to partner at the monthly Basingstoke assembly balls, her two eldest brothers were already settling down in life. James, as planned, had entered the Church, and was now the vicar of Sherborne St John. He lived, however, in Mr Austen's other parsonage house at Deane, with his wife, Anne Mathew; in 1793, their first child, Anna, was born. Edward, having returned from his Grand Tour at the end of 1790, fell in love with Elizabeth Bridges, one of the many daughters of a Kentish baronet, Sir Brook Bridges, and the

Bridges family provided a small house near Godmersham in which Edward and Elizabeth could begin their married life. Soon Jane was able to travel independently into Kent for visits to her brother and his wife, and the children who rapidly appeared on the scene, and thus make a whole new circle of acquaintances outside her Hampshire neighbourhood. Whenever Jane and Cassandra were apart from each other on such family visits, they wrote very full and chatty letters; much of the available biographical information about Jane, limited though it is, comes from such letters of hers as were preserved by Cassandra.

THE FIRST THREE NOVELS

During the decade of the 1790s these domestic changes had begun to broaden Jane's horizons and provide her with new information and ideas that she gradually wove into her literary compositions. At this time she had no intention of publication, but wrote for her own pleasure and for the amusement of her family, to whom the stories were read out in the evening around the fireside. After copying out her early comic stories into Volumes the First, Second and Third, she experimented with a very short novel-in-letters on a serious adult theme; the letters reveal the scheming of a coldhearted, gold-digging young widow who callously enjoys breaking up happy families with her manipulative lies and flirtations, while at the same time trying to force her teenage daughter into an unhappy marriage. Jane did not give a title to this story, but it is known today as *Lady Susan*, the name of the villainess, and it is assumed that she wrote it in about 1793–4. It seems that she made her first attempt to write a full-length novel in 1795, with another story-in-letters about two sisters, which she called *Elinor and Marianne*; and as soon as she had finished this, she started writing *First Impressions* in 1796—the original version of *Pride and Prejudice*. Mr Austen was so pleased with his daughter's work that he thought it should be published, and when this second story was finished, in the autumn of 1797, he wrote to the London publisher Cadell offering to send him the manuscript. Unfortunately, Mr Austen did not explain that the novel was a very witty comedy of manners, so it is perhaps not surprising that Cadell did not even bother to ask to see the manuscript but told his clerk to reject the offer forthwith. Luckily for us, Jane was not discouraged; she put *First Impressions* aside for the time being, and instead went back to *Elinor and Marianne*, changing it into what we now know as *Sense and Sensibility*.

Later in 1797, Mrs Austen, with her two daughters, went to Somerset to stay for some weeks in Bath with her brother and his wife, Mr and Mrs Leigh-Perrot (he had taken the second surname in compliance with a family inheritance), who lived during the winter months in a tall town house, No. 1 Paragon Buildings, on the eastern edge of the city and overlooking the River Avon in the deep valley below. Mrs Austen had lived in Bath for two years before her marriage, and Jane and Cassandra may have passed through it on some earlier occasion, but the year 1797 is the first time Jane is known to have visited this tourist resort, which was so popular in the eighteenth century. Here she would have been introduced by her aunt to the busy daily routine of Bath society, which gave her the background information needed for the composition of *Northanger Abbey* (or *Susan*, as it was then simply called) in the following year.

THE BATH YEARS

Bath, in fact, soon became Jane Austen's home, for at the end of 1800 Mr Austen quite unexpectedly decided that he would give up his active clerical duties as rector of Steventon and Deane, and retire to Bath. All his sons were settled in their different ways of life: James's wife, Anne, had died suddenly in 1795, leaving him with their one little girl, Anna, and in 1797 he had married an old friend of the Austen family, Mary Lloyd, by whom in due course he had another two children, James-Edward and Caroline. James would now move his family into Steventon rectory and take over his father's duties; he was not ambitious, and perfectly happy to remain a country clergyman to the end of his days. Edward and his Elizabeth, at Godmersham, already had six children and would eventually have eleven; Elizabeth herself had many brothers and sisters, so Edward's web of relationships by marriage fixed him firmly in his place among the other rich Kentish landowners.

Instead of taking Holy Orders, Henry had joined the Oxfordshire Militia and done very well, becoming Captain and Adjutant of the regiment; he now intended to resign his commission and move to live in London, where he planned to set himself up as a private banker and army agent for the sale and purchase of commissions. He had married his widowed cousin, Eliza de Feuillide, at the end of 1797, but they had no children. Frank was now a post-captain in the Navy, and provided he survived wartime service, was therefore assured of steady promotion; he was still single, but a captain's salary would enable him to marry and support a family in reasonable comfort. Charles was still only a lieutenant in the Navy, but under wartime conditions he also could expect fairly rapid promotion.

This meant that Cassandra and Jane, now aged twenty-eight and twenty-five respectively, and perilously close to being viewed by contemporary standards as confirmed old maids, were left at home with Mr and Mrs Austen, both elderly and not in the best of health. It may have been the Leigh-Perrots who urged them to come to Bath, perhaps suggesting, on the one hand, considerations of health and, on the other, that their daughters would be more likely to find suitable husbands in the busy city than in the sparsely populated countryside. Jane had enjoyed dancing and flirting lightly with various partners for the past eight winter seasons, but was still unmarried and unengaged. There had been a short and intense flirtation in the winter of 1795–6 with Tom Lefroy, a visiting nephew of the Reverend George Lefroy of Ashe; but the senior Lefroys had taken fright at the idea of a formal engagement between such a young and penniless couple, and sent Tom off to London before he could commit himself. How deeply Jane's feelings may have been involved is not known; but even if she did shed some tears at hearing of Tom's sudden departure for London, only a few months later she started writing *First Impressions*, which is certainly not the product of a broken heart. Family tradition, however, recalled that she had been very upset when told by her parents of their impending departure from Steventon.

BATH, THE TOURIST SPA

The city of Bath had been a health spa and tourist resort for nearly two thousand years, ever since the invading Romans had found the local Celtic population worshipping the goddess Sul, who presided over the fast-flowing thermal springs that gushed out at the base of the hills just above the river valley of the Avon. The Romans channelled and piped the springs and created a luxurious bathing complex, around which their city of Aquae Sulis (the Waters of Sul) grew; over the succeeding centuries the great stone bath-houses fell into ruin and a medieval city was built on top of them, but some of the springs remained visible and were used in a lesser way for medicinal bathing. Queen Anne came to Bath at the beginning of the eighteenth century in the hope of a cure for her ailments, and it was her visit that brought the city into favour as a resort for those seeking both health and pleasure. Richard 'Beau' Nash, a shrewd, suave adventurer, arrived in Bath from his native Wales in 1702, and made himself into the Master of Ceremonies and the arbiter of taste and fashion. He codified rules for social behaviour within the city, and inaugurated the winter season for visiting gentry; gambling, balls, parties, concerts and plays kept the healthy enjoying themselves, while invalids hoped to be cured by bathing in the hot springs and drinking the mineral water.

Local landowners then took the opportunity of

developing their property with large and handsome houses built in Bath's golden limestone, and throughout the eighteenth century new terraces, crescents and squares climbed ever further up the hillsides away from the damp, airless river valley, until the new Bath could fairly be described as a town of hills and a hill of towns. Most of the houses were built on speculation for the tourist trade, to be let as lodgings for short periods, and by the middle of the century anyone who wished to be considered fashionable had to spend at least a few weeks every year 'taking the waters' at Bath. The season ran from September to May, as the three summer months were considered too hot for town life.

However, Bath's very success in attracting tourists led to its gradual decline as a resort; when the *nouveaux riches* began to arrive in the later part of the eighteenth century, the fashion leaders promptly moved on to try sea-bathing at Weymouth or Brighton, leaving Bath to become a place of residence for retired people of the middle-ranking professional classes. By the beginning of the nineteenth century visitors began to think that the city, though still beautiful in itself and with a multitude of expensive shops, was nevertheless dull and depressing, now inhabited largely by single people who were either confirmed invalids or ugly old maids and who were preyed upon by professional gamblers or fortune-hunters.

BATH AND THE WEST COUNTRY
The Austens arrived in Bath in May 1801 and took a short lease on No. 4, Sydney Place, a small terraced house facing Sydney Gardens, on the

newer eastern side of the city. Here they lived for the next three years, making excursions in the summers to various little seaside resorts on the south Devon coast; it seems probable that in 1801 they visited Sidmouth and Colyton, in 1802 they were certainly at Dawlish, and in 1803 and 1804 they visited Lyme Regis and the surrounding countryside. Jane seems to have been particularly pleased with Lyme and neighbouring Charmouth, and years later made it the setting for part of the action of *Persuasion*.

In 1803 Captain Frank Austen was posted to the port of Ramsgate in Kent, to command the local Sea Fencibles (a kind of maritime home defence force) on that vulnerable coastline, and presently became engaged to Mary Gibson, whose family lived in the town. Mr and Mrs Austen and their daughters travelled to Kent that summer to stay with Edward and his family at Godmersham and meet Mary Gibson at the same time; and Ramsgate gave Jane some ideas in due course for the creation of her fictional Sanditon.

The Bath years were busy but not particularly happy for Jane; her letters show that she was no longer dancing in the Assembly Rooms, but constantly occupied with the duller social round of little card parties and tea-drinking visits amongst other genteel widow and spinster families. There were no signs of any eligible husbands for herself and Cassandra in the city; a family tradition was recorded in later years that on one of the summer holidays a mutual attraction had arisen between Jane and some unnamed gentleman who was visiting the sea coast at the same time, but that he had died suddenly before he could return to become an accepted suitor. In the winter of 1802, certainly, while she and Cassandra were on a visit to their brother James back in the family rectory at Steventon, Jane received a proposal from Harris Bigg-Wither, the plain and awkward younger brother of some girlhood friends of hers, and heir to a pleasant country estate near Basingstoke. Perhaps from feelings of friendship or gratitude, she accepted his proposal in the evening; but by the next morning had evidently decided that worldly benefits would not outweigh the disadvantages of a loveless marriage, and so retracted her consent.

There were disappointments, too, with her literary interests; in 1803, with the encouragement and assistance of her brother Henry, she had sold the manuscript of her 1798 story, *Susan*, to the London firm of Benjamin Crosby & Co., who had even advertised it as being in the press and forthcoming, but then never published it. It may perhaps have been at this time, under the initial enthusiasm of having her story accepted, that she started another novel, now known as *The Watsons*; but she wrote only a few chapters before laying it aside, and never returned to finish it.

The lease of No. 4 Sydney Place expired in the autumn of 1804, and the Austens moved to No. 3 Green Park Buildings, rather nearer the centre of Bath. Only a few months later, in January 1805, Mr Austen died quite suddenly after two days' illness; and even though her sons rallied round with promises of financial support, Mrs Austen's income, as a widow, was much reduced. It was agreed that in future she would stay with her sons and their families during the summer, and return to Bath to live in rented accommodation over the winter.

FAMILY VISITS

For the next few months Jane's life was unsettled, as she, her mother and Cassandra wound up their home in Green Park Buildings and roamed around the south of England in the course of paying these family visits. They stayed for a few months in a lodging house in Bath, No. 25 Gay Street, and then went to Steventon and Godmersham; from there they had an autumn holiday at Worthing, on the Sussex sea coast, where they met their old friend Martha Lloyd, the elder sister of James's wife Mary. Martha had been living with her widowed mother for many years, but now that Mrs Lloyd had died, Martha chose to join forces with her Austen friends in preference to becoming her sister's pensioner at Steventon. The Austen ladies, and Martha, returned to Bath in the spring of 1806, and lodged for the time being in Trim Street.

In the summer of 1806 Mrs Austen and her daughters finally left Bath and set off again on another round of visits, starting with a short holiday at Clifton before calling upon her cousin the Reverend Thomas Leigh at Adlestrop in Gloucestershire. Mr Leigh was a rich old widower, living with his spinster sister, Elizabeth, at Adlestrop rectory, and had recently called in the famous landscape gardener Humphrey Repton to improve the layout of the garden and parkland that lay between the rectory and the nearby Adlestrop House, where Mr Leigh's nephew lived. Repton charged five guineas a day for his professional services, as Mr Leigh evidently informed his guests; and Jane made a mental note of this information, using it later in *Mansfield Park*.

From Adlestrop the house party moved on to Stoneleigh Abbey, in Warwickshire. This was an estate owned by a different branch of the Leigh family, which had unexpectedly come into the possession of the Reverend Thomas Leigh, and he was anxious to see the extent of his new inheritance. The house was a strange mixture—it had originally been built in the sixteenth century on the site of an old abbey, as the name implies, but early in the eighteenth century the then owner had remodelled the west wing into a new principal front in the Palladian style, while leaving the rest of the rambling Elizabethan house unaltered. Mrs Austen was fascinated by the place, and wrote a long letter to her daughter-in-law Mary Lloyd, James's wife:

> . . . every thing is very Grand & very fine & very Large—The House is larger than I could have supposed—we can *now* find our way about it, I mean the best part, as to the offices (which were the old Abby) Mr Leigh almost dispairs of ever finding his way about them—I have proposed his setting up *directing Posts* at the Angles—I expected to find everything about the place very fine & all that, but I had no idea of its being so beautiful, I had figured to myself long Avenues, dark rookeries & dismal Yew Trees, but here are no such melancholy things . . . I will now give you some idea of the inside of this vast house, first premising that there are 45 windows in front, (which is

26

quite strait with a flat Roof) 15 in a row—you go up a considerable flight of steps (some offices are under the house) into a large Hall, on the right hand, the dining parlour, within that the Breakfast room, where we generally sit, and reason good, tis the only room (except the Chapel) that looks towards the River,—on the left hand the Hall is the best drawing room, within that a smaller, these rooms are rather gloomy, Brown wainscoat & dark Crimson furniture, so we never use them but to walk thro' them to the old picture Gallery; Behind the smaller drawing Room is the State Bed chamber with a high dark crimson Velvet Bed, an *alarming* apartment just fit for an Heroine, the old Gallery opens into it—behind the Hall & Parlour a passage all across the house containing 3 staircases & two small back Parlours—there are 26 Bed Chambers in the new part of the house, & a great many (some very good ones) in the Old . . .

From Stoneleigh the Austens journeyed on into Staffordshire, to stay for several weeks with Mrs Austen's nephew the Reverend Edward Cooper and his family, in his rectory of Hamstall Ridware; so far as is known, this is the furthest north that Jane ever travelled. When she returned south, it was to her native county of Hampshire, and to a new home in Southampton.

SOUTHAMPTON
The idea that Mrs Austen and her daughters

should settle in Southampton had come from Frank Austen. He had married his fiancée, Mary Gibson, in July 1806, and did not want his young wife to be lonely while he was away on his next voyage; it was therefore agreed that they would all live together in Southampton, which was conveniently near the naval dockyard at Portsmouth. Frank found a house to rent in Castle Square, which had a fine garden running down to the old medieval walls of the town and a view across Southampton Water to the Isle of Wight on the other side of the estuary. Here Jane lived for the next two years. Visiting Portsmouth in Frank's company enabled her to see the High Street, the garrison chapel, the ramparts and the dockyard, and to bring all these memories into *Mansfield Park*: 'The day was uncommonly lovely. It was really March; but it was April in its mild air, brisk soft wind, and bright sun, occasionally clouded for a minute; and every thing looked so beautiful under the influence of such a sky, the effects of the shadows pursuing each other, on the ships at Spithead and the island beyond, with the ever-varying hues of the sea now at high water, dancing in its glee and dashing against the ramparts with so fine a sound . . . .'

THE CHAWTON YEARS

Family considerations once again influenced the lives of Mrs Austen and her daughters—this time, the death in childbed of Edward's young wife, Elizabeth, in the autumn of 1808. Edward was suddenly left to care for eleven motherless children, the eldest of whom was his daughter Fanny, not yet sixteen years of age. Anticipating his need to call upon his mother and unmarried sisters for assistance, he offered Mrs Austen a home on his other Hampshire estate of Chawton, near Alton. Thus it was that in the summer of 1809 Mrs Austen, with Jane, Cassandra and their faithful friend Martha Lloyd, all moved into a rather old-fashioned but comfortable small house in Chawton village, which became known to the family as 'Chawton Cottage'. Five minutes' walk away was Chawton Great House, the Elizabethan manor where Edward and his children now came to stay for the summer months of every year, when frequent contact was enjoyed between the Cottage and the Great House. Chawton was less than twenty miles from Steventon, so James could ride over to visit his mother quite easily; Frank's wife, Mary Gibson, with her babies, was also living in Alton while he was away on a long voyage to China; and soon Charles Austen returned from naval service in the West Indies, bringing his wife, Fanny Palmer, and their two children with him. The Great House became a focal point for the Austens, for if Edward himself was not living there, he was happy to lend it to either Frank or Charles whenever they were on leave from their naval duties. Henry was living in London, fifty miles away, running his successful banking partnership of Austen, Maunde & Tilson, but as his bank had a branch in Alton, it was convenient for him to pay visits that combined business with family reunions.

FIRST PUBLICATION

Unfortunately there is a gap in Jane's surviving correspondence between July 1809 and April 1811, and so it will probably never be known just when it was that her family persuaded her to try again to get one of her manuscripts published. She had attempted to retrieve her manuscript of *Susan* from the negligent Benjamin Crosby & Co., but could not afford the ten pounds they demanded as the original purchase price. Having failed with *Susan*, this time she submitted *Sense and Sensibility* to the London publisher Thomas Egerton of Whitehall, probably in the autumn of 1810; he was prepared to take it for publication upon commission—that is, at the author's expense—and it must have needed all her family's encouragement for Jane to accept this offer, because she was so sure its sale would not repay the expense of publication that she put aside some money from her very moderate income to meet the expected loss.

However, when *Sense and Sensibility* appeared in the autumn of 1811 it received some quite favourable reviews, and the first edition was sold out by the summer of 1813, providing Jane with a final clear profit of about £140. In the meantime she had returned to the text of *First Impressions*, made some alterations and contractions, and changed the title to *Pride and Prejudice*. Egerton had no doubt that this would sell well, and so on this occasion bought the copyright from her for the sum of £110 in the autumn of 1812. It was published at the end of January 1813, and indeed proved so popular that a second edition followed within a few months. Jane's name did not appear on the title page of either of the books, since at that date it was considered very unbecoming and undignified for a respectable lady to be seen to write novels for money and for general publication;

30

her first book was therefore said to be 'By A Lady', and the second was 'By the Author of "Sense and Sensibility"'.

Now that Jane was settled in a permanent home again, and had gained the self-confidence of a published author, she wrote her next two novels at top speed and without any different drafts or revisions. She was working on *Mansfield Park* in the autumn of 1812, and by the New Year of 1813 was already halfway through it, probably finishing it before the year was out. Egerton was evidently not enthusiastic about this story, so much more subdued in tone than *Pride and Prejudice*, and did not offer to buy the copyright but once again published on commission, bringing the book out in the spring of 1814. The title page showed it as being 'by the Author of "Sense and Sensibility" and "Pride and Prejudice"', and no doubt this was sufficient recommendation for it to sell well, with a profit to Jane of £350.

No sooner had Jane sold *Mansfield Park* than she immediately started on *Emma*, in January 1814, and finished this, without any problems, at the end of March 1815. Her brother Henry had always acted on her behalf when negotiating with publishers, and this time he offered the manuscript to John Murray of Albemarle Street, who took it on commission. During Jane's visit to London, Henry fell dangerously ill, and she had to stay longer than she intended in order to nurse him; but this enforced change of plan led to a quite unexpected event—a visit to a royal palace.

Although her books were all published anonymously, Henry could never resist proudly acknowledging his sister's name whenever he heard her works praised in London society, so here at least her authorship was an open secret. It so happened that Dr Baillie, who attended Henry in his illness, also numbered the Prince Regent among his patients, and was therefore able to tell Jane that the latter was a great admirer of her novels, that he often read them and that he had a set in each of his residences. In turn, Dr Baillie told the Prince that Miss Austen was now in London; with the result that the Prince sent one of his staff, the Reverend James Stanier Clarke, librarian of Carlton House, to meet her and take her on a conducted tour of the Prince's small but highly luxurious London palace. During the visit to Carlton House, Mr Clarke suggested that Jane should dedicate her next novel to the Prince Regent; this put her in something of a quandary, as she thoroughly disapproved of the Prince's extravagant and immoral lifestyle. However, a dedication was obviously expected. She just had time to add this to *Emma*, and she sent a pre-publication copy to Carlton House in mid-December 1815. This copy, specially bound in red morocco gilt, is now preserved in the Royal Library at Windsor Castle.

Jane was still full of inspiration after finishing *Emma*, and started *Persuasion* in August 1815. However, it may be that the worry of Henry's illness later that year and his bankruptcy in the spring of 1816 had rendered her susceptible to infection, for it was at this time, early in 1816, that she first felt the symptoms of what became her terminal illness. It is difficult to be certain, but from the comments she made about her illness it seems probable that she was suffering from

Addison's disease, a form of kidney failure that can be caused by tubercular infection. By the summer she was weakening, and had trouble during July and August in finishing *Persuasion* to her satisfaction, having to rewrite the last two chapters. She was also revising the manuscript of *Susan*, which Henry had bought back on her behalf from the firm of Benjamin Crosby & Co. Another novel called *Susan* had been published in recent years, so Jane changed her heroine's name to 'Catherine'; but she seems to have been disheartened by finding the story, as she thought, so much out of date, and put it aside again.

For the rest of 1816, Jane's state of health fluctuated, but overall the trend was always downwards. In the New Year of 1817 she had a period of remission, and while she felt hopeful of recovery she started another novel, now known to us as *Sanditon*. But the symptoms of ill health soon reappeared, and she began to spend more time in bed, still trying to write when she felt strong enough. She put the manuscript aside for the last time on 18 March, having drafted the first twelve chapters of what was evidently planned to be a long and most amusing story.

In May 1817 Cassandra took Jane to Winchester, so that she could consult Dr Lyford, one of the surgeons at the County Hospital in the city, and they lodged at No 8, College Street for some weeks. Given the state of medical knowledge at the time, Dr Lyford could have no real hope of curing her; but, as her brother Henry later wrote: 'She supported, during two months, all the varying pain, irksomeness, and tedium, attendant on decaying nature, with more than resignation, with a truly elastic cheerfulness. She retained her faculties, her memory, her fancy, her temper, and her affections, warm, clear, and unimpaired to the last.' The end came in the early hours of 18 July 1817, and she was buried in Winchester Cathedral a week later.

Henry took it upon himself to get Jane's last two manuscripts published, and John Murray brought them out together at the very end of the year. It seems to have been Jane's custom to write her stories first and choose their titles afterwards, so the titles we know these two by, *Northanger Abbey* and *Persuasion*, must have been chosen by Henry; and he added a 'Biographical Notice of the Author' as a preface to *Northanger Abbey*. *The Juvenilia* and the two unfinished works, *The Watsons* and *Sanditon*, were not published in full until the twentieth century.

Jane's life, short though it was—she was not yet forty-two when she died—nevertheless spans one of the most interesting periods in British history, and a brief consideration of the United Kingdom's place in world events, and some aspects of the social life in her day, will help to place her novels more specifically in context of both time and place.

ROYALTY AND THE COURT

George III, a tall, fair, florid young man, with prominent blue eyes and a somewhat receding forehead and chin, had succeeded to the throne at the early age of twenty-two, in October 1760. The following year he married Princess Charlotte of Mecklenburg-Strelitz, a little German principality not much bigger than an English county; and despite his and Charlotte's plain looks—she was small and skinny, with a wide mouth and flat nose, and her courtiers tittered a few years later that 'the *bloom* of her ugliness was going off'—between them over the next twenty years they produced a family of fifteen handsome fair-haired sons and daughters. George was the first of the Hanoverian line of kings to care more for his British kingdom than for his German inheritance, and was proud that he had been born and educated in England. Although his tutors had not discovered any outstanding intelligence in him, he had strong interests in architecture, music, astronomy, agriculture and gardening, and all who knew him

35

agreed that he had a kind heart and an innate rectitude, and was anxious to the point of obstinacy to follow the course which he believed to be righteous.

In accordance with the King's preference for the country, the Royal Family lived at Windsor Castle instead of in London, and any one of his subjects who cared to go to the Castle could see the King walking on the terrace there in the summer evenings, his little wife in a black silk cloak and plain straw bonnet beside him, and the long train of their children and their attendants following on behind. Life at Windsor was very plain and quiet, with music parties in the evenings but no lavish entertaining or late nights. One of the King's favourite pastimes was to inspect the large farms that he had created in Windsor Great Park, to ensure that they were being well managed, and to drop in unannounced at the labourers' cottages to chat jovially to his tenants. Some of the cartoonists nicknamed him 'Farmer George' and mocked him for his modest and unostentatious lifestyle, but his genuine kindness and interest in the well-being of all those around him became something of a legend.

Unfortunately the King had inherited from his distant Stuart ancestors the rare metabolic disorder of porphyria, which produces apparently inexplicable physical pains and sometimes bouts of mental derangement as well. His first lengthy attack occurred in 1788, which led to talk of a Regency, but the King recovered before the necessary constitutional arrangements could be made. He had further attacks in 1801 and 1804, and the drastic but useless treatments prescribed

36

by his various doctors left him so frail that, in 1809, the jubilee celebrations to mark the fiftieth year of his reign had to be held early, in case the King did not survive until the end of the year. James Austen and his family went to a jubilee ball at the Basingstoke assembly rooms on 24 October, and on the next day, the actual anniversary of the King's accession, Mr William Digweed gave a supper in his barn at Steventon for all the inhabitants of the parish.

In 1810 the King had another attack, brought on by his grief over the lingering death from tuberculosis of his youngest daughter, Princess Amelia, aged only twenty-seven. This time it was obvious that he could never recover; indeed, by the summer of 1811 it seemed that the King's death was imminent and his loyal subjects were preparing for national mourning, so Jane Austen went shopping in Alton on her mother's behalf to buy the necessary lengths of black bombazine. In the event he lived for another nine years, but he spent them, deaf and blind, secluded in his apartments in Windsor Castle.

THE REGENCY

The heir to the throne, George-Augustus-Frederick, Prince of Wales from his birth, officially became the Prince Regent on 6 February 1811, and the title given to this period has now come to identify a flamboyant era of British history, the Regency. Although George III was a most affectionate father to his sons while they were children, he could not maintain easy relationships with them as they grew older, and—sober and respectable himself—was horrified at the wild and extravagant lifestyle that the Prince of Wales adopted almost before he was out of his adolescence. The Prince was tall, fair and handsome, universally agreed to be charming, witty and intelligent, and in later life became a patron of literature, music and the arts; he was also irresponsible and deceitful, gluttonous and drunken, squandering his princely allowance on fine clothes, expensive mistresses and grandiose building projects at Carlton House in London and his seaside residence, the Pavilion at Brighton. In his youth he was nicknamed 'The First Gentleman of Europe', but as years of over-eating led to gross obesity, cartoonists would depict him as 'The Prince of Whales'.

In 1785 the Prince secretly married Mrs Maria Fitzherbert, a twice-widowed lady rather older than himself, a commoner and a Roman Catholic, and therefore unacceptable on more than one count as the wife of the heir to the throne. The Hanoverian dynasty had become rulers of Britain earlier in the eighteenth century specifically because they were Protestants; and in 1772 George III had passed the Royal Marriages Act, by which the Crown's consent was needed for the marriage of all the British descendants of George II, and stipulating also that such marriage partners must be Protestants. At the time, one parliamentarian had said that it should be called 'An Act to encourage fornication and adultery in the descendants of George II'. The Prince's marriage was therefore illegal in civil terms and could not be publicly acknowledged.

At his father's request, and in order that his debts might be paid off by Parliament, the Prince bigamously, but officially, married his cousin, Princess Caroline of Brunswick, in 1795. The marriage was doomed from the start—whereas the Prince admired cultured, elegant, intelligent ladies, the unfortunate Caroline was short, ungracefully podgy and notorious for neglecting her personal hygiene. All too soon she showed herself also to be a tactless chatterbox, and eccentric and improper in her behaviour. Their daughter, the Princess Charlotte of Wales, was born nine months to the day after the wedding, and the couple immediately separated. The Princess of Wales was given a house on the outskirts of London, and the baby Charlotte was brought up under the supervision of the Prince and his parents.

The Prince's political opponents sided with the Princess, making it their business to portray her as a wronged and innocent wife, and for some years, until her own behaviour became too notorious to be concealed, public sympathy was on her side. In February 1813 Caroline's advisers composed a letter to the Prince, reiterating her grievances, and arranged for it to be published in the newspapers; and a few days later Jane Austen wrote to her friend Martha Lloyd:

> I suppose all the World is sitting in Judgement upon the Princess of Wales's Letter. Poor Woman, I shall support her as long as I can, because she *is* a Woman, & because I hate her Husband—but I can hardly forgive her for calling herself 'attached & affectionate' to a Man whom she must detest . . . I do not know what to do about it;—but if I must give up the

Princess, I am resolved at least always to think that she would have been respectable, if the Prince had behaved only tolerably by her at first.

FOREIGN AFFAIRS

For most of the eighteenth century the European powers were jockeying and fighting for territory and trade all over the rest of the known world, and for decades Britain had been almost continually at war with France and Spain. When George III came to the throne in 1760, the provinces of Quebec and Montreal, in what is modern Canada, had just been wrested from French settlers, so much of the eastern side of North America came under British control; however, the Spanish-American empire stretched from California to Argentina, and the West Indian islands were constantly changing hands between the Spanish, French, British and Dutch. The costs of driving the French and Spanish out of the Atlantic side of North America had been met by the British taxpayer, and the thirteen American colonies on this eastern seaboard had contributed nothing. The British government decided that the time had come for the Americans to pay for their own defence, and that this money should be raised by local taxation, as was the practice in England. The Americans, who did not have any Members of Parliament to argue on their behalf in the House of Commons, took the view that there should be no taxation without representation.

Disagreements and demonstrations rumbled on for the next few years, until the American colonists took up arms against the British in 1773 in the War of Independence. The situation was at first something of a stalemate—as the Americans had no fleet, they could not stop the British from landing wherever they wished on the eastern seaboard, but Britain equally could not provide or supply an army large enough to put down the rebellion. The colonists fought doggedly, and the formally drilled British troops, unsuited for the conditions of guerrilla warfare, lost as many battles as they won. The Americans published their Declaration of Independence in July 1776, and the Spanish, Dutch and French all took advantage of the situation to provide ships and troops to assist the Americans, so compelling the surrender of the British at Yorktown, Virginia, in 1781. The remaining British garrisons were evacuated, and a peace treaty was formally signed at Versailles in 1783, with the recognition of American independence. Some sixty thousand colonists, the United Empire Loyalists, who had disagreed with the idea of rebellion, moved northwards from the new American republic to join other British settlers in Canada.

So far as is known, the Austens did not have any particular personal interest in the American War of Independence, but any backwash of hostilities towards the West Indies would certainly have worried them. These scattered islands, strategically situated between the two American continents, had been settled by Europeans early in the seventeenth century, and ever since then many of the younger sons of the English nobility and landed gentry had gone out there to try to make their fortunes by developing plantations and exporting their crops back to the United Kingdom.

The Civil War in the middle of the century increased the flow when defeated Royalists fled to the West Indies to escape Cromwell's new Puritan republic at home. The plantations were worked initially by English convicts and later by slaves brought from the West Coast of Africa, and by the middle of the eighteenth century a flourishing triangular trade had developed: rum, sugar, cotton, cocoa and coffee from the West Indies and the eastern seaboard of North America came to English ports—Bristol, Liverpool and London in particular—and the proceeds of their sale went to purchase trade goods such as metalware, textiles, weapons and alcohol, which were wanted in Africa. The ships went out to Africa, exchanged these goods for the slaves brought to them by Arab slave traders, and took these slaves across the Atlantic to work on the plantations and thus produce more rum, sugar, cotton, cocoa and coffee. It was understood that the profitable production of these crops was dependent upon the use of slave labour.

The Austen family's connections to this part of the world were threefold: Mrs Austen's brother, Mr James Leigh-Perrot, had married Jane Cholmeley, whose family had a plantation in Barbados; Mr Austen himself was for some years one of the trustees of a plantation in Antigua, on behalf of the son of an old Oxford University friend of his; and two of Mr Austen's Kentish nephews, William and George Walter, went out to Jamaica and died there, in 1787 and 1779 respectively. No doubt it was memories of these family links which led Jane to bestow Antiguan estates upon Sir Thomas Bertram in *Mansfield Park*.

42

Much nearer to Jane's home in Hampshire, the first gathering storm clouds of European unrest appeared across the English Channel, when on 14 July 1789 the Parisian mobs stormed the old prison fortress of the Bastille, a hated symbol of an oppressive government. This date is now taken as the start of the French Revolution. At first some English people were sympathetic towards the idea of a change of government in France, especially those who had been accustomed to look with a favourable eye upon the American War of Independence in the previous decade. All too soon, however, the motto of *'Liberté, Egalité, Fraternité'* became nothing but a bloodstained mockery as the paranoid revolutionary leaders massacred and guillotined without trial anyone whom they declared to be an enemy of the state. Many French families fled across the Channel to England, hidden in fishing boats, while others were rescued by the British fleet. One colony of *émigrés* formed in Reading, some of them settling next door to Mrs La Tournelle's Abbey House school, and the contemporary comment was made that 'very many lived literally on the produce of their own industry; the gentlemen teaching languages, music, fencing, dancing; whilst their wives and daughters went out as teachers or governesses, or supplied the shops with those objects of taste in millinery or artificial flowers for which their country is unrivalled'. Although Jane and Cassandra were no longer at the Abbey House by this date, this interesting information would have come to the Austen family in the columns of the local newspaper, the *Reading Mercury*.

In January 1793 Louis XVI of France was

guillotined. His queen, Marie Antoinette, soon followed him to the scaffold. The Comte de Feuillide, husband of Jane's cousin Eliza, was among the many who went to the guillotine in 1794. Eliza had earlier managed to escape to England, and was able to make a new home in London for herself and her little son, Hastings; but the Comte's cruel death brought the horrors of the revolution right into the peaceful rooms of Steventon rectory, leaving Jane with an abiding hatred of republican beliefs.

A few days after the death of the King, the new French Republic declared war on Britain, and for the next twenty years—half of Jane Austen's lifespan—battles were fought between all the European nations, by land and sea, across the globe from America to India. The outbreak of war changed the life of Jane's sister, Cassandra; she was engaged to be married to the Reverend Tom Fowle, one of her father's old pupils, but he went as chaplain with the British expeditionary force sent out to defend the West Indies in 1795, and died there of yellow fever. Cassandra never found anyone to replace Tom in her affections, and died an old maid fifty years later. Jane's brother Henry, who had originally intended to enter the Church like James, rushed to the defence of his country; he tried first to enter the regular army, but—perhaps in deference to his parents' wishes—settled instead for a lieutenancy in the Oxfordshire Militia, and for the next few years moved with his regiment round the coast of England, ready for defence in case of a cross-Channel attack.

At the turn of the new century there was a brief break in the hostilities between Britain and France,

44

when the Revolutionary Wars came to an end. In 1799 the young Corsican soldier Napoleon Bonaparte overthrew the republican government and seized power, calling himself First Consul of France. Napoleon assured Britain that he wished for peace. An armistice was agreed in the autumn of 1801, and the Peace of Amiens (named for the town where the treaty had been signed) was in force for the next eighteen months. The English started to demobilize their armed forces, and both Frank and Charles Austen signed off from their respective ships and were able to join their family in Bath for some months. Napoleon, however, used the time for rearming and declared war again in the spring of 1803, putting the south coast of England once more under threat of cross-Channel invasion—a threat not finally lifted until Admiral Nelson defeated the combined French and Spanish fleets at the Battle of Trafalgar in the autumn of 1805. The war in Europe continued until Napoleon's forced abdication in 1814, followed by a brief flare-up in the spring of 1815 that was finally quenched on the midsummer battlefield of Waterloo.

NORTH AMERICA IN THE NINETEENTH CENTURY
In 1811, while the Napoleonic Wars were at their height, resentment again arose between Britain and America over the fact that, while Britain was blockading all the European ports of those countries allied to the French cause, American trading ships—officially neutral—were trying to evade this blockade, and also encouraging British seamen to desert to them. There was a faction in the American government that wished to continue

45

territorial expansion and take Canada from Britain, and Florida from Spain, as well as ousting the western Indian tribes from the lands beyond the Mississippi; they were anti-British on the excuse that Britain was supporting the Indians. The views of this faction, plus others who felt genuine resentment over the Royal Navy's policy of stopping and searching American ships suspected of trading with France or of carrying deserters, led to America declaring war against Britain on 18 June 1812.

The Americans attacked Canada and captured York (as Toronto was then called), the capital of Upper Canada, on the shores of Lake Ontario, and the frontier war became a seesaw of raiding parties, with the British burning Washington in August 1814. The situation was again stalemate, and in December 1814 it was agreed by the Treaty of Ghent that both sides would revert to their pre-war territories. However, the battle of New Orleans was fought in January 1815 because the news of the cessation of hostilities had not yet reached America—the transatlantic crossing took at least six weeks. The boundary between the United States of America and Canada was finally agreed, in the middle of the nineteenth century, as being the 49th Parallel.

This war with America led to one of Jane Austen's rare political comments, in a letter to her friend Martha Lloyd:

[Henry's] veiw, & the veiw of those he mixes with, of Politics, is not chearful—with regard to an American war I mean;—they consider it as certain, & as what is to ruin

46

us. The Americans cannot be conquered, & we shall only be teaching them the skill in War which they may now want. We are to make them good Sailors & Soldiers, & gain nothing ourselves.—If we *are* to be ruined, it cannot be helped—but I place my hope of better things on a claim to the protection of Heaven, as a Religious Nation, a Nation inspite of much Evil improving in Religion, which I cannot beleive the Americans to possess.

OTHER CONTINENTS

Meanwhile, on the other side of the world, Australia was still largely unexplored. The Dutch had discovered much of the western and northern coasts in the 1640s, which they called New Holland. Captain Cook, for Britain, charted the eastern coast, and in 1770 he founded the new settlement of Botany Bay in what later became New South Wales. Following the American Declaration of Independence, it was no longer possible to punish British convicts by transporting them to North America; and after much discussion it was decided that they should go instead to New South Wales, to colonize this empty land that was rich in natural resources. On 13 May 1787, a convoy of nine ships, known in Australian history as the First Fleet, and carrying about 800 convicts, set out from Portsmouth under the leadership of Captain Arthur Philip, and disembarked at Sydney Cove on 26 January 1788. When the First Fleet returned to England, they brought the news that the settlers had discovered 'a creature there shaped like a hare, with short fore-legs, the hind-

47

legs much longer, as big as a sheep, called Kangouras, and eats like mutton'; and in May 1794, an advertisement appeared in the London *Times*: 'Lately arrived in the *Rose*, East Indiaman, a most wonderful living Male Elephant, and to be seen in a commodious room, over Exeter Change, in the Strand. Admittance 1 shilling each. Likewise is lately added to the Grand Menageries, as above, two very singular and most astonishing Kanguroos, male and female, from Botany Bay. Admittance 1 shilling.' When Cassandra was staying with Henry in London in February 1801, it would seem, from a reference in one of Jane's letters, that she visited the menagerie to see these exotic animals.

British colonization of the Indian subcontinent was already well advanced and going from strength to strength. The East India Company, originally a consortium of rich London merchants anxious to promote trade with the Far East, had established five settlements on the Indian coast in the previous century, serviced by their own private fleet of fast-sailing merchant ships—the 'East Indiamen' of the advertisement above. The Company's good relations with the local Moghul emperors allowed trade to develop and the settlements to thrive. Competition from the French and Spanish had been largely eliminated by the middle of the eighteenth century, and when the Moghul empire collapsed the vacuum in the power structure enabled three of the settlements—Calcutta, Madras and Bombay—to grow into large districts or presidencies, each of which maintained its own private army commanded by professionally trained British officers. India became known as the place where impoverished young men could go out as junior employees of the East India Company and, by trading privately in the intervals between fulfilling their paid duties, they stood a good chance of becoming very rich indeed. They would then be nicknamed a 'nabob' (a corruption of a Hindi word meaning a prince, or very rich man), and would return to England to buy a town house in London and an estate in the country, and so enter the ranks of landed gentry. The drawbacks to this happy pipedream were the long and dangerous sea voyages between Britain and India, and the high death-rate among Europeans living in the presidencies. It was a known, if unspoken, fact that in Calcutta a man could be ostensibly healthy in the morning, dead by nightfall and buried in the European cemetery the next day. It was also, of course, possible that riches might not after all materialize, as had been the case with Jane's uncle, Tysoe Hancock.

Africa, like Australia, was still largely unexplored, but the Dutch East India Company had created the settlement of Cape Colony on the tip of southern Africa, the Cape of Good Hope, and until the Suez Canal was constructed in the nineteenth century all ships making the months' long voyage to India or Australia had to stop off there for re-victualling. One of Cape Colony's products was the rare and excellent Constantia wine that is mentioned in *Sense and Sensibility*, when Mrs Jennings offers a glassful to the distraught Marianne Dashwood. The Colony was seized by the British in 1795, and eventually became a British possession in 1814. In 1796 Henry Austen was thinking of joining the newly raised 86th Regiment, which had been ordered to sail for the Cape and was stationed there for three years before going on to India. As Jane was hoping he would not succeed in this plan to join the regular Army and leave England, she must have been relieved when he entered the Oxfordshire Militia instead.

THE CHANGING ENGLISH COUNTRYSIDE
In George III's reign Great Britain was a cleaner, greener, quieter and more beautiful land than it is today. There are no official figures for the population during the eighteenth century, but it is estimated that in the 1760s the inhabitants of England, Scotland and Wales probably totalled some eight million, the bulk of whom lived in the countryside and were engaged in agriculture or related trades. In 1801 the first official census showed a figure of about ten million, with a further five million in Ireland, now joined to Great Britain by the Act of Union. London, as always, was the biggest city, with a population of just under one million, and a worldwide trade served by the sailing ships that anchored in the Thames at the Pool of London. Outside London the next biggest cities were the northern manufacturing towns of Liverpool, Manchester, Leeds and Sheffield, with Birmingham and the port of Bristol also growing fast. Between these urban centres lay many other smaller provincial cities and prosperous market towns, which served a network of villages; each village had its substantial mansion or manor house, its church and parsonage, its stone, brick or timbered farmhouses, wind- and water-mills, and a knot or straggle of cottages in a few narrow lanes, all surrounded by meadows and cornfields. Once a

week, on market days, the villagers and farmers would trudge or jog-trot their carts into the nearest town to sell their home produce, exchange local gossip, and perhaps seek new employment or—the younger ones—meet a potential marriage partner at the same time.

Between the villages there were still large areas of rough waste or common-land, purple with heather, golden with gorse, or green with marsh and scrub—though the growing enthusiasm amongst country squires for agricultural improvements meant that these wastes were gradually being enclosed by the planting of new hedgerows and strips of woodland and so brought into cultivation. Roads were unmetalled potholed tracks, blindingly dusty in summer, and rutted and muddy in winter. The ensuing difficulty in travelling meant that all these small communities were to a large extent isolated and self-sufficient.

TRAVEL AND TRANSPORT
Journeys were undertaken at an average speed of seven miles an hour, either on horseback or in a carriage drawn by one or more horses. The horse was the only motive power on the roads in Jane Austen's lifetime and for many years afterwards, and farmers, blacksmiths, farriers, saddlers and harness-makers, inn-keepers and coach-masters all provided for its needs and relied upon its strength. However, despite the proverbial phrase 'as strong as a horse', the animal is not in fact capable of sustaining exertion for any great length of time, and needs frequent pauses for rest and food. In *Northanger Abbey*, on the return from the second trip to Clifton, 'Mr Morland's horse was so tired he

51

could hardly get it along'; and when General Tilney and his party leave Bath for Northanger, 'they set off at the sober pace in which the handsome, highly-fed four horses of a gentleman usually perform a journey of thirty miles'—which journey has to be broken into two fifteen-mile stages with a two-hour rest at Petty France. At Mansfield Park Mrs Norris boasts of her kindness towards Sir Thomas's coach-horses: 'And when we got to the bottom of Sandcroft Hill, what do you think I did? You will laugh at me—but I got out and walked up. I did indeed. It might not be saving them much, but it was something, and I could not bear to sit at my ease, and be dragged up at the expense of those noble animals. I caught a dreadful cold, but *that* I did not regard.'

In this scene Mrs Norris also mentions the bad state of the roads between Mansfield and Sotherton, in the middle of winter: 'I thought we should never have got through them, though we had the four horses of course . . . when we got into the rough lanes about Stoke, where what with frost and snow upon beds of stones, it was worse than anything you can imagine. . . .' Road maintenance was then the responsibility of the parishes through which the road passed; local rates were raised for the purpose, and each year the parish had to appoint two officials, Surveyors of Highways, to supervise the works of maintenance and repair. In the past, parish councils had rightly complained that non-resident travellers added to the wear on the roads but contributed nothing towards their upkeep, and in the seventeenth century Turnpike Trusts were created as a means of combating this problem. A group of local gentlemen, the Trustees, would arrange for a stretch of the main road, where it passed through their parish, to be closed off at each end and at intermediate cross-roads by means of heavy gates (turnpikes), with a little toll-house beside each gate; anyone wishing to use that section of road had to pay a toll for the gate to be opened and the tolls collected were then used for the maintenance of the road. This system worked fairly well, and during the eighteenth century the quality of main roads gradually improved, thus enabling carriages to travel far more quickly and smoothly. Many of today's main roads still follow these turnpiked routes, now hidden under tarmac, and some toll houses survive at the roadside and can be identified by their large front windows, from where the gatehouse-keeper could look up and down the road and be ready for the passing traffic.

Country lanes, however, were still left unimproved, as Jane Austen's nephew, James-Edward Austen-Leigh, remembered, when he wrote in 1869:

The lane between Deane and Steventon has long been as smooth as the best turnpike road; but when the family removed from the one residence to the other in 1768, it was a mere cart-track so cut up by deep ruts as to be impassable for a light carriage. Mrs Austen, who was not then in strong health, performed the short journey on a feather bed placed upon some soft articles of furniture in the waggon which held their household goods. In those days it was not unusual to set men to work with shovel and pickaxe to fill up ruts and holes in roads seldom used by carriages, on such special occasions as a funeral or a wedding.

On the main roads the public conveyances were basically of three kinds: stage coaches, mail coaches and road-wagons. These last were vast and slow, creeping along at three miles an hour; with ten very broad wheels and pulled by eight horses, they carried heavy goods, luggage and those passengers too poor to pay for coach travel. Mail coaches, as their name implies, were run by the government as part of the general postal service. Their prime business was to carry the mailbags across the country, but they were allowed to take up to four passengers without personal luggage. They had four horses, were driven by a coachman with a guard sitting beside him and carrying a blunderbuss (large-bore short-barrelled shotgun) as a defence against highwaymen, had right of way on the road, and were expected to travel at never less than seven to eight miles an hour. In 1784 the mail coach service could do the 116-mile journey from London to Bath in less than thirteen hours, which was considered a really astonishing speed. During the French wars they were also used for the official dissemination of news: in 1801, when the Peace of Amiens was agreed, the coaches were placarded 'Peace with France', and the drivers all wore a sprig of laurel, as an emblem of peace, in their hats. On other occasions, to announce the news of British victories, the coaches were decorated with oak branches, laurels and ribbons.

Stage coaches were run by commercial firms; they were drawn by four or six horses, and were supposed to take six passengers inside and an unspecified number sitting on the roof, and there was also a very large wicker basket fixed to the back of the coach into which the passengers' luggage was placed. The passengers on the roof had no seats, but dangled their feet over the edge while holding on by a small ring or handle, bouncing around with every jolt; in 1782 one young German visitor, riding from Leicester to Northampton on the roof, was so frightened that he took the opportunity to crawl into the basket behind, along with the luggage. This, he soon found, was all right while the coach was going uphill, but downhill the trunks and parcels began to fall about and hit him until he got back on the roof—'quite shaken to pieces and sadly bruised'— as the lesser of two evils. There was no official limit to the number of people carried on top, and the top-heaviness of over-crowded coaches often led to accidents; in 1795 the Gosport coach was carrying eleven on the coach and box, plus the driver, and nine in the basket, when it overturned. Drunken sailors frequently fell off the roof, and in winter passengers on top might be found frozen to death at the end of a long cold journey; such calamities were reported in the newspapers with decent regret but no word of surprise.

The horses pulling these coaches also suffered greatly, and this, too, was taken as being a matter of course. Private gentlemen like Sir Thomas Bertram or General Tilney would treat their animals well, but the horses used in public service vehicles were regarded as so many machines, from which the greatest amount of energy had to be extracted in order to keep the coaches running to time. The horses were changed at every stage of the journey—distances about seven to ten miles apart—and were expected to work two stages a day, out and back to their own stable, with some rest days allowed. In practice, to pull a heavy-laden coach over rough roads and in all weathers while keeping to a strict time schedule meant constant whipping and utter exhaustion for the horses. On fast stages, like the Hartford Bridge Flats on the Hampshire/Surrey border, where the road was remarkably smooth and flat, the horses were expected to gallop for six or seven miles at a stretch, and the working life of a coach-horse was accepted as being no more than three years. In 1816 a firm of coach-masters set up in London to run a service to Brighton, fifty-two miles away, at a guaranteed travelling time of six hours, galloping all the way—but the firm folded after fifteen horses died in one week.

Travel by stage coach had other drawbacks besides the long, cold, jolting journeys, as a newspaper pointed out in 1791: 'By the common stage, you are classed with company of every description, and who may very frequently turn out very disagreeable. You are also paid no attention to at the inns where you stop, although you pay exorbitant for refreshment, and are frequently insulted by the indecent behaviour of the coachman . . . ' It was for these reasons that single ladies did not usually travel on stage coaches, and after Mr Austen's death in 1805 his sons had to make themselves available to escort their mother and sisters if so required. Towards the end of her life, in 1814, Jane Austen did go to London alone; but this was in the local Alton coach and some of

56

the other passengers were known to her, and she was able to assure Cassandra the next day that 'they were all very quiet & civil'.

The journalist of 1791 recommended as the alternative to the stage coach: 'If two or three passengers choose to travel together, they may, by travelling in a post-chaise, not only avoid all these inconveniences, but suit their own convenience in point of time, and be at less expence—besides meeting with genteeler treatment at the inns on the road.' Post-chaises were owned by innkeepers, who hired them out together with horses and postboys (postillions) to ride them; '. . . they are good carriages with four wheels, shut close . . . hold three persons in the back with ease; are narrow, extremely light, well hung, and appear the more easy, because the roads are not paved with stone . . . the postillions are not only civil but even respectful. . . .' Travelling post, however, was very expensive, as the rate was a minimum of one shilling per horse per mile, plus a tip to the postboy and tips to all the inn servants along the way. In *Sense and Sensibility*, when the Steele sisters travel from the West Country to London, Nancy, 'with quick exultation' tells Mrs Jennings: '. . . we came post all the way . . . Dr Davies was coming to town, and so we thought we'd join him in a post-chaise; and he behaved very genteelly, and paid ten or twelve shillings more than we did.'

For private owners there were as many different types of carriages available as there are cars today; and just as today people are judged by society according to whether they drive a Rolls-Royce, a Porsche, a BMW or a Volkswagen, so in Jane Austen's time the type of carriage a family used

57

clearly identified their place on the social ladder. 'Carriage' was the generic term, and other names—for example, coach, chaise, gig—were specific. They might have four wheels or two; have a completely solid body (a 'closed' carriage), have a solid body with a collapsible leather hood, or be without any form of hood or covering (an 'open' carriage); might be drawn by anything from one humble donkey up to six thoroughbred horses; and might be driven either by the owner or by a coachman or postillion. The heavily built coach, the oldest style of vehicle, and the largest and most expensive, could take up to six people inside, and so was the choice for family transport—the Bennets, the Bertrams and the Musgroves all have a coach, with a coachman to drive it. As roads improved, it became feasible to build smaller carriages: a chaise was much lighter and carried only three people, with a postillion riding the nearside horse; a chariot had the same body as a chaise, but was coachman-driven from a box-seat fixed on top of the body. The John Dashwoods have a chariot, as does the dowager Mrs Rushworth; and in 1784 Mr Austen bought a chariot for the benefit of his wife and daughters, which was sold in 1801 when the family left Steventon.

Of the other larger vehicles, the German landau, invented about 1800, was as big as a coach, but had a leather hood which opened in two halves from the centre; the landaulette was smaller, with the body of a chariot and a single hood which collapsed from front to back; the barouche, with a single hood, and carrying four people inside and two on the box, was likewise invented in Europe

58

and did not come to England until about 1800. Henry Crawford drives a barouche, and on the trip to Sotherton Court Aunt Norris, Fanny, Mary Crawford and Maria Bertram sit inside with the hood down, and Maria glowers jealously at the sight of Henry driving and flirting with Julia as she sits beside him on the box. In 1804 the barouche-landau was invented as a combination of the two carriages, and Mrs Elton constantly boasts that her rich brother-in-law Mr Suckling owns one, though we never actually see it arrive at the vicarage in Highbury; and Anne Elliot becomes 'the mistress of a very pretty landaulette' following her marriage to Captain Wentworth.

The small open carriages were owner-driven, and at the end of the eighteenth century the two-seater phaeton, or 'Highflyer', with a small body perched high above four large wheels and drawn by two or more horses, had been very popular with sporting young men who wished to display their skill at driving this dangerously designed vehicle. A lower-slung, less lethal but still very smart carriage was the two-wheeled two-horse curricle, and in Jane Austen's novels the richer of her young men drive curricles—Willoughby, Darcy, Henry Tilney, Rushworth. A gig—two wheels and one horse—was the cheaper small carriage used by most people, and the undergraduates James Morland and John Thorpe both drive them. John Thorpe boasts to Catherine about his second-hand gig, trying to pretend it is nearly as smart as a curricle: 'Well hung; town built; . . . curricle-hung you see; seat, trunk, sword-case, splashing-board, lamps, silver moulding, all you see complete; the iron-work as good as new, or better.' Ladies could drive a pony-phaeton (a small, low-slung and consequently much safer version of the 'Highflyer'), a gig, a whiskey (a small, lightly built gig, so called because it 'whisked' along), or the basic minimum of a donkey-cart. Mrs Gardiner looks forward to going round the park at Pemberley in 'a low phaeton, with a nice little pair of ponies'; and in real life the much less well-off Mrs Austen had a donkey cart to trot into Alton for shopping expeditions.

Travellers in open carriages were of course at the mercy of wind and weather, and Mrs Allen dislikes them because: 'A clean gown is not five minutes wear in them. You are splashed getting in and getting out; and the wind takes your hair and your bonnet in every direction.' In the next generation of fiction, Anne Brontë's unhappy governess Agnes Grey arrives at her employer's house after a long cold drive in a gig: 'I was somewhat dismayed at my appearance on looking in the glass—the cold wind had swelled and reddened my hands, uncurled and entangled my hair, and dyed my face of a pale purple; add to this my collar was horribly crumpled, my frock splashed with mud . . . .' Closed carriages could have every luxury the owner wished—hot bricks on the floor to keep feet warm, sheepskin rugs across the knees, and silver chamber pots for use on long journeys.

Road accidents were frequent. Even the slow broad-wheel wagons could have their calamities, for farmboys would ride on the shafts, and they might easily slip off and be crushed by the huge wheels behind. If a frightened saddle horse bolted uncontrollably there were two options for a rider— to jump off and hope to fall lightly, or to hang on and hope to be flung clear when the horse itself crashed. Jane Austen's great friend Madam Lefroy of Ashe was killed in 1804 when she threw herself off a runaway horse. When horses were harnessed to a carriage, it was easy enough for them to overturn it through fright or bad temper, and a Scottish girl remembered the constant trouble they had with their four handsome carriage-horses, two bays and two greys. They worked very well once started, but to make the start was the difficulty. One bay merely indulged in a few plunges, but the other regularly lay down, and it took all the ostlers and half the post-boys at every inn, with plentiful applications of a long whip, to bring him to his feet again; he was cured of this trick afterwards by having lighted straw put under him. The two greys were merely awkward, one setting out to the right and the other to the left, instead of going straight forward—and to add to the tumult her nervous mother kept screaming at the top of her voice all the time, standing up and trying to unlock the carriage door to get out.

In October 1806 there was a fatal accident at Leatherhead in Surrey, and the Austens would have read the inquest report in the *Hampshire Chronicle*. The Princess of Wales and two of her ladies-in-waiting, Lady Sheffield and Miss Harriet Cholmondeley, had been visiting Surrey and were returning to London in an open barouche-landau, the impatient Princess urging the post-boys who drove the four horses to travel at top speed. The horses took a corner too fast and too wide, the off-wheels ran up the roadside bank and the carriage overturned. The three ladies were flung out; Miss Cholmondeley was picked up bleeding copiously from mouth and ears and died a few minutes later. As Leatherhead is said to have been the basis for Jane Austen's fictional Highbury, this accident may have some echo in Mr Woodhouse's dread of the dangerous corner at the turning into Vicarage Lane.

Another hazard on the road was that of robbery; during the summer of 1793 a highwayman was hiding in the woods in the neighbourhood of Overton, only a few miles from Steventon, and for several months robbed passing carriages or late-night travellers. He was never caught, but the offer of a large reward had the effect of making him leave the district. The Austens would have been well aware of this local danger, because their friend Mrs Bramston of Oakley Hall was robbed when driving home on the night of 6 June; she later wrote: 'I have been very much frightend lately, by being Stopd returning from drinking tea with Mrs Lefroy, by a footpad, who put his pistol Close to me & said he would blow out my Brains if I did not give him my Money I lost 8 Guineas which I did not like at all, beside its having made my head Ache ever since & I now Start at my own Shadow but am getting better . . . .'

SPAS, TOURING AND PICNICS

For those who felt that the risks and discomforts of travel were outweighed by the benefit of change from their own surroundings, or believed their health required a course of spa therapy or sea bathing, there were a variety of options available. One of the earliest ideas for a holiday, dating back to the sixteenth century, was that of travelling round to visit other people's country houses; and since the outbreak of war with France in 1793 had made the Grand Tour impossible, the would-be tourist now looked inland and started to admire the scenery of the United Kingdom instead, particularly the hills and mountains of Wales, the north of England and Scotland. It therefore became an accepted arrangement to make a tour to these beauty spots with country house visits on the way, and this is what the Gardiners do, taking Elizabeth Bennet with them. Their first plan had been to go to the Lake District, but it turns out that Mr Gardiner's business commitments mean that there is no time to go further north than Derbyshire, and they have to content themselves with 'the celebrated beauties of Matlock, Chatsworth, Dovedale, or the Peak'—and, of course, Pemberley. Elizabeth is embarrassed at the thought and tries to evade this visit: 'She felt that she had no business at Pemberley, and was obliged to assume a disinclination for seeing it. She must own that she was tired of great houses; after going over so many, she really had no pleasure in fine carpets or satin curtains'—but once she has learnt from the chambermaid in the inn at Bakewell that the Darcy family are not yet 'down for the summer' from London, she agrees with her aunt's wish to make the visit; and, in the course of their tour of the house guided by Mrs Reynolds, the house-keeper, hears much about Mr Darcy's kindness.

Of the mineral water spas, Bath was the oldest, and the one best known to Jane Austen as she had actually lived there; but when she and her parents visited Kent in 1788 they may perhaps have spent a day or two at Tunbridge Wells on the way. These wells, famous for their iron-impregnated water, had first become known in the seventeenth century, but the spa-town did not grow up around them until much later. The springs here were not thermal, and not nearly so copious as those at Bath; hence the water was used for medicinal drinking rather than bathing. Nevertheless, Tunbridge Wells had all the necessary spa attributes of assembly rooms, theatre, libraries, luxury shops, paved promenades and a bandstand in the centre of the little town, as well as elegant lodging-houses and pretty walks and rides, and the advantage of being only thirty-six miles south of London. It had been very fashionable in the middle of the eighteenth century, but was now starting to decline as the fashion leaders moved elsewhere. Mrs Thorpe, the not very rich widow from Putney—then a village on the southern outskirts of London—brings her daughters here, and Isabella can awe the naive Catherine by her ability to compare the balls of Bath with those of Tunbridge. The town also had its own souvenir industry, 'Tunbridge ware'—trinkets decorated with patterns or pictures made in coloured woods such as cherry, plum or yew. Harriet Smith keeps her *Most precious treasures* concerning Mr Elton in a 'pretty little Tunbridge-ware box'.

Other inland spas were created during the eighteenth century, whenever some enterprising landowner found a spring on his property and claimed that the water had medicinal properties, and they all had their periods of local fashion and prosperity. Clifton, on the outskirts of Bristol, had its hot wells, the waters obviously coming from the same underground source as those at nearby Bath;

but Clifton's popularity waned when it was realized that the hot wells might be contaminated by Bristol's sewage. Cheltenham and nearby Leamington were growing in popularity in Jane Austen's day, and when she felt herself ailing in 1816 she went for three weeks to Cheltenham to drink its waters. For those who lived further north, a trip to the warm waters of Matlock or Buxton in Derbyshire might be more convenient than a longer journey to Bath. In the early nineteenth century the Duke of Devonshire started to develop the village of Buxton by building an enormous crescent containing three hotels and all other tourist amenities.

However, the medical belief now was that sea air and bathing in salt water would cure many diseases, and seaside resorts were becoming more popular than inland spas. The warm climate of the Dorset and South Devon coast led to the growth of Weymouth, Lyme Regis and Sidmouth in particular, with the smaller villages of Dawlish, Teignmouth and Torquay doing their best to catch up. Weymouth became fashionable, and consequently expensive, in the 1780s, when the Royal Family first visited the town. Fanny Burney in her diary reported the King's holiday there in 1789:

> The loyalty of all this place is excessive; they have dressed out every street with labels of 'God save the King'; all the shops have it over the doors; all the children wear it in their caps—all the labourers in their hats, and all the sailors *in their voices*; for they never approach the house without shouting

it aloud—nor see the King, or his shadow, without beginning to huzza, and going on to three cheers. The bathing-machines made it their motto over all their windows; and those bathers that belong to the royal dippers wear it in bandeaux on their bonnets, to go into the sea; and have it again, in large letters, round their waists, to encounter the waves. . . . Nor is this all. Think but of the surprise of His Majesty when, the first time of his bathing, he had no sooner popped his royal head under water than a band of music, concealed in a neighbouring machine, struck up 'God save great George our King'.

Weymouth was still fashionable in the early nineteenth century, and it is here that Tom Bertram strikes up a friendship with the frivolous Mr Yates.

The most famous seaside resort in Sussex was then and is still Brighton, originally called Brighthelmstone, which at the end of the eighteenth century was only a fishing village; it began to develop in the 1750s when its local resident Dr Russell wrote a book advocating sea-bathing, and then rocketed into fashion and popularity when the Prince of Wales chose the village as a holiday resort and spent several decades there, building and rebuilding what had originally been a large farmhouse until he had succeeded in converting it into his vision of an Oriental palace, the exotic Brighton Pavilion. Other villages on the Sussex coast followed Brighton's example, though on a smaller scale and without the benefit of royal patronage, and by the beginning of the nineteenth century the less-wealthy visitor to Sussex could choose between Hastings, Eastbourne, Bognor, Littlehampton and Worthing for a seaside holiday. Jane herself stayed for some weeks in Worthing, in the autumn of 1805, and her memories of this holiday, plus visits to the Kentish resort of Ramsgate in earlier years, no doubt gave her the local colour for the creation of *Sanditon*.

On the colder Kent coast, Margate was the first place to use bathing-machines, in 1750; and soon the neighbouring Ramsgate overtook Margate to become the most fashionable of the Kentish seaside bathing places; it is to Ramsgate that Tom Bertram goes for a week in September, to walk on the pier and stay with his friends the Sneyds in the newly built Albion Place on the top of the cliffs. There were also budding resorts on the East Anglian coast, and Mr John Knightley takes his family to Southend in Essex, only 40 miles from London, rather than Cromer in Norfolk which is 130.

A change of scene could be enjoyed for less time and money by shorter day trips and picnics in the neighbourhood, though in Jane Austen's novels such picnics always seem to result in disappointment. Sir John Middleton delighted in them: '. . . in summer he was for ever forming parties to eat cold ham and chicken out of doors . . .' and one of these is planned for Whitwell, '. . . a very fine place about twelve miles from Barton, belonging to a brother-in-law of Colonel Brandon . . . The grounds were declared to be highly beautiful, and Sir John, who was particularly warm in their praise, might be allowed to be a tolerable judge, for he had formed parties to visit them, at least twice every summer for the last ten years. They contained a noble piece of water; a sail on which was to form a great part of the morning's amusement; cold provisions were to be taken, open carriages only to be employed, and every thing conducted in the usual style of a complete party of pleasure'—but this party has to be cancelled at the last minute when Colonel Brandon is called away to London. The first trip by the Thorpes and Morlands to Clifton and Blaise Castle has to be abandoned halfway there for lack of time, to everyone's annoyance; the visit by the Bertrams and Crawfords to Sotherton Court leads towards Maria's seduction by Henry; the strawberry-picking party in the gardens of Donwell Abbey leads to a secret quarrel between Frank Churchill and Jane Fairfax, and the picnic to Box Hill the next day ends for Emma literally in tears; while the trip from Uppercross to Lyme, which was intended to be merely an overnight stay, ends in disaster the following morning with Louisa's accident on the Cobb.

LONDON
It was the custom for the landed gentry to stay in London for some part of the winter season—roughly January to April—'for a few weeks' annual enjoyment of the great world', as do Sir Walter and Elizabeth Elliot; though on the other hand Lady Bertram, 'in consequence of a little ill-health, and a great deal of indolence, gave up the house in town, which she had been used to occupy every spring, and remained wholly in the country . . .'

The Austens had neither the money nor the inclination to participate in the smart London season, and in consequence Jane's knowledge of London was limited to the districts where there were already family connections. Her first trip to the city was probably with her parents in 1788, when they called upon Mr Austen's sister Philadelphia Hancock, who was living in Marylebone, then the northern outskirts of London; in later years Jane went to stay with her brother Henry, who had his banking premises in the central commercial district of Covent Garden, and who lived at different times in Brompton and Chelsea, then separate villages on the south-western side of the city.

In Jane's lifetime London was still a compact entity, and its limits could practically all be seen from the topmost gallery of St Paul's Cathedral: it was bounded on the west by Park Lane and the Edgware Road, and the West End or Mayfair district began at Hyde Park Corner and was bordered by Hyde Park on one side and Piccadilly and Green Park on the other. Bond Street, Piccadilly, the Mall and St James's Street had the finest shops and were the smartest streets in which to stroll, and fashionable young men were referred to as 'Bond Street loungers'. St James's Palace, the King's official London residence, was an unimpressive, rambling old Tudor building of smoke-stained brick; Buckingham House was also used by the Royal Family, but this too was small and rather old-fashioned, not yet enlarged and re-built into the royal residence which it now is. Not far away the Prince of Wales had his own London residence at Carlton House, which Jane visited in 1815 at the Prince's invitation.

From Westminster the riverside was built up along to Billingsgate and the docks in the east, then northwards to the City Road and the Marylebone Road and so back to the Edgware Road. On the north-east side of the City housing was creeping out towards the villages of Islington and Hackney, and a foreign visitor noticed: 'Many of the new houses are inhabited by bankers and rich merchants, who establish themselves there, with their families, they however keep their counting houses in the city, where they transact business . . . their daily journeys, a distance sometimes of several miles, would appear insupportable in any other country, but it agrees very well with the active habits so common to all classes of the English nation.' It was not only the active habits of the rich merchants that led them to live several miles away from their counting houses in the City, but the fact that so many of the urban trades produced noise, smoke and nauseating stenches. In the early nineteenth century, in Goswell Street, not far north of the City proper, all the following offensive trades or businesses were operating within a circumference of two hundred yards: manufacturers of Prussian blue dye, soap lees man, soap boiler, tallow melter, dye house with steam engine, burying ground, night man, horse boiler, drug grinder, starch maker, skinner's distillery, two or three hog butchers and a soda manufactory. The burying ground would probably have been no more than a tiny patch of earth barely covering the uncoffined bodies of beggars; the night-soil man stored barrels of human excrement scraped out of neighbouring cesspits, before selling them on as agricultural manure; most of the other trades were concerned in the rendering down of rotting animal carcasses into their component parts of hair, hides, fat and bones. The boiling down of fat to produce the tallow that was then re-melted and turned into either candles or soap was considered to produce the most disagreeable smell of all.

In the smart West End of London new residential development was constantly in progress, creating the symmetrical terraces, squares and crescents of the Georgian and Regency periods. Such new houses were all of the same basic layout, which had proved to be admirably suited for urban living; the typical site was a terrace, made up of long narrow strips of ground running back from the street, with the house in front, a garden or courtyard in the middle, and a coach-house and stable at the far end, served by a subsidiary lane parallel to the front street. (This subsidiary lane, together with the accommodation for horses and carriages, was collectively described as 'the mews'.) The house was set back from the roadway by the basement area which gave light to the kitchen windows and opened on to storage vaults underneath the pavement. Whatever the size of the house, the basic plan was always the same—one room at the back and one at the front on each floor, with a passage and staircase at one side. At the lower levels of basement, ground and first floors there might be a second back room extending into the garden space, making the plan L-shaped rather than simply rectangular. European visitors, who were more accustomed to living horizontally, in flats or apartments, were puzzled by the English

71

insistence upon building vertically: 'These narrow houses, three or four storeys high—one for eating, one for sleeping, a third for company, a fourth underground for the kitchen, a fifth perhaps at top for the servants—and the agility, the ease, the quickness with which the individuals of the family run up and down, and perch on the different storeys—give the idea of a cage with its sticks and birds.'

These foreign visitors were however impressed by the wide, straight streets, flanked by footpaths paved with broad flagstones that were evenly laid and constantly swept; rainwater was not allowed to flood the gutters but was channelled from roofs into downpipes and so into the great common sewer under the middle of the street, and there were paved crossings from one side of the street to the other. On both sides of the street were posts upon which oil lamps were hung—these were numerous and always lit before sunset. Oxford Street was particularly admired by visitors, and one kindly German lady described it when she wrote home to her children as:

> a street taking half an hour to cover from end to end, with double rows of brightly shining lamps, in the middle of which stands an equally long row of beautifully lacquered coaches, and on either side of these there is room for two coaches to pass one another . . . the pavement can stand six people deep and allows one to gaze at the splendidly lit shop fronts in comfort . . . first one passes a watchmaker's, then a silk or fan store, now a silversmith's, a china or glass shop . . .

confectioners and fruiterers . . . pyramids of pineapples, figs, grapes, oranges and all manner of fruits are on show . . . right through the excellently illuminated shop one can see many a charming family scene enacted: some are still at work, others drinking tea . . . entertaining a friendly visitor . . . joking and playing with their children.

Oxford Street also contained the huge hall called the Pantheon, as its façade was copied from the Pantheon in Rome. It had been erected in 1771 at a cost of £90,000, and was famous for its balls and riotous masquerades; the Georgian building has long since disappeared, but the site today is still known as the Pantheon, and a modern building now houses a Marks & Spencer store.

There were three large theatres in London at that time—the King's Theatre in the Haymarket, the Theatre Royal in Drury Lane and the Opera House in Covent Garden—and the smaller Lyceum in the Strand. Whenever Jane stayed with Henry, he always took her to the theatre, and her letters mention most of the best actors and singers of the day. The play *Lovers' Vows*, which Jane uses to such good effect in *Mansfield Park*, had first been performed at Covent Garden in October 1798 and remained very popular for some time thereafter, but it is not known when Jane herself actually saw it. Astley's Amphitheatre, where John Knightley takes his family together with Robert Martin and Harriet Smith, was open during the summer months and housed an equestrian circus.

If walking, shopping and theatre-going proved

too exhausting, a pastrycook's shop could offer refreshment: at one near Leicester Square the walls were covered with glass cases, 'in which all kinds of preserved fruits and jellies are exhibited in handsome glass jars; in the middle of the shop, however, there stood a big table with a white cover containing pyramids of small pastries and tartlets and some larger pastries and sweetmeats; wine glasses of all sizes, with lids to them, and full of liqueurs of every conceivable brand, colour and taste were attractively set out in between ...'

On the western outskirts of London was the village of Kensington, where in the seventeenth century William III had lived in the small Kensington Palace, as an escape from the smoke and smells of London itself. George III did not use this royal residence, and so was agreeable to allowing the public to walk in the gardens, which again delighted the foreign visitor:

... many other people were strolling in the spacious gardens, daily open to all, by the King's good grace. Here one may wander between tall trees and lovely shrubs, or by the pond over hilly ground, or across meadows, book in hand, towards a resting place where charming vistas of near and distant verdure, or flower beds, alternate with the instructive pleasure of reading. Many inhabitants of London who have no country seats of their own, in summer move into Kensington houses for the sake of the good air, the gardens and the fine prospect.

In *Sense and Sensibility*, the only one of Jane's

novels in which any part of the action takes place in London, Mrs Jennings and Elinor Dashwood walk in Kensington Gardens one fine Sunday in March; and Jane Austen herself mentions in a letter in April 1811 that she had had a pleasant walk in the Gardens—'everything was fresh & beautiful'.

SOCIAL RANKS

The nobility and gentry of English society fell into an order of precedence, descending from the King, which had developed over many hundreds of years. The hereditary peers of the realm came first under the monarch—dukes, marquises, earls, viscounts and barons. Then came the baronets, whose titles were hereditary but who were not ranked as peers and so could not sit in the House of Lords, the Upper Chamber of Parliament. Below them were the knights, whose titles were not hereditary, as the honour of knighthood was bestowed upon one particular man for some special reason; and finally the landed gentry—the untitled country squires of varying degrees of wealth and gentility.

It was said that there were the great who lived profusely, the rich who lived plentifully and the middle class who lived well. The richest group of landowners, invariably titled, were nicknamed the Upper Ten Thousand; their members went into Parliament, kept town houses in London and took the lead in their several societies. The lesser landed proprietors, who might have no more than a thousand acres, seldom went further from home than their county town, like Mr Musgrove in *Persuasion*, but each was the leader in his own parish.

This middle class of lesser landed gentry shaded into the professional classes—soldiers, sailors, clerics, lawyers, doctors—and below them were the urban merchants, farmers and wealthy tradesmen, who could always hope that their businesses would prosper to an extent where they, too, could purchase a country estate and rise in the world to become landed gentry. Such farmers and tradesmen were usually looked down upon by the established gentry: in *Emma*, Emma thinks that as Robert Martin grows older 'He will be a completely gross, vulgar farmer—totally inattentive to appearances, and thinking of nothing but profit and loss', and she disapproves of the Cole family because 'they were of low origin, in trade, and only moderately genteel'. Tradesmen in particular were seen as being 'muckworms', supposedly vulgar in thought and speech, unwashed—'smelling of the shop'—uneducated, and badly dressed. But as English society has always been fluid, within a generation or two of amassing wealth, purchasing an estate and acquiring education, such lower-class origins could easily be forgotten. Indeed the Coles, having done well in their business, are already living in a style second only to that of Emma and her father. When Jane Austen came to write her novels, she never attempted to portray any landowner of higher rank than Mr Darcy, the grandson of an earl, nor anyone richer than the foolish Mr Rushworth, with his £12,000 a year income from the Sotherton Court estate. She herself was of the middle rank and knew it, and drew pen-pictures of that same middle-rank society which she saw around her— the country baronets, squires and parsons.

MASCULINE OCCUPATIONS

Most of the leading male characters in Jane Austen's novels are landed gentry, and in the Georgian period it was accepted that of the several sons of a family the eldest son inherited the paternal estate intact, and the second son could hope to inherit some land or money from his mother's side of the family. All other younger sons, and the second son if he had no inheritance, would have to make their own way in the world, and would be expected to do so by entering the Navy or the Army, taking Holy Orders, or being called to the Bar, in roughly that order of choice. Gentlemen could become physicians and surgeons, but apothecaries and attorneys were definitely lower class. To be a banker or rich merchant—say in the East India Company—was acceptable, but nothing further down the commercial scale would do; Bingley's sisters, having been to their smart ladies' seminary in London, are desperately trying to forget that 'their brother's fortune and their own had been acquired by trade', and laugh snobbishly at the idea that Jane Bennet has one uncle who is an attorney in Meryton and another who is a London merchant living near Cheapside: the City of London was held to be the very centre of vulgarity.

Estate management in itself could be a full-time occupation for a gentleman, and this is seen most clearly in the case of Mr Knightley and his Donwell Abbey lands.

> As a magistrate, he had generally some point
> of law to consult John about, or, at least,

some curious anecdote to give; and as a farmer, as keeping in hand the home-farm at Donwell, he had to tell what every field was to bear next year . . . the plan of a drain, the change of a fence, the felling of a tree, and the destination of every acre for wheat, turnips, or spring corn . . . of moving the path to Langham, of turning it more to the right that it may not cut through the home meadows . . .

His tenant at Abbey Mill Farm, young Robert Martin, comes to him for advice regarding marriage with Harriet Smith, and he is also required to join Mr Elton, Mr Weston and Mr Cole at the regular parish meetings, held at the Crown in Highbury, to deal with local government business.

The larger landowners would delegate the day-to-day business of farming and parish politics to a bailiff or steward, but it was still incumbent upon them to give personal attention to the well-being of their dependants on the estate. Mr Darcy is said by his housekeeper Mrs Reynolds to be '. . . the best landlord, and the best master, that ever lived. Not like the wild young men now-a-days, who think of nothing but themselves. There is not one of his tenants or servants but what will give him a good name.' General Tilney, though not a kind-hearted man, nevertheless accepts the responsibilities of owning 'as considerable a landed property as any private man in the county' by keeping his estate well-managed, employing many of his villagers and providing them with the most up-to-date working conditions in the servants' quarters of Northanger

Abbey.

In real life, the Duke of Devonshire in his palatial Chatsworth had a household of 180 persons, for whose sustenance on average five bullocks and fifteen sheep were killed every week, and he paid £5 a year in pensions to every poor family in the neighbourhood. In the winter, when there was less work in connection with crops and flocks, it was the mark of a good landowner to find something else for his labourers to do that would keep them gainfully employed; and when the weather grew bad and fuel was scarce, the landowner would use his large kitchens to cook thick soup for regular distribution to the poorest villagers. The Austens' friend Mrs Chute of the Vyne noted in her diary every year the purchase of vast quantities of beef, potatoes and peas for this purpose.

Apart from seeing that the farms on his estate were in the hands of efficient tenants, the eighteenth-century owner might spend much thought and money upon landscaping the park— that area of land immediately surrounding the manor house or mansion. In the previous century this ground had been laid out with geometrically patterned beds of flowers, shrubs or evergreens divided by gravel paths and surrounded by clipped yew or box hedges, often with a small canal—an area of ornamental water—symmetrically in the centre, and the whole enclosed by high brick walls. Beyond the walls, avenues of trees planted in straight lines would radiate from the house in several directions. The park and gardens of Mr Rushworth's Sotherton Court seem to be of this date and style.

By the middle of the eighteenth century this geometric formality was seen as old-fashioned, and when the landscape gardener Lancelot 'Capability' Brown (1715–83), so nicknamed because of his favourite phrase that a garden or park had 'great capability of improvement', was called in, he swept away the parterres and smoothed the land out, bringing bare grassy lawns right up to the windows of the house, with clumps and belts of trees to provide a changing series of views. This extreme simplicity, however, could result in large handsome stone mansions appearing to be set incongruously in the midst of bleak open fields. In the next generation Humphrey Repton (1752–1818) believed that a house should be an integral part of its landscape. He reintroduced parterres and terraces near the buildings, and created visual interest by planting shrubs on bare riverbanks and cutting peepholes in belts of trees to provide vistas through. At Adlestrop in Gloucestershire, where Jane Austen's Leigh cousins lived, Repton merged the hundred-acre park of Adlestrop House with the garden of the adjoining rectory; the entrance to the rectory was moved and a road diverted, and '. . . a lively stream of water has been led through a flower garden, where its progress down the hill is occasionally obstructed by ledges of rock . . . it falls into a lake at a considerable distance, but in full view both of the mansion and the parsonage, to each of which it makes a delightful, because a natural, feature in the landscape'.

NAVAL AND MILITARY LIFE

During the eighteenth century the British Royal Navy had become the best in the world, an island nation's symbol of security and prosperity, and popularly regarded as invincible. British ships sailed all the oceans—from Canada via the Caribbean to South America, end to end of the Mediterranean, and round the Cape of Good Hope to India and China—defending and enlarging colonial trade, and always, of course, patrolling the Channel to ensure that no invader dared to cross this temptingly narrow strip of sea. Life at sea was hard and dangerous for the sailors of any nation, and more men died of disease than were killed in action, but overall the British Navy had better ships, officers and crews than any other European power, and it was the firm popular belief that one British sailor was a match for half a dozen Frenchmen.

Younger sons of the landed gentry, and other adventurous boys like William Price, seized the opportunities afforded by the Revolutionary and Napoleonic Wars to join the Navy in the hope of gaining both honours and prize-money. The official arrangement was that any hostile ship which the Navy captured, together with its cargo, was sold to the British Government, and the proceeds were divided amongst the victorious crew. Captains and admirals could certainly expect to grow rich, and even the lower deck could gain appreciable sums. Captain Wentworth, by 1814, has amassed prize money to the sum of £25,000, and so is able to contemplate buying his own landed property and living in married comfort thereafter. Admiral Croft, too, has a sufficient fortune to plan on buying some estate in Somerset, and so rents Kellynch Hall while he looks around the county to choose at his leisure. Admiral

81

Crawford had evidently been a younger son of the previous generation, since it is his nephew Henry who inherited the family property of Everingham while still a schoolboy.

Jane Austen's brothers Frank and Charles were away on active service for many years during this wartime period, Frank in the Mediterranean and the Baltic, and Charles first of all in home waters and then in the West Indies; and both, in due course and long after her death, rose to become admirals. While in Spain and in pre-revolutionary France naval officers had to be members of the nobility, in England rank and promotion could be gained by men of much humbler origin; it was well known that Admiral Nelson's father was a country parson in Norfolk. As the loving and admiring sister of naval officers, when Jane Austen came to write *Persuasion* she must have enjoyed making Sir Walter Elliot display his conceit and stupidity by saying that the Navy was '. . . the means of bringing persons of obscure birth into undue distinction, and raising men to honours which their fathers and grandfathers never dreamt of . . . A man is in greater danger in the Navy of being insulted by the rise of one whose father, *his* father might have disdained to speak to . . .'

In peacetime the regular, or standing Army, was always deliberately kept small in order to reduce governmental expenditure, and by the 1790s it had dwindled to something like fifteen thousand men in the United Kingdom and another thirty thousand serving overseas. As there was then no civil police force, the Army was sometimes used also to restore order in the streets if unruly mobs rioted—as Henry Tilney teased his sister and

Catherine Morland:

> . . . she immediately pictured to herself a mob of three thousand men assembling in St. George's Fields; the Bank attacked, the Tower threatened, the streets of London flowing with blood, a detachment of the 12th Light Dragoons (the hopes of the nation), called up from Northampton to quell the insurgents, and the gallant Capt. Frederick Tilney, in the moment of charging at the head of his troop, knocked off his horse by a brickbat from an upper window.

Apart from the London-based fashionable regiments of the Household Cavalry—the Lifeguards, who formed the Sovereign's Escort, and the Royal Regiment of Horse Guards (the Blues)—the Army was not so highly regarded for a career as the Navy. The Royal Military Academy at Woolwich, on the outskirts of London, had been founded in 1741 for the military education of gentleman cadets, and is mentioned in *Mansfield Park*, when Mrs Price wonders if Sir Thomas Bertram can arrange for William to be admitted to the Academy—but presumably Sir Thomas finds it simpler to send William off to sea. Promotion in the Army depended less upon ability than upon 'influence'—that is, favouritism—and money. Commissions could be bought and sold like any other commodity, irrespective of the age and capability of the young men concerned, and some rich fathers bought their sons commissions while they were still at school, in order that the pay should be their pocket money. The rank and file were largely recruited from the rogues and vagabonds who could settle to no other useful trade—as the Duke of Wellington later said, from the scum of the earth. However, the King's second son, the Duke of York, presently became Commander-in-Chief, and he used his administrative abilities to correct abuses and increase recruiting at this time of emergency, when England was threatened by a French invasion.

The militia regiments, which were only called up when hostilities threatened, were recruited on a county basis, and were intended purely for home defence, not being obliged to serve abroad as was the regular Army. There was no formal conscription, but each village was supposed to supply a certain quota of able-bodied men for its local militia force, to serve as long as the emergency might require. Most of the officers were drawn from the younger sons of the local gentry, and the colonel was usually some landowner of the county. The militia was called up now in 1792 and the regiments were deployed along the south and east coast of England, and in Ireland as well, when it seemed likely that the French might invade there. In the summer months the troops lived in tented camps in the open countryside, and in the winter they were quartered wherever accommodation could be found for them in the nearby towns and villages.

It is the arrival of a militia regiment in Hertfordshire that starts to thicken the plot of *Pride and Prejudice*, and no doubt Jane was aided in her composition of this novel by her brother Henry's tales of his service with the Oxfordshires. As public relations exercises, to demonstrate to the civilian populace how efficiently they were being defended, every so often the militia would be paraded for review by a visiting general, and would spend a day marching, drilling and firing at targets, or engaging in mock skirmishes. These reviews were held on some open hillside or common land, and made thrilling entertainment for the local residents; hence Mr Bennet sardonically promises Kitty: 'If you are a good girl for the next ten years, I will take you to a review at the end of them.'

The Volunteers, first raised in 1794, were a second line of home defence, composed of those men who could not serve full-time but were prepared to undertake some weeks of military training and guard duties every summer. In 1804, when there was another invasion scare, Jane's brother Edward Knight formed his villagers into the Godmersham & Molash Company of the East Kent Volunteers, and went off with them to take their turn in guarding the Channel coastline.

CLERICAL LIFE

In the eighteenth century there was no need for a young man to feel that he had a vocation for a clerical life—to be a clergyman in the Church of England was viewed merely as a suitable profession for an educated gentleman, and the main problem was to find a parish rich enough to enable the parson to live like any other country landowner. At that time there were no fixed salaries for the clergy, whose income had instead to be made up from several sources—mainly from tithe payments (the right of the parson to receive one-tenth of the annual gross product of all the cultivated land in the parish) and the produce of farming their own glebe lands (an area of land belonging to the church to be used for the benefit of the incumbent), with surplice fees (customary payments for baptisms, marriages and burials) in addition. Small rural parishes could offer only very humble monetary rewards—in the 1770s the Steventon living was valued at £100 p.a. and Deane at £110, and as the parishes were adjoining, Mr Austen had the Archbishop of Canterbury's approval to hold them in plurality—that is, be rector of both of them at the same time. He used his own education and augmented his income by taking pupils into his home at Steventon, tutoring them in Greek and Latin with a view to university entrance later on.

A clergyman was not expected to devote himself full-time to his duties, as the basic requirements were only that he should attend his church on Sundays to take morning and evening service, with or without preaching a sermon, and that he should hold Holy Communion services at least three times a year. Weddings and funerals could be arranged also for Sundays, though baptisms of sickly infants sometimes needed to be carried out more urgently. Visiting the sick was expected, and also attendance at the formal parish meetings held at Eastertime and at irregular intervals during the rest of the year, when all the local landholders were supposed to assemble to settle clerical and parish business matters.

In practice, the advowson (the right of presenting a clergyman to a living) was viewed as a form of property ('an incorporeal hereditament' was the technical term), and as such could be bought and sold between gentlemen in order to provide for their sons and nephews. This led to advertisements such as one in *Jackson's Oxford Journal*:

> To be sold by Auction by Hoggart and Phillips, Old Broad Street, London: the next presentation to a most valuable living in one of the finest sporting counties. The vicinity affords the best coursing in England, also excellent fishing, extensive cover for game, and numerous packs of fox-hounds, harriers, etc. The surrounding country is beautiful and healthy and the society elegant and fashionable.'

Not surprisingly, young clerics in such livings as these, 'buckish' parsons as they were called, spent most of their time in field sports, paying a curate a minimal wage to carry out the essential duties.

Mr Austen was undoubtedly a good and conscientious parson, who took his duties seriously and was hardly ever absent from his parishes, and on the whole the Hampshire clerics of Jane's time seem to have been quite adequately virtuous to suit their calling. Elsewhere, however, there could be found clergymen so feeble as to be inaudible in church and incapable of visiting their parishioners; so deranged as to shut themselves up in the parsonage and never be seen at all; or so drunken as to be discovered on Sunday mornings lying under the gooseberry bushes in the garden while the bells were ringing for church. It was in reaction to this kind of neglect and abuse of clerical duties that the Wesley brothers, John and Charles, started their campaign for Evangelical Revival, which later in the eighteenth century came to be nicknamed

'Methodism'.

The clerics in Jane Austen's novels demonstrate the Church of England as she saw it at this period: Edward Ferrars drifts into ordination as a last resort, and is very lucky that Colonel Brandon comes to his rescue by presenting him to the living of Delaford, small though it is; Mr Collins, having been presented to Hunsford by Lady Catherine, considers his prime duty is to flatter her, with parochial duties taking second place; Henry Tilney sees no need to spend more than two or three days a week in his family living at Woodston. In the three later novels, as the effect of the Evangelical Revival was felt in educated society, Edmund Bertram means to reside full-time in his parish of Thornton Lacey, to Mary Crawford's annoyance; Mr Elton, though personally conceited and spiteful, is nevertheless conscientious in his duties at Highbury; and Charles Hayter intends to be a resident and dutiful curate at Uppercross so that the old Reverend Dr Shirley can retire in peace after forty years' service there.

MALE EDUCATION AND PURSUITS

The boys who would grow up to follow these gentlemanly careers received by our standards a very narrow education. Small boys were taught reading, writing and elementary arithmetic by their parents or by a governess; some might then be tutored in a private household, like Mr Austen's pupils at Steventon rectory; and others, like Edward Knight's sons, might be sent to board at a preparatory school from about eight to thirteen, followed by five years at a public school, and university thereafter. The curriculum was still very limited, consisting mainly of Latin and Greek classical texts in prose and verse, with some modern history leading on from that of the ancient world; geography ('use of the globes'), French and Italian were usually taught as extras, along with handwriting, dancing, drawing and miscellaneous lectures on scientific topics. Conditions at the old-established public schools were invariably spartan—at Winchester the boys got up at 5.30 in the morning, and in winter and summer alike washed under the pump in the courtyard, dressed only in shirt and trousers, before attending a chapel service and receiving an hour or more's tuition before breakfast.

Discipline was ferocious, for most headmasters still held to Dr Johnson's view that 'Children, not being reasonable, can only be governed by fear', and flogged their pupils as a matter of course. It is perhaps hardly surprising that at more than one public school rebellions broke out, some so fierce they could only be quelled by bringing in soldiers. At Eton, where 170 boys sat together in the one big classroom known as Upper School, rotten eggs were thrown at the headmaster Dr Keate after he had flogged twenty boys for defying him, and he promptly retaliated by flogging another sixty. High rank made no difference—at Harrow the Duke of Dorset was always beaten twice, once for the offence and once for being a Duke. It was said that one headmaster, who was accustomed to punish boys every morning according to a list provided, muddled his lists and whipped the Confirmation class before the error was corrected.

In Jane Austen's own family, her father and several of his Austen cousins had been educated at

Tonbridge School, but her brothers James, Edward and Frank all sent their sons to Winchester, while two other cousins went to Eton. She seems to have disapproved of Westminster, for in her novels the foolish Robert Ferrars and the heartless Henry Crawford have both been educated there. Edmund and Tom Bertram were at Eton, and the Merchant Taylors' school in the City of London is probably where John Thorpe went, as his younger brother is still a pupil there. Sir John Middleton and the Musgroves and Hayters have probably been to some old-established West Country school, such as King's at Bruton, or Blundell's at Tiverton. Edward Ferrars was privately tutored in the home of the Reverend Mr Pratt, at Longstaple near Plymouth, where he falls into the clutches of the scheming Lucy Steele. Jane does not tell us where the Knightley brothers were educated, but Eton or Winchester would have been the likeliest.

Unless a youth went straight from school into the Army or Navy, he would normally continue his studies by taking a university degree—which was certainly required in the case of any candidate for Holy Orders. At this time Scotland had four universities but England only two, Oxford and Cambridge; we are told that Edward Ferrars, Edmund Bertram, James Morland and John Thorpe went to Oxford, and probably Henry Tilney and Mr Collins were there too; it seems likely that Darcy and Wickham were at Cambridge. The universities, like the public schools, taught little besides classics, and once the war with France started in 1793 it was no longer possible for young men to make the Grand Tour as part of their tertiary education. Men like Mr John Knightley, who wished to become barristers, would enter one of the Inns of Court in London—that is, the societies or quasi-colleges which provided for the study of the law and had the exclusive right of calling their graduates to the Bar—and would then live and work in the Holborn and Bloomsbury districts of London in order to be near the central law courts.

In terms of leisure activities, from September to April most country landowners would spend much of their time engaged in field sports, mainly hunting and shooting. A landowner might keep a pack of hounds purely for the amusement of himself and his friends in the locality, as did Lord Osborne in *The Watsons* and the real-life Mr Chute of the Vyne in Hampshire. A few very dashing ladies might make an appearance in the hunting-field, but it was not normally considered a pastime suitable for females. We do not hear of Mr Knightley or Mr Darcy taking part in these sports, but Sir John Middleton hunts—probably stags as well as foxes, as he lives in the West Country—and shoots, and Marianne meets Willoughby on the hillside when he is out with his gun and two pointers. The Bertrams, father and sons, shoot their pheasants in Mansfield Wood, and Henry Crawford sends for his hunters from Norfolk so that he can ride them in Northamptonshire while he is staying at Mansfield parsonage. Mr Rushworth bores Maria Bertram with 'repeated details of his day's sport, good or bad, his boast of his dogs . . . his zeal after poachers . . .'; and John Thorpe, similarly, boasts to Catherine Morland of his outstanding brilliance at both hunting and shooting. Horse-races were usually held in late summer or early autumn—Tom Bertram is away from Mansfield during July and August at a race meeting and then a seaside visit—and most provincial towns had a small race-course, where the local gentry would organize a festive race week ending with a ball at which their daughters could make a debut.

In *Pride and Prejudice*, 'Mr Gardiner, though seldom able to indulge the taste, was very fond of fishing . . .' and evidently Darcy is too, for he invites Mr Gardiner to fish in the Pemberley trout stream and offers to supply him with fishing tackle. In London, tough young men would take fencing and boxing lessons from professionals, and those who lived near the coast might swim and row. Yachting was just starting to become popular— hence the sea trip at Weymouth where Jane Fairfax was endangered—and in 1815 the Yacht Club was formed at Cowes in the Isle of Wight, earning its title of Royal when the Prince Regent joined in 1817. Cricket is said to have originated at the Hampshire village of Hambledon in the middle of the eighteenth century, and matches between the Hambledon Club and All England XIs were already being organized during Jane's lifetime.

MALE FASHIONS

The fashions in masculine clothes changed only slowly during Jane Austen's lifetime, but in the end there were considerable differences in appearance between the boys and men of 1760 and 1820. In the earlier years of the century the basic male suit consisted of a knee-length coat with long and bulky skirts, a long waistcoat, and close-fitting knee-breeches worn with stockings and buckled shoes.

The coat gradually evolved by alterations in its cut, removing the skirts in front and dividing those at the back into two tails that would fall more conveniently when the wearer was on horseback, and likewise diminishing baggy sleeves and wide cuffs to a far neater outline. The waistcoat dwindled accordingly to fit inside a smaller coat. In the 1790s the breeches lengthened to become tight pantaloons worn tucked into short boots, and in the early nineteenth century the pantaloons became looser and evolved into trousers worn with shoes. Boys' clothes too followed this process of simplification, though in later years more specifically childish costumes emerged, in a style distinct from that of adults.

In 1783, when Edward Austen was formally adopted by Mr and Mrs Thomas Knight II, a group silhouette was painted by William Wellings to commemorate this event, which shows the teenage Edward with his long hair tied back and wearing the same style of coat and breeches as his father and Mr Knight. In the following year, when an unnamed schoolboy ran away from home to join the Navy, his anxious parents advertised for him as: '. . . complexion remarkably fair and ruddy, round visage, large blue eyes, white eyebrows, and long light hair hanging loosely upon his shoulders. He was dressed in a dark chocolate-coloured coat with white sugar-loaf buttons, white striped dimity lapelled waistcoat, fustian breeches and white cotton stockings.' By the end of the century small boys had short cropped hair and were wearing 'skeleton suits'—loose nankeen cotton trousers with a high waist that buttoned on to a very short jacket, with a small frilly shirt collar protruding at the top of the jacket.

There were always elderly gentlemen who preferred to cling to the fashions of their youth, and Mr Francis Austen, a wealthy lawyer in Sevenoaks and Jane's aged great-uncle, was such a one. He had been a smart man early in the eighteenth century, wearing a bushy wig and a suit of light grey trimmed with narrow gold lace edgings, and retained this 'perfect identity of colour, texture & make to his life's end', his only concession to modernity being to discard the gold lace. In the middle of the century men's coats and waistcoats were often made in rich fabrics elaborately patterned, with much silk embroidery added to the cuffs, the seams and the tails, and this lavish style lingered on for years as dress for formal occasions. When Sir William Lucas of Meryton was presented at St James's Court, before the opening of *Pride and Prejudice*, he would have had to appear in something like 'a brown and blue striped silk coat and breeches, with a white silk waistcoat, the suit elegantly embroidered with silver and bouquets of flowers', and with lace ruffles on the shirt front and cuffs. By the end of the century, an elderly gentleman well dressed for everyday life— as might be Mr Bennet—would wear 'a white kerseymere waistcoat and small-clothes [breeches], dark blue coat, white silk stockings with very glittering shoe and knee buckles, frilled shirt, and white plaited [pleated] stock buckled behind, his hair powdered with a queue [pigtail].'

Young men first started to wear their hair cut short in the 1790s, and a tax on hair-powder in 1795 meant that many people gave up using it. Some people, however, still preferred to use powder and pay the tax—in 1802 the Prince of Wales was wearing a striped green velvet coat embroidered with silver flowers, and a powdered wig with curls and queue. In Jane Austen's early novels, most of the gentlemen would have had long hair, powdered and tied back in a queue with a large bow of black ribbon—Mr Bennet certainly wears his hair like this, as he talks of his 'powdering gown'; and the bills left behind at Northanger Abbey by Eleanor Tilney's future husband show an entry for hair-powder. Robert Watson quarrels with his wife as to whether or not he should re-powder his hair for the evening; and the old-fashioned Mr Woodhouse would doubtless have maintained this style of his younger days. Sir Walter Elliot sneers that Admiral Baldwin has 'nine grey hairs of a side, and nothing but a dab of powder at top'.

The overall tendency was for men's clothes to grow plainer in style and fabric and more comfortable for everyday wear, as most men spent much time out of doors and on horseback. In the nineteenth century, a young West Country squire, a real-life version of Charles Musgrove, was wearing 'a green jockey or hunting coat, yellow buckskins and brown tops, buff waistcoat, a yellow and red silk handkerchief round his neck, and a broad frilled shirt'. A newspaper of 1804 lamented the slovenliness of modern young men: 'Slouched hats, jockey waistcoats, half-boots, leather breeches, cropped heads, unpowdered hair . . . the present race of Bucks without blood, Beaux without taste, and Gentlemen without manners!' By 1814 a smart gentleman would have 'a coat of light blue, or snuff [light brown] colour, with brass

95

buttons, the tail reaching nearly to the heels; a gigantic bunch of seals dangled from his fob, whilst his pantaloons were short, and tight at the knees; and a spacious waistcoat, with a voluminous muslin cravat and a frilled shirt, completed the toilette.' Sir Walter Elliot could have looked just like this.

FEMININE OCCUPATIONS

The daughters of the landed gentry families would probably have had only the minimum of formal instruction before leaving home—in many cases while still in their teens, like Catherine Morland and Marianne Dashwood—to marry country gentlemen in their own rank of society. Until well into the nineteenth century education was not considered necessary for girls. In fact, it was felt to be rather a hindrance to their settlement in life, as they would be regarded with suspicion if thought clever or bookish. Jane Austen was well aware of this attitude, and wrote teasingly in *Northanger Abbey*: 'Where people wish to attach, they should always be ignorant. To come with a well-informed mind, is to come with an inability of administering to the vanity of others, which a sensible person would always wish to avoid. A woman especially, if she have the misfortune of knowing anything, should conceal it as well as she can.'

Most girls were educated at home, either by their parents or by a governess with the assistance of visiting tutors, but the sum total was the same: needlework, both for necessity and for pleasure; simple arithmetic; fine hand writing, which was considered a very elegant accomplishment; enough music to be able to sing and play some country dances on the forte-piano or harpsichord for family entertainment; a little drawing; some French fables to recite; reading the Bible, Shakespeare, other poetry and some respectable novels such as *Sir Charles Grandison*; and some very scrappy ideas of history and geography. Mrs Austen herself had probably had no more education than this; but luckily for her children, her own natural intelligence and that of Mr Austen, together with his teaching ability, ensured that Jane and Cassandra were encouraged to read and study at home far more than might have been the case in other families. Music and drawing masters visited Steventon rectory for the children's benefit, and all through her life there are references in Jane's letters to the books which the family bought or borrowed—novels, poetry, biographies, histories, travels and political essays— keeping themselves up to date in every way with current events.

It was sometimes either desirable or else necessary for a girl to be educated at a boarding school—as was the illegitimate Harriet Smith, whose father is prepared to support her but wishes to remain anonymous, or Anne and Mary Elliot, sent away when their mother died. In the Austens' case, there were hardly any young girls amongst the Steventon neighbours, and Jane and Cassandra may well have been sent to Mrs La Tournelle's Ladies' Boarding School at the Abbey House in Reading for the sake of giving them some youthful company. Unfortunately, Jane did not herself record any memories of her schooldays, but another girl, Mary-Martha Butt (later the authoress Mrs Sherwood), who was there in the 1790s, not long after the Austen sisters, left some quite detailed recollections of the school at that time. From this description it can be seen that the Abbey House school matches well that run by Mrs Goddard in Emma's Highbury: '. . . a real, honest, old-fashioned Boarding-school, where a reasonable quantity of accomplishments were sold at a reasonable price, and where girls might be sent to be out of the way and scramble themselves into a little education, without any danger of coming back prodigies'.

Much higher up the social scale was the school run by the Misses Stevenson in Queen's Square, in London's newly developing Bloomsbury district. It was known as the 'Ladies' Eton', and charged fees of one hundred guineas a year. While Jane and Cassandra were at the Abbey House, their future sister-in-law Elizabeth Bridges was at the Queen's Square school—and this too may well be reflected in Jane's later comment in *Emma*: ' . . . a seminary, or an establishment, or anything which professed, in long sentences of refined nonsense, to combine liberal acquirements with elegant morality upon new principles and new systems—and where young ladies for enormous pay might be screwed out of health and into vanity . . .', for the academic curriculum here was minimal, and the prime object was to instil Decorum, Manners and Deportment. Every movement of a pupil's body in entering and quitting a room, in taking a seat and rising from it, was duly criticized. An old coach without wheels was kept propped up in the back of the house, to enable the young ladies to practise ascending and descending with calmness and grace, and without any unnecessary display of ankles. They were also expected to acquire 'the great Art of Society—the art of properly paying and receiving visits, of saluting acquaintances in the street and drawing-room; and of writing letters of compliment, [of displaying] perfect womanly gentleness and high breeding, [and that] peculiar suavity, the tact which made everybody in a company happy and at ease— most of all the humblest individual present.' Jane may perhaps have amused herself by imagining that this was where Charlotte Palmer was a pupil, because her mother Mrs Jennings still keeps hanging over the mantlepiece 'a landscape in coloured silks of her performance, in proof of her having spent seven years at a great school in town to some effect.' Bingley's sisters, too, 'had been educated in one of the first private seminaries in town', but Miss Bingley's rudeness to Elizabeth hardly seems in keeping with the ethos of the Ladies' Eton.

In *Persuasion*, Jane lists female occupations as the 'common subjects of housekeeping, neighbours, dress, dancing, and music'. Her contemporary readers would have understood what lay behind this succinct phrase, but for us much enlargement is needed. Housekeeping alone was then a full-time occupation in its own right, and although ladies would of course delegate the actual heavy work to servants, the mistress of an average landed gentry household was nevertheless in modern terms something like the manageress of a small hotel. She had to engage, instruct and supervise domestic servants; home-produce as many foodstuffs and household goods as possible, and buy in, probably with difficulty and at considerable expense, any that could not be made at home; make, mend and keep clean the family's clothes, with the assistance of dressmakers and washerwomen; keep her domestic accounts and not run into debt; educate her young children and engage governesses for them; be a sociable hostess to maintain good relations with the neighbouring gentry; and, in all likelihood, undertake all these necessary duties while being in an almost constant state of pregnancy. It was also part of the lady of the manor's duties to provide Christmas gifts of baby clothes, blankets, shawls, coats, stockings and flannel petticoats to the villagers, and to organize a dame school where the children might learn to read and write. When Marianne Dashwood married Colonel Brandon, 'she found herself at nineteen, submitting to new attachments, entering on new duties, placed in a new home, a wife, the mistress of a family, and the patroness of a village'; and at Hunsford, whenever any of the cottagers 'were disposed to be quarrelsome, discontented or too poor', Lady Catherine de Bourgh 'sallied forth into the village to settle their differences, silence their complaints, and scold them into harmony and plenty'.

The Morland family have ten children in their Fullerton parsonage, and Mrs Morland's time 'was so much occupied in lying-in and teaching the little ones, that her elder daughters were inevitably left to shift for themselves'—and it seems that all she can do for Catherine is to teach her a little French and to sew well; writing and accounts (arithmetic) she is taught by her father; and there is no mention of any governess being employed. When she becomes engaged to Henry Tilney: ' "Catherine would make a sad heedless young house-keeper to be sure," was her mother's foreboding remark; but

100

quick was the consolation of there being nothing like practice.' At Longbourn, Charlotte Lucas has to go home because she is wanted about the mince pies; but when Mr Collins enquires which of his fair cousins has prepared the dinner, Mrs Bennet 'assured him with some asperity that they were very well able to keep a good cook, and that her daughters had nothing to do in the kitchen'. Lady Bertram is, of course, too indolent to do anything except tangle her embroidery, and the unnamed house-keeper at Mansfield Park must have had to assume responsibility for all the domestic tasks and fend off interference from Mrs Norris into the bargain. Ever since her mother died, Elizabeth Elliot has been 'presiding and directing' at Kellynch Hall, 'doing the honours and laying down the domestic law . . .', while Mary Musgrove, hypochondriacal and lazy, spoils her little boys and puts too much trust in her flighty, extravagant nurserymaid Jemima.

In real life, young Mrs Whatman, wife of a wealthy paper-maker in Kent, kept a household manual in which she wrote out complete instructions for all her female servants. The housemaid, for example:

> . . . must be an early riser, because the ground floor should be ready against the family come down stairs. In summer, when the stoves take less time, and there is also less dust and dirt, the Housemaid should dry rub some part every morning, as the floors get sooner dirty in summer from the insects, and if they are well dry rubbed all summer, they will keep well with very little

attention in the winter, which cannot be given at that time of the year in a morning, but may occasionally when the family drive out. . . . Drawingroom: The blinds always closed in the morning and window up. Kept dusted, and the chairs and sofas dusted occasionally, and the mahogany rubbed. The covers shook. The girandoles Mrs. W. always cleans herself. They should never be touched, nor the pictures . . . When the fire is light and the stove cleaned, something must be laid down to prevent the carpet from being dirtied, as it is nailed down.

Apart from the cleaning of the house, the general domestic washday was an exhausting chore which was undertaken as rarely as possible. The more wealthy a family was, the more changes of linen its members were supposed to possess—a weekly wash implied a poor household, whereas middle-rank families would aim for a large wash every six weeks or even every quarter. Washing, drying and ironing had to be spread over several days—soaking on Monday, washing on Tuesday, folding and starching on Wednesday, ironing on Thursday and airing on Friday—and this programme presupposed that the weather was fine enough to get the bed-linen and clothes dry to schedule; if not, the kitchen quarters would be full of damp sheets and underwear hanging on airers for days on end, with the corresponding disruption to meals and the normal domestic routine. In April 1816 Jane Austen wrote in a rather embarrassed tone to her niece Caroline, younger daughter of her brother James: 'We are almost ashamed to include your Mama in the invitation, or to ask *her* to be at the trouble of a long ride for so few days as we shall be having disengaged, for we *must* wash before the Godmersham party come & therefore Monday would be the last day that our House could be comfortable for her. . . . We do not like to *invite* her to come on Wednesday, to be turned out of the house on Monday . . . .'

Like many ladies, the Austens' friend Martha Lloyd kept a manuscript book in which to collect favourite recipes—cookery entered at one end, and home hints at the other—and so very probably when they were all living together at Chawton, Jane Austen used simple cosmetics of Martha's making: hard pomatum, from beef and mutton suet, beeswax and scent essence; coral toothpowder, from prepared powdered coral and cuttlefish bone mixed with powdered cassia bark and coloured pink; cold cream, from spermaceti, white wax, oil of sweet almonds and rosewater; rose pomatum, from roses, lard and white wax; and milk of roses, from rosewater and sweet almond oil. Martha's book shows too that it was quite usual to make one's own writing-ink and shoe-blacking at home; to clean silks and gauzes with a mixture of honey, soft soap and whisky or gin; to whiten silk stockings by hanging them up in the fumes of burning sulphur; to mix one's own varnish for small tables; and to whitewash rooms, tinting with indigo for a blue wash, and with Dutch pink or spruce ochre for a buff wash.

In rural communities there might be no physician within reach, and so simple home doctoring remedies, whether for herself or for others, were also a very necessary part of a lady's knowledge.

103

Martha Lloyd included in her book various medical recipes, for complaints such as worms, fever, whooping cough and toothache—though whether any of them were actually effective is another matter. Quinine had been brought to Europe in the seventeenth century, and it was known that a decoction of willow bark (the source of salicylic acid, from which aspirin was later developed) could decrease fever and bring some pain relief, provided that the patient could stomach the bitter taste. However, the only efficient painkiller was opium, and this was therefore freely used, despite the recognized risk of addiction; Martha's advice for toothache was to make a pill of opium and camphor with spirits of wine and plug the hollow tooth with it. Laudanum was a solution of opium in alcohol, taken a few drops at a time, and in 1798, when Mrs Austen had an upset stomach, the Basingstoke physician recommended her to take twelve drops of laudanum when she went to bed, as a composer (sedative), and Jane carefully measured it out for her.

For those ladies who did not settle down as mistress of a country house or parsonage, but who married soldiers and 'followed the drum', life could be just as busy, besides being far more dangerous. In the summer of 1797, Lord Dorchester, a soldier for more than fifty years, retired to Hampshire and rented Kempshott House; and Mrs Bramston at Oakley Hall wrote to her friend:

. . . we had to dinner the other day our new Neighbours from Kempshott, Lord & Lady

Dorchester . . . he is a General-like-looking Man & She a Genteel-looking Woman but you may perceive on her countenance an Impression that conveys to your Mind an Idea that She had had many Misfortunes & I believe that is the case, she has made Eight voyages almost all with a young Family & in them experienced every danger incident to the Sea, at one time their Ship was many days stuck between Ice—a most hazardous situation, Shipwreckd on a desert Island where they stayd a fortnight, one day & night split on a Rock, in one Voyage they changed their Ship four times from Accidents . . .

FEMALE FASHIONS

Women's fashions changed radically during this period of George III's reign. Both Jane Austen's grandmothers had died before she was born, but had they been alive in 1775 they would probably still have been wearing the fashions of thirty years before—'sacques and négligés of very rich silks, caps with lappets, huge breast and sleeve bows, gauze aprons, kerchiefs and ruffles, and extremely high heeled shoes'. These heavy silk gowns hung loose from the shoulders and were draped over a wide hooped petticoat, and the gauze apron was intended to be not functional but purely decorative. For a few years the hooped petticoats grew wider and wider, and at mid-century, though dying out of use in everyday life, became fossilized as the correct style for Court dress.

In the second half of the eighteenth century dresses still had bunchy skirts, though no longer supported by hoops, and were made in softer fabrics rather than the stiff brocaded or embroidered silks. When Jane Austen's mother married in 1764, she wore a highly practical dress of red woollen fabric, cut trimly in the style of a riding habit; and according to family tradition, the young couple's income was so limited that Mrs Austen had no new gown for two years, relying on this red wool dress for her daily wear. It ended its life by being cut up into a jacket and breeches for the eight-year-old Frank—the future admiral—to wear when he went hunting on his chestnut pony, Squirrel.

In the 1770s a fashion arose for building the hair up into a huge pile above the head, by means of 'a large triangular thing called a cushion to which the hair was frizzed up with three or four enormous curls on each side; the higher the pyramid of hair, gauze, feathers and other ornaments was carried the more fashionable it was thought'—and this whole creation was greased with scented pomatum and sprayed with hair powder. 'Such was the labour employed to rear the fabric that night caps were made in proportion to it and covered over the hair, immensely long black pins, double and single, powder and pomatum and all, ready for the next day.' These 'heads' were not 'opened' for a week or more at a time with, naturally, horribly unhygienic results: a lady in Bath 'recollected perfectly one Sunday in church, seeing a mouse peep out of one of the curls of a lady sitting in the pew before her, and its little tail appearing now and then, as it meandered to and fro, no doubt well fed with so much powder and pomatum.'

In 1783 a middle-aged lady returned to her family home from a failed marriage, and her young cousin remembered:

> She arrived in a post chaise with a maid, a lap dog and a canary bird, and boxes heaped upon boxes, till it was impossible to see the persons within . . . she was a large woman elaborately dressed and highly rouged . . . the hair was then crimped or frizzed, and formed about the face in the shape of a horse shoe; long stiff curls fastened with pins hung round the neck, and the whole was well pomatumed and powdered with different coloured powders; a high cushion was fastened on the top, and over that either a cap adorned with artificial flowers and feathers to such a height as sometimes rendered it difficult to preserve the equilibrium, or a balloon hat; this latter was a fabric of wire and tiffany of immense circumference, fixed on the head with huge pins, and standing trencher wise, quite flat and unbending in its full proportions, the crown being low, though like the cap, richly set off with feathers and flowers. The lower part of the dress consisted of a full petticoat, generally flounced, short sleeves, and a very long train; but instead of a hoop there was a vast pad at the back, and a frame of wire in front, so as to throw out the neck handkerchief till it resembled the craw of a pigeon.

Balloon hats remained fashionable, and the Austens' neighbour Mrs Bramston of Oakley Hall wrote to her friend Mrs Hicks, when the latter was in London in 1787:

> . . . I think from the descriptions you have
> been so good to give me I shall be able to
> make myself a Hat that will do . . . however
> if I should find myself mistaken I will
> trouble you to purchase me one. . . . you will
> I am afraid think me very particular about
> my dress but indeed I am not but as I have
> not seen any of the present fashions I like to
> be drest like other people. . . .

As with men's clothes, female wear became
simpler as the time passed, with soft cotton fabrics,
especially white muslin and lawn, being made into
less voluminous garments. The hair was no longer
built up into a pyramid, but allowed to fall in loose
curls and only powdered for formal occasions. This
is the style that enables Willoughby to cut off a
long lock of Marianne's hair, as it lies tumbled
down her back. By the end of the century the
fashion of the very short waist arrived from France,
with a light sash or ribbon tied immediately under
the breasts, and remained popular for the next
twenty years; dresses were now at their skimpiest,
nearly always white, and made of the thinnest of
fabrics, and hair was styled to be short and curly.
Some ladies took to wearing fashion-wigs—black
in the morning and dressed in short curls, and for
evening long fair hair elaborately styled.

Plumper ladies found it necessary to keep their
figures under control by means of stays, to the
disapproval of a journalist of the time:

> The bosom, which Nature planted at the

bottom of her chest, is pushed up by means of wadding and whalebone to a station so near her chin that in a very full subject that feature is sometimes lost between the invading mounds. . . . Not only is the shape thrust out of its proper place but the blood is thrown forcibly into the face, neck and arms. . . . Over this strangely manufactured figure a scanty petticoat and as scanty a gown are put.

These very skimpy dresses posed their own problems, as an energetic teenager of 1801 recalled:

> . . . the most uncomfortable style of dress was when they were made so scanty that it was difficult to walk in them, and to make them tighter still, invisible petticoats were worn. They were wove on the stocking loom, and were like strait waistcoats . . . but only drawn down over the legs instead of over the arms, so that when walking, you were obliged to take short and mincing steps. I was not long in discarding mine and shocking my juvenile acquaintance by my boldness in throwing off such a fashionable restraint.

It was also, of course, necessary to provide some warmth for the wearers of these flimsy dresses, and wraps, cashmere shawls, large neck-handkerchiefs and large fur muffs all came into use. The spencer, a short-waisted close-fitting jacket with long sleeves, appeared in the 1790s, and in the cold

June of 1808 Jane Austen told Cassandra that '. . . my kerseymere Spencer is quite the comfort of our Evening walks'. The pelisse—a long coat or over-dress, buttoning down the front—was invented a few years later, and a cloak could be worn over the pelisse in very cold weather. One January morning in 1809, when the Austens were in Southampton, the Misses Williams came to call, '. . . each in a new Cloth Mantle & Bonnet . . . [Miss Williams's] being purple, & Miss Grace's scarlet'—which Jane evidently felt was rather beyond the bounds of good taste.

Predictably, the older generation strongly disapproved of the fashions and behaviour of the young, and in 1813 an elderly lady complained in print:

> On lately entering a ball-room I beheld a group of little girls with bare heads and bosoms, gossamer gowns, and lilliputian fans . . . the gentlemen, too, seemed equally metamorphosed. I knew indeed that lace and embroidery were no longer seen, but I was not aware that the frocks [plain coats] and unpowdered heads which I saw in the morning would be deemed proper for an evening appearance. . . . The gentlemanly bow and the low curtsey are looked for in vain . . . on leaving the ball room some of the men attend to their partners so far as to wrap their shawls and tippets around them, give them their arm as far as the head of the stairs, shake hands, and say, 'Good night. If I had my hat I would see you down.'

In their childhood in the 1770s to 1780s Jane and Cassandra would have worn dresses with a natural waistline and wide bunchy skirts; the hair was long and loose, hanging in curls, though restrained to some extent by a large mob-cap, and the wide coloured sash worn round the waist had ribbons to match in the cap. By the end of the eighteenth century the dresses for little girls had become as plain, high-waisted, low-necked and skimpy as those of their mothers, and their hair was likewise cropped very short and layered to fit the shape of the head. One Scottish girl, Elizabeth Grant, remembered that she and her sisters had all been dressed alike, with pink gingham or yellow nankin frocks in the morning, and white calico for the afternoon, cotton stockings at all times, and not a ribbon, curl or ornament to be seen. In 1810, when she was thirteen, and first taken out to an adult party in London, she had a new frock of soft clear muslin, very full and with several deep tucks, her hair was freshly cut and brushed flat and smooth with rose-scented oil, and her sole ornament was a cairngorm cross dangling on a gold chain. When she was given a pound to spend, she bought herself a pea-green silk parasol with a carved ivory handle; no doubt, like Mr Parker's daughter Mary at Sanditon, she walked about with it very gravely, fancying herself quite a little woman.

Jane and Cassandra had neither the money nor the inclination to turn themselves into fashion freaks, and although from time to time Jane mentions in her letters the purchase of lengths of new material to be made up into gowns, she also frequently talks of dyeing and altering her present gowns to make them last another year or so. We

111

know that she spent money on silk stockings, white gloves and pink persian (a lightweight silk used for underskirts or linings); that a new gown had lost its colour in its first wash; that her stuff (woollen fabric) gown was a great comfort in December weather; and that on various occasions during her life she bought white, blue, pink, brown, yellow and lilac materials to be made up into gowns. Of this lilac gown she added that she intended to trim it with black satin ribbon, and that 'With this addition it will be a very successful gown, happy to go anywhere.' She also spoke rather disapprovingly of the wife of a neighbouring Hampshire clergyman, as being 'at once expensively & nakedly dress'd' in lace and muslin at a dinner party in winter; and in her very last recorded letter, written in May 1817, she jokes about the previous year's fashion for very short skirts.

COSMETICS

Cosmetics, as well as hairstyles, are all part of female fashion, and here again the appearance of women's faces changed quite radically during Jane's lifetime. In the earlier part of the eighteenth century the fashion was for powdered hair, and a dead-white face with dark eyebrows, rouged cheeks and red lips. This style was achieved by using the proverbial 'powder and paint'—'paint' was ceruse, a mixture of powdered white lead and vinegar, which was brushed on to give the skin a mask-like coating. The powder itself could be more white lead, or kaolin clay or talc, all ground very fine. The eyebrows were trimmed and blackened or else disguised by gluing on false brows made of strips of mouse-skin. Powdered white lead was also the main ingredient in most rouges and lip salves, and its lead content could ruin the skin and complexion rather than preserving it. It was said that the noted Irish beauty Maria Gunning, later Lady Coventry, had died from lead poisoning in 1760 owing to her continued use of cosmetics.

Black 'patches' were also stuck on the face, either to provide a visual contrast against the white mask or more practically to cover up pimples; they were cut out of black velvet, taffeta or silk, and were usually circular, but sometimes more elaborate shapes such as stars and crescents, or even birds and trees, were created. The patches were kept in special little elegant patch boxes, with a mirror inside to aid the application. Patches continued to be used well into the eighteenth century; and in 1818 an old lady remembered how, when she was about fifteen, she had possessed herself of her mother's patch box, and not content with one or two black spots to brighten her complexion, had stuck on a whole shower, and thus speckled had set out on a very satisfactory walk, with everyone she met staring at her admiringly—or so she had thought.

Not surprisingly, such harsh cosmetics led to all sorts of skin troubles, and the apothecary John Gowland invented his Gowland's Lotion about 1740. He advertised this as 'clearing the skin of pimples, tetters, ringworms, freckles, tan, redness of the nose &c, and inducing a clear and cool healthful white and red'. His claim was that the application of the lotion released a top layer of scurf from the skin, which could then be wiped off, allowing the skin beneath to breathe again and

113

recover its natural bloom. In fact his lotion contained not only bitter almonds and sugar, but also a small quantity of corrosive mercuric chloride, which removed the top layer of skin—in modern terms, ladies who used it were giving themselves a chemical peel. Gowland's Lotion nevertheless continued to be sold for decades, and Sir Walter Elliot believes that it has quite carried away Mrs Clay's freckles.

Cosmetic necessities for a rich young lady in the 1760s, Lady Caroline Russell, were listed as: powder, dressing pins, combs, *pomades à baton* (sticks of scented fat for greasing the skin and hair), a swansdown powder puff, a top knot and tresses of false hair, jars of jasmin-scented soft pomade, a knife for removing the powder and paint, and a supply of bear's grease—this latter was used as base for home-made creams and rouges, although lard was a more usual and cheaper substitute.

By the 1780s the crude contrasts of 'powder and paint' were going out of fashion, and cheeks were now simply dusted with talc and only lightly rouged, perhaps with a red leather imported from Brazil; the colour of the lips was strengthened with carmine or with lipsticks made from ground and coloured plaster of Paris. Nevertheless, newspapers still carried advertisements for cosmetics such as:

Lady Molyneux's Italian Paste, prepared by Mrs Gibson of Hatton Garden in London . . . so well known to the Ladies for enameling the Hands, Neck and Face, of a lovely white; it renders the most rough or brown Skin,

114

smooth and soft as Velvet; nor will the most severe frost crack the skin . . . also Lady Molyneux's Liquid Bloom, which in a Moment gives to Pale Cheeks the Rose of Nature, and which the most nice Eye cannot possibly suspect for Art, nor will it come off the cheek be the Face ever so hot.

Toothbrushes and toothpowder had been invented, and in 1784 Mr Charles Sharp, perfumer, of Fleet Street, London, advertised the Prince of Wales's Tooth Powder, along with Royal Tincture of Peach Kernels for the teeth and gums. He also sold Olympian Dew, which he claimed was used by the Queen of France and her court ladies. Apparently it rivalled Gowland's Lotion, inasmuch as Mr Sharp claimed it cleared skin of freckles, pimples, tan and every deformity, instantly made wrinkles disappear and gave a loveliness to the countenance.

Even though powder and paint were no longer used, a pale complexion was still admired, hence Miss Bingley's sneer that Miss Eliza Bennet was grown so brown and coarse—to which Darcy chivalrously replies that he 'perceived no other alteration than her being rather tanned,—no miraculous consequence of travelling in the summer'. Patent soaps were now advertised, such as Burgess's Lilac Flower Soap, said to be made with milk extracted from the flower and so producing a complexion beautifully white, soft and smooth.

There is no evidence that either Jane or Cassandra ever used such cosmetics, and with her pink cheeks Jane would certainly never have needed rouge. Sir Walter Elliot regrets the fact that Lady Russell does not use cosmetics: 'Morning visits are never fair by women at her time of life, who make themselves up so little. If she would only wear rouge, she would not be afraid of being seen; but last time I called, I observed the blinds were let down immediately.'

SOCIAL ACTIVITIES

With servants available to undertake the household chores, the landowner and his family could spend a considerable amount of time enjoying a wide variety of recreations, both public and private. The most socially important of these was dancing, for this was the chief way in which young people could become acquainted with each other in a respectable and carefully chaperoned environment. Modern readers are sometimes puzzled as to why dance scenes have so prominent a place in Jane Austen's novels; but in her lifetime the dance floor was the best, and indeed almost the only place, where marriage partners could be identified and courtship could flourish. Marianne Dashwood is thrilled by the idea of Willoughby's male energy when she hears he danced all night and was up again four hours later for a day's hunting; Henry Tilney teases Catherine that country dancing can be considered as an emblem of marriage; despite Elizabeth Bennet's sharp comments to Darcy in their first dance together, when she is exasperated by his silence, he has already a 'tolerable powerful feeling towards her, which soon procured her pardon'; Mr Rushworth and Maria Bertram, 'after dancing with each other at a proper number of balls', announce their

116

engagement; and it is at the ball at the Crown in Highbury that Emma first realizes that Mr Knightley is an attractive man—'His tall, firm, upright figure . . . not one among the whole row of young men who could be compared with him . . . .'

The name 'country-dance' has nothing to do with country as opposed to town, but comes from the French 'contre-danse', describing the way in which the dancers start by standing up facing each other in two long rows, men on one side and girls on the other. The leading couple would then move off down the row, the other couples falling in behind them; there was no fancy footwork involved, but the dancers would weave their way in a variety of patterns across the floor, linking arms or hands with their partners as the figure required—the 'allemande' figure involved 'a great deal of going hand in hand, and passing the hands over each other's heads in an elegant manner'. Scottish reels and strathspeys and Irish jigs became popular in the 1790s, and hornpipes were very fashionable in the following decade, in honour of the country's naval victories. Music in waltz time had come to England from the Continent in the late 1790s, when certain aspects of the dance, notably its entwining arm movements and the turning of the lady under her partner's arm, received leering comments in the newspapers: 'The Balls at Southampton are exceedingly lively, and well-attended. The young Ladies are particularly favourable to a German Dance, called *the Volse*; for squeezing, hugging, &c, it is excellent in its kind, and more than one Lady has actually fainted in the middle of it.' The idea of a couple clasping each other even more closely, with one hand on

117

the other's waist, was held to be positively indecent, and this style of waltzing did not become acceptable until after 1815. The quadrille, a dance specifically for four couples, was brought to England from Paris by the fashionable Lady Jersey in 1815, and quickly became the rage; early in 1817 Jane Austen's eldest niece, Fanny Knight, sent her some quadrille music to play, which Jane thought was 'pretty enough, though . . . very inferior to the Cotillions of my own day'.

Dances could be public, in a town's assembly room with admission by subscription, or private, when the landowner invited his personal friends and neighbours; they might also be entirely impromptu, when a family rolled back the carpet after dinner, and some older lady of the party played so that the young people could dance up and down the room—as Anne Elliot does for the Musgroves at Uppercross Hall. With or without dancing, music was an important part of family entertainment in the evening, and girls were usually taught to play the harpsichord, piano, harp or guitar, while men learnt the violin, flute and cello. Catherine Morland cannot bear to learn to play, and Fanny Price is too frightened even to try; Emma is too lazy to practise sufficiently and is honest enough to admit that Jane Fairfax is by far the more proficient; while of the Bennet sisters Mary plays with 'a pedantic air and conceited manner . . . Elizabeth, easy and unaffected, had been listened to with much more pleasure, though not playing half so well'. Singing was also part of domestic entertainment, since this too was something in which both sexes could join, as when Willoughby sings duets with Marianne, and Frank

118

Churchill with Jane Fairfax.

Theatre-going was primarily an urban entertainment for the winter months, but during the summer theatrical companies would tour smaller towns and villages, performing if need be in a large barn, and it was the practice for the chief personage of the district to give a handsome sum for tickets and to attend with a large party. This naturally led to the desire for amateur theatricals in the home, and those who could afford it indulged themselves in this respect on a grand scale. The Duchess of Marlborough had her private theatre at Blenheim in 1788, and, nearer home to the Austens, Lord Barrymore built a theatre, said to hold as many as seven hundred, at his riverside villa at Wargrave-on-Thames in Berkshire, where he and his friends presented *The Rivals* in 1791: 'It was a small and beautiful theatre, all glittering with gilding, with two tiers of boxes principally filled with the neighbouring nobility; the play was performed by gentlemen, the female characters being actresses from London.' It is more than likely that Jane's aunt and uncle, Mr and Mrs Leigh-Perrot, whose country house was in the parish of Wargrave, attended the performance and told their Steventon relations about it. The young Austens themselves performed plays at Christmas time from 1782 to 1789, and James Austen's versified prologues and epilogues for these productions survive.

Whist clubs were popular with gentlemen, and meetings would usually be held at some local inn; card parties at home provided quiet domestic entertainment for older people, and Emma is always happy to invite Mrs and Miss Bates, together with Mrs Goddard, to come and play quadrille (the name was applied both to the dance for four couples and to a card game for four people) with her father. Loo, Cassino, Brag, Vingt-un, Piquet and Commerce are all mentioned in the novels; and at Mansfield Park, the game called Speculation is used by Jane Austen with symbolic effect, when Mary Crawford's reckless gambling with the cards foreshadows her unsuccessful attempt to capture Edmund Bertram. Other parlour games such as lottery tickets, backgammon and spillikins could be played by all ages; and at Hartfield a Scrabble-type game ensues when Frank Churchill and Emma start playing with the alphabets she had written out for her little nephews, and Frank unkindly torments Jane Fairfax with anagrams of words that have emotional meanings for her. Billiards was more usually played by men, but it was not unknown for ladies to participate as well.

CULTURAL PURSUITS

For more private entertainment there were always books and newspapers to read, though in both cases they were not so freely available as they are today. Books were expensive—in 1816 *Emma* cost a guinea, which was the weekly salary upon which a poor curate might have to keep himself and his family—and commercial libraries would solicit subscribers whose payments went towards maintaining a constant supply of new books of all kinds. Private book clubs were also set up, whereby a group of friends would subscribe to buy books specifically requested by members of the club, amongst whom they would be distributed at the

120

end of the year. The normal practice was for a book to be published in several volumes, so that different members of the family could all read it at the same time—hence at Netherfield Miss Bingley, trying to attract Darcy's attention, chooses a book only because it was the second volume of the one he was reading.

Novels, especially the romantic tales of mystery and horror that were then so popular—*The Mysteries of Udolpho, The Romance of the Forest, The Midnight Bell* and *The Castle of Wolfenbach*, to name but a very few—were considered by the serious-minded to be conducive to frivolity and immorality, especially among female readers; but the Austens were 'great Novel-readers & not ashamed of being so', and there are numerous references in Jane's letters to the novels which the family bought or borrowed. *Udolpho* was a well-known spine-chiller, and the scene of the black curtain behind which something terrible was apparently concealed was remembered by many readers as the highlight of the story. Henry Tilney assures Catherine that his hair was standing on end the whole time he was reading it; and in real life a Scottish girl recalled:

As my father would not let us read any of the romances or novels he had in his library, [my sister] subscribed to the circulating library at Melrose, and read the books in her own room, and having Mrs Radcliffe's most horrible romance of the *Mysteries of Udolpho*, she would read so much of it to me in mine before going to bed . . . taking care, however, to leave off before the dreaded hour of twelve when ghosts were supposed to wander abroad . . . but on this night we were so much interested, and curious about a certain black curtain, behind which it was suspected there was some mysterious spectacle, that we forgot to look at our watches to notice the hour. . . when we observed it was past twelve . . .

and suddenly their pet dog started to growl furiously and a strange rumbling noise came nearer and nearer. The two girls hid under the bedclothes till broad daylight. It then transpired that the terrifying noise had been caused by a conscientious servant who was rolling empty beer barrels out of the cellar last thing at night.

Apart from these popular works mentioned in *Northanger Abbey*, many of the characters in Jane Austen's novels read constantly and intelligently; Darcy continues to add to his own library at Pemberley, which has been accumulated over several generations; Fanny Price likes biography and poetry; Lady Russell likes 'all the new poems and states of the nation', but Elizabeth Elliot is very bored by them; and Emma at least makes lists of the books she means to read some day. There are lending libraries at Meryton and Sanditon; and, as in real life, at Portsmouth and Lyme Regis.

Newspapers were likewise small—four pages of minute type—and expensive, and were issued weekly or twice-weekly; initially it was only the London paper the *Daily Universal Register*, later re-christened *The Times*, which appeared every day. Jane seems to think that newspapers were more the province of the gentleman than the lady, perhaps because they printed mostly political and commercial news and ladies were not supposed to be interested in such matters—though Anne Elliot follows the fortunes of Admiral Croft and Captain Wentworth by dint of studying the naval events reported in the papers. London papers could be sent down to the country, and it was a generous kindness on the part of the subscriber to pass his paper on to the neighbours when he had finished with it. It seems that Mr Holder at Ashe Park gave his to the Austens at Steventon; and in Portsmouth Mr Price walks off to return the one he has borrowed from a neighbour.

LETTERS, DIARIES, JOURNALS

Letter-writing was an essential part of social life, both to maintain family connections and to act as mini-newspapers—anyone living in or visiting London, for example, was supposed to send all the latest gossip out to the provincial friends, and such letters would then be lent even further round the local community. Writing paper was expensive, and the usual amount devoted to any letter was one quarto sheet, about fifteen inches long by nine inches wide, folded over to make two leaves—four pages—each about seven and a half inches by nine. There were no ready-made envelopes, so the name and address of the recipient was written in the middle of the fourth page, and the paper then folded in on itself several times, both vertically and horizontally, until it was reduced to a small packet. One flap of the packet was finally tucked inside the other, and the tuck fastened by either an adhesive 'wafer' (a small circle of dried glue, which was moistened and pressed into place) or by a blob of sealing-wax. This was the standard-size letter upon which postal charges were based, and if any extra sheets of paper were used the cost rose accordingly. No pre-paid postage stamps yet existed, and the postal charges were paid by the recipient, not the writer, so it was necessary to cram as many lines of writing as possible on to this one sheet, 'crossing' the paper if necessary—that is, once the sheet had been completely filled, giving it a quarter-turn and writing again at right-angles to the previous lines. Miss Bates says of Jane Fairfax's letters, '. . . in general she fills the whole paper and crosses half.' The custom of 'crossing' died out later in the nineteenth century as both paper and postage became less expensive.

In London there was a local twopenny post, which provided six deliveries a day, one penny being paid by the sender and one by the recipient. The postmen wore blue coats with red facings, and went on their rounds with a bell and a bag to collect letters. Outside the London area, however, postage rates were charged by a combination of the size of the letter and the distance travelled; the minimum charge, for a single-sheet letter, was three pence for up to fifteen miles, rising in rapid stages to eight pence for over 150 miles.

Steel pen-nibs were not invented until the 1830s, and in Jane Austen's time everything was written with quill pens. A quill, being soft and flexible, splayed out in use and needed constant trimming and re-cutting—hence a 'penknife' originally meant the small folding knife carried about by the writer for this purpose. Miss Bingley officiously offers to 'mend' Darcy's pen for him, but he prefers to do it himself. Caroline Austen, one of

Jane's nieces, remembered: 'Her handwriting remains to bear testimony to its own excellence; and every note and letter of hers, was finished off *handsomely*—There was an art *then* in folding and sealing—no adhesive envelopes made all easy—some people's letters looked always loose and untidy—but *her* paper was sure to take the right folds, and *her* sealing wax to drop in the proper place –.' When Fanny Price writes her first letter to her brother William, kind Edmund 'sent him half a guinea under the seal'—that is, he hid the small, thin half-guinea coin under a thick blob of wax, so that it could only be discovered when William broke the seal to open the letter. The letter is delivered to William free of charge, because Sir Thomas Bertram is able to frank it—marking it 'Free' and signing his name on the outside, below the address—a privilege enjoyed by Members of Parliament on behalf of their constituents.

Apart from letters, both men and women kept 'pocket-books'—very small printed diaries with room for just a few words on the page, what we would now call engagement diaries—and some of them also had larger plain volumes in which they kept a 'journal', recording their private opinions and daily life in as much detail as they pleased. It seems that Jane Austen used pocket-books, but unfortunately they were probably all thrown away after her death.

DRAWING AND PAINTING
Drawing and painting were usually female pastimes, but the subject was part of the curriculum for military and naval training, so that officers would be able to reconnoitre a town and its

fortifications and produce some sort of visual impression from which a plan of attack could be decided. There were also civilian gentlemen who simply enjoyed sketching as they travelled about on holiday, or who drew out their own ideas for landscape gardening if they could not afford to call in Mr Repton. Colonel Brandon and Captain Wentworth would probably have had some artistic training during their service in the Army and Navy, and Henry Tilney and his sister Eleanor are both accustomed to drawing landscapes. Edward Ferrars admits he cannot discuss picturesque landscapes in any way that would satisfy Marianne; but in the Dashwood family Marianne is the musician and it is Elinor's drawings which are 'affixed to the walls of their sitting room' at Barton Cottage. Emma, as with her music, has been too impatient and too lazy to learn to draw properly: 'Her many beginnings were displayed. Miniatures, half-lengths, whole-lengths, pencil, crayon, and water-colours had been all tried in turn.' Catherine Morland has never had any lessons, and Mrs Elton gladly pretends that her wifely duties leave her no time for drawing or music. In real life, the Austens' friend Mrs Chute of the Vyne pleased her husband by painting portraits of his favourite foxhounds.

NEEDLEWORK AND HANDICRAFTS
More specifically female recreations were the various kinds of needlework popular at the period; fine sewing could be put to practical use, in making clothes for the family or for charitable recipients, but embroidery was more often merely a way of filling in the time on wet days. In 1788 the Austens' neighbour Mrs Bramston chattered on to her

friend:

> I have worked an Apron in that pattern we
> had of Mrs Greens I enlarged it by placing
> the wave at a greater distance from the
> Scollop & the Chain too which makes it a
> proper border for an Apron I run three
> rows for the wave & did the Flowers in
> Goble Stitch or to use a more Genteel word
> Coventry Stitch you cannot think how well it
> looks it has so much the appearance of Lace
> I hope you have not begun yours in any
> other pattern . . .

Little girls were taught to sew by making samplers
in cross-stitch, and this simple form of stitch could
be used on a larger scale, with thick wool on coarse
canvas, to produce small rugs or bedside carpets.
There was at one period a fashion for copying
paintings in satin stitch, with the brush-strokes
being meticulously reproduced in the stitchery.
Knotting was even more time-consuming,
consisting as it did of making knots at regular
intervals in a length of thread, which was then sewn
down, either in outline or to fill in the motifs of a
design, to produce something of a lace-like effect
overlying the fabric below. Netting—creating a
mesh of varying size—was undertaken by both men
and women, according to whether the product was
required for female accessories and trimmings, or
for sporting use as in fishing nets or rabbit snares.
Isabella Thorpe's friend Miss Andrews 'is netting
herself the sweetest cloak you can conceive', and
Bingley classes netting purses as one of the normal
'accomplishments' of young ladies. Knitting, at this

time, seems to have been considered rather low-class, or else only for old ladies such as Mrs Bates and, in real life, Mrs Austen, who in 1813 suddenly became enthusiastic about knitting gloves. Crochet was not introduced into England until nearly the end of Jane Austen's life, and it is not mentioned in her works.

The 'filigree work', or 'rolled-paper work' that Elinor Dashwood and Lucy Steele do together in the evening at Barton Park was a form of papercraft considered especially suitable as an art for ladies of leisure. A piece of stiff paper or parchment was cut into strips about an eighth of an inch wide; the edges were sometimes gilded, sometimes tinted a red colour. These strips were then rolled and pinched into the shapes of leaves, swags, hearts and so on, and glued on to the article to be decorated, and the spaces left between these decorations were then filled in with tightly rolled smaller strips of paper stuck on as close together as possible. Patterns were sold specially for this purpose—the *New Lady's Magazine* for 1786 issued a series of twelve sheets of patterns and some sixty motifs in all, and the *Gentleman's Magazine* for 1791 commented that an enormous number of tea-caddies with filigree-paper panels were now being decorated by young ladies.

SOCIAL LIFE

Even within the family, modes of address were very formal, and husbands and wives—in public at least—spoke, and referred, to each other as 'Mr Bennet' or 'Mrs Bennet'; while children called their parents 'Sir' and 'Ma'am' as well as 'Papa' and 'Mama'. Outside the family, Christian names

128

were used to distinguish younger brothers or sisters: Tom is 'Mr Bertram' as he is the elder son, and 'Mr Edmund Bertram' indicates that he is the younger—likewise 'Miss Bertram' and 'Miss Julia Bertram'. To address or refer to some unrelated person by their Christian name alone signified either that the person was a child or an inferior, or else that the speaker was over-familiar and vulgar. Even engaged couples hesitated at first to use each others' names; Frank Churchill much resents the way in which Mrs Elton calls his fiancée 'Jane' and tells his step-mother Mrs Weston: 'You will observe that I have not yet indulged myself in calling her by that name, even to you.' In the 1790s it was permissible to call or refer to a man by his surname alone, as 'Willoughby' or 'Bingley', but twenty years later Mrs Elton's use of 'Knightley' is considered a vulgarity.

Respectable young women could have no profession except matrimony, hence girls were expected to marry as soon as possible after they made their debut into society in their late teens; they joked together about gentlemen who wore red, blue or black coats—that is, soldiers, sailors or parsons. Nevertheless, courtship was very difficult—unrelated young men and women were not supposed to be left alone together in private, and when in public the slightest expression of interest in or concern for a member of the opposite sex—'being particular'—could be taken by the onlookers as an indication of matrimonial intentions. Conversations therefore had to be exceedingly discreet at all times and much had to be interpreted from facial reactions alone—stares, frowns, blushes, tears. A curtsey or a bow could be

129

a wordless and non-committal acknowledgement of some verbal comment, while to shake hands was not so much a sign of greeting or leavetaking, but more a mark of unusual affability or intimacy: Henry Crawford insists on taking Fanny's hand as he leaves Mansfield Park—'he would not be denied it'. We have forgotten all this, and in forgetting have lost some of the humour in the scenes Jane Austen creates; her contemporary readers would have realized very early on that Emma's interest in Mr Elton is going to be misinterpreted by him, and would have found far more tension in these chapters than we now do, as they waited gleefully for the bubble to burst. Likewise, in chapter fifteen of *Northanger Abbey*, they would have been well aware, as the naive Catherine Morland was not, that John Thorpe was clumsily announcing his intention to call at Fullerton to ask her father's permission to marry her.

There was also an inflexible law which forbade correspondence between marriageable persons not engaged to be married. Elinor knows that Willoughby has been permitted to cut off a lock of Marianne's hair, but it is not until she sees her sister writing to inform him of their arrival in London that she concludes they must be engaged, however secretly. Jane Bennet cannot write direct to Bingley to tell him that she is now in London, but can only correspond with his sisters; and as they wish to nip this romance in the bud, they are careful *not* to give him her news. Darcy's explanatory letter to Elizabeth has to be clandestine, and she does not consider replying to it. Henry Crawford cannot write to Fanny Price, so

130

it is his sister who has to pass on his suggestion of a wedding in London at the very smart church of St George's in Hanover Square. It is only extreme emotional stress which induces Captain Wentworth to write his secret note to Anne, and she cannot write back but has to wait for an opportunity to speak to him in order to accept his proposal. It is essential for Jane Fairfax to visit the post office every morning by herself, so that no one else in Highbury knows that she is in secret correspondence with Frank Churchill.

Another handicap in the race towards the altar was that of a dowry for the bride. Georgian marriage was viewed as a financial partnership, with the bride's father contributing a sum that would assist in paying for the upkeep of her future children, go towards running her matrimonal home and provide her own income if she were left a widow. Thanks to Mr Bennet's irresponsibility, Elizabeth and Jane will have only £1,000 apiece, and they will not even receive this sum until after their mother's death; but luckily for them, both Bingley and Darcy are sufficiently rich to be able to marry impoverished girls. Lady Bertram had had £7,000 as her dowry, and this was considered £3,000 short of what she should have had to enable her to become a baronet's wife; while Fanny Price, being penniless, was by contemporary standards unbelievably lucky in having attracted the attention of Henry Crawford with his £4,000 a year, and should have jumped at the chance of marrying him. Sir Walter Elliot's extravagance means that he can give Anne only a small part of the £10,000 dowry that was her right, but as Captain Wentworth has £25,000 prize money in hand he can afford to marry her nevertheless.

Once a couple had come to an understanding and their parents had also given consent, it was a serious matter to break off the engagement. But while such an act was absolutely forbidden to a gentleman, it was just permissible for a lady: when Sir Thomas Bertram realizes that Mr Rushworth is a fool and that Maria has no love for him, he offers to act for her and release her.

When the wedding could finally be planned, the more elegant way to get married was by special licence, since some young ladies, like the romantically minded heroine of *The Rivals*, could not bear the idea of their banns being 'cried three times in a country church, and have an unmannerly fat clerk ask the consent of every butcher in the parish to join John Absolute and Lydia Languish, spinster! Oh that I should live to hear myself called spinster!' Mrs Bennet insists: 'You must and shall be married by a special licence.' The actual wedding ceremony would be quiet and private, with only very close friends and relations in attendance; lavish weddings with many bridesmaids and guests did not become popular until later in the nineteenth century, when the Victorians wished to make displays of conspicuous consumption.

The newly wed couple would probably go straight to the husband's house, and a 'wedding trip' or 'bridal tour' would be undertaken a week or so later; the tour often included visits to relations on both sides of the family, in order to introduce their new son- or daughter-in-law to them. It was considered proper for the husband to purchase a new carriage for this purpose, and also to

132

re-furnish at least some of the rooms in his house in honour of his bride. It was also quite usual for the couple to take some female relation of the bride's along with them on the tour—Julia Bertram accompanies Maria and Mr Rushworth to Brighton, and Mrs Jennings thinks it was unkind of Lucy Steele, now Mrs Robert Ferrars, not to take Nancy with her to Dawlish.

When the newly weds returned home after the bridal tour, they were unlikely to find themselves lonely in some many-roomed mansion, for in all probability several other members of the bridegroom's family lived under his roof and might well continue to do so for years. His mother was supposed to leave once he was married: 'Mrs Rushworth was quite ready to retire, and make way for the fortunate young woman whom her dear son had selected;—and very early in November removed herself, her maid, her footman, and her chariot, with true dowager propriety, to Bath . . .'; but in those families who could not afford the upkeep of several establishments, she would have to stay on and accept second place in the household after her new daughter-in-law. The groom might have any number of siblings still living with him, and the bride likewise might have to bring along some widowed mother or unmarried sister of hers; there could also be spinster or widowed aunts on both sides of the family for whom the younger generation would have to accept responsibility. This is why the young Lucas sons were so glad to see their rather plain eldest sister Charlotte marry Mr Collins, as otherwise they would have had to support her throughout her life. In real life, this is exactly what happened to the widowed Mrs Austen and her two daughters; Edward Knight provided them with accommodation in the Chawton cottage, and the other sons contributed financially towards their upkeep.

Georgian or Regency wives would expect to have a baby within the first year of marriage, and probably every fifteen or eighteen months thereafter. Mrs Austen's first three sons were born in 1765, 1766 and 1767; it seems probable she then had a miscarriage in 1768, brought on by the move from Deane to Steventon; the next four children arrived in 1771, 1773, 1774 and 1775; and her last was in 1779 when she was forty. Indeed, to have only eight children was quite a modest family by the standards of the time, when a woman could feasibly produce two dozen children between puberty and menopause. Family planning is a twentieth-century luxury, thanks to the availability of contraceptives; condoms, made from sheep or pig intestines, had been invented in the seventeenth century, but these were used by rakish young men-about-town as a protection against infection from prostitutes, rather than for contraception in a respectable family environment. Total abstinence was the only sure safeguard against unwanted pregnancies—as Jane wrote, when hearing that her Kentish friend Mrs Deedes had just had her eighteenth child: 'I hope she will get the better of this Marianne, & then I wd. recommend to her & Mr D. the simple regimen of separate rooms.'

The death of young women in childbirth was common, and three of Jane Austen's brothers lost their wives in this way—Edward's Elizabeth died

134

following the birth of her eleventh child, Frank's Mary died likewise at her eleventh and Charles's Fanny at her fourth. The death rate for the children themselves was highest in the first five years of life, mostly from stomach complaints caused by incorrect feeding and aggravated by drastic doctoring. Once a child had survived to its teenage years, it might have a fairly reasonable life expectation; smallpox was now diminishing thanks to Jenner's discovery of vaccination, but tuberculosis could ravage a family and appendicitis would be fatal. Medical treatment consisted almost entirely of administering emetics, purges and enemas internally, with blistering and blood-letting externally; there was no anaesthesia or antisepsis for surgery, which could therefore easily result in infection and death. Dental treatment was minimal, consisting usually of extraction, again without any form of anaesthetic—by the age of forty-nine Mrs Austen had lost most of her front teeth, which understandably made her look old. Some dentists attempted to provide false teeth, made of ivory or porcelain, but these were for cosmetic rather than functional purposes; and cork pads, called 'plumpers', were held in the mouth between the gums and cheeks, in order to disguise or prevent, however temporarily, the sunken, wizened appearance of the face that inevitably followed once many teeth had been lost.

There are few references to this painful side of life in Jane Austen's novels—deaths, when they need to be mentioned, have usually occurred offstage at some earlier date; we are never told, for example, how Emma's mother came to die when still only in her thirties. There are some shadows lightly sketched in—Tom Bertram's accident and subsequent fever make his physician 'apprehensive for his lungs', and Jane Fairfax's family history makes the sympathetic neighbours in Highbury fear that she too will die young of tuberculosis. But on the whole, Jane's families may look forward to enjoying a happy, busy life in the country, with haymaking parties in midsummer to eat syllabubs and cream tarts, harvest suppers with an impromptu ball if a villager could play the fiddle, fruit-storing in autumn, ale-brewing in October, Christmas parties with beef and mince pies; and they may hope, like the Musgroves, to live to see their grandchildren growing up around them.

MEALS AND FOOD

The mealtimes and pattern of the day for Jane Austen and her characters were considerably different from ours, bound as most of us are to commute to day-long commercial employment. The agricultural labourers might rise with the dawn, but the landowner's family probably rose about seven or eight, and pursued a variety of early-morning tasks before breakfasting at ten. Edward Ferrars walks into Barton village to inspect his horses; Anne Elliot and Henrietta Musgrove walk down to the beach at Lyme; and Edmund Bertram has a long talk with Fanny Price plus a discussion, more quarrelsome, with Tom— all before breakfast. In real life, Jane herself, when in London in September 1813, was up and dressed and downstairs by half-past seven in the morning in order to finish a letter, at eight she was to have a discussion with Henry's house-keeper, and at nine she was going to walk out for a shopping

136

expedition to get that over before breakfast.

Once breakfast was finished at about eleven o'clock, the 'morning', by contemporary standards, lasted right through until about four o'clock in the afternoon or even later, when a large and lengthy dinner was served. There was no fixed luncheon in the middle of the day, but as it was courteous to offer refreshment to morning callers, who by definition would arrive between roughly eleven o'clock and three o'clock, any combination of cold meat, sandwiches, cake and seasonal fruits might be served on a tray at what we would now consider to be lunch-time. When Anne Elliot comes to stay at Uppercross Cottage, it is almost one o'clock, but she refers to the time as being still early in the morning, and Mary Musgrove then eats some cold meat before the sisters walk out to call at Uppercross Hall.

The dinner-hour varied according to the family's place of residence and social status—town or country, fashionable or conservative—and indeed changed quite considerably during Jane Austen's short lifetime alone. Earlier in the eighteenth century dinner had been at three, and another sit-down cooked meal, supper, ended the day about nine. At Barton Cottage dinner is at four, and also at Hartfield; at Mansfield parsonage it is four-thirty; when Mrs Jennings is in London she dines at five; General Tilney dines at five even in the country; and the Bingleys—obviously influenced by the ultra-fashionable Miss Bingley—at Netherfield dine as late as half past six. After dinner the family moved into the drawing-room, where tea with cold snacks or cakes was served about seven or eight; and for those who chose to sit up with cards or music until later in the evening, there might yet be a supper tray brought in about eleven o'clock or midnight, with wine and further cold food. Guests could be invited to join the family for the complete dinner, or else to come later on just for the tea. Mr Woodhouse, of course, prefers an earlier dinner and a cooked supper, in the fashion of his youth.

The style of dining was *à la française*—that is, all the food was laid out on the table at the same time, to be ready as the diners walked in; the dishes would vary in number from five to twenty-five, according to the grandeur of the occasion, and they were placed symmetrically around a large centrepiece. There would always be soup, large joints of meat and large whole fishes, as well as every kind of seasonal game and poultry, vegetables, sauces and pickles, and savoury and sweet puddings. The host would start the carving, and thereafter the guests helped themselves and each other from the nearest dishes, or else sent one of the attendant menservants to fetch a dish from elsewhere on the table. Rich families would have a footman to stand behind every chair, but more modest households would have to make do with whatever menservants they could muster—the Reverend Dr Philip Williams, a Hampshire cleric, wrote crossly to his daughters about a dinner he had attended where there was only one 'miserable joskins' (clumsy yokel) who was supposed to wait upon eight people.

It was not expected that everybody should eat everything. Individuals would choose the dishes they preferred, and once the guests had had as much as they required from this first course, the

138

table was cleared and the second course brought in—still the same number of separate dishes, both sweet and savoury, but tending now towards the lighter and sweeter side, with fruit tarts, custards and jellies. When the second course had been dealt with, the table was cleared yet again and the dessert brought in—nuts and fruits, fresh or preserved, with ice creams and other confectionery, together with sweet dessert wines. The youngest children of the family, who would not sit up for such adult dinners, were now brought down in their best clothes from the nursery to be introduced to the guests and given some little share of the dessert dainties. Mrs Norris, of course, is bitterly envious of the quality of the dinners the Grants serve, and consoles herself by the 'conviction of its being impossible among so many dishes but that some must be cold'. At the Coles' dinner party, when Frank Churchill and Emma are sitting side by side, their conversation is interrupted by 'the awkwardness of a rather long interval between the courses . . . but when the table was again safely covered, when every corner dish was placed exactly right, and occupation and ease were generally restored', they were able to return to their flirtatious gossip.

The dishes served at these dinners were also rather different from what we would now expect to eat. With no refrigeration or rapid air transport, foods were of necessity locally produced and their availability was entirely dependent upon the weather and the seasons. Nothing edible was ever wasted, and recipes existed for using every part of the animal—tripe, udder, testicles, pigs' ears, cocks' combs, all could be prepared in some way

139

for the dinner table. The first green peas of the summer were a great luxury, and it was a point of honour and competition between neighbours to have them ready to eat on 4 June, the King's birthday. Only rich landowners like General Tilney or Mr Darcy could afford heated greenhouses to produce cucumbers, pineapples, melons, grapes, nectarines and peaches throughout the summer; lesser squires would have to content themselves with the seasonal outdoor-grown cherries, apples and pears, and soft fruits, and their wives would hasten to bottle, pickle, candy, dry or otherwise preserve the surplus for use during the coming winter. Not even riches could provide meat and fish that were out of season, and when Catherine visits Northanger Abbey in March there would have been no venison, pheasants or plovers, no cod or mackerel; but, as a consolation during this cold spring month, pork could be eaten fresh, and other delicacies would be tame rabbits and early lambs.

Chocolate, tea, coffee, sugar and rice were all imported and consequently expensive, as were fine French wines. Oranges and lemons came from the Mediterranean countries and so arrived either half-ripe or else rotten, and were used for peel and juice in prepared dishes or drinks rather than eaten raw. Confectioners in large towns could afford to import and store Norway ice to use in the preparation of ice creams and cold drinks, but such luxuries were unobtainable in the countryside. Fish could only be eaten fresh by those people who lived near the sea or inland waters; but in 1801 sardines were first introduced to England, as being 'a fish cured in a peculiar manner, highly esteemed as a sandwich, and deemed of superior flavour to

140

the anchovy'.

In the smaller country towns tea parties were popular in winter, starting at about seven o'clock and taken as a formal meal in the dining room. The tortoiseshell tea caddy held the place of honour, containing black and green tea, with a cut-glass bowl in the centre for the expensive lump sugar. All the ladies were asked their tastes: 'Is the tea to your liking, ma'am? Do you prefer green to black? Is yours sweet enough?' All this took time, but was considered the essence of politeness, as there was much formality, even among old neighbours.

SERVANTS
Among the gentry even the average family would need to employ a number of servants to enable it to maintain its expected place in society, and the wealthier the family the greater the number. The ratio of servants to income was well understood in Jane's day, and is reflected in her novels: Mrs and Miss Bates can only afford the one little maid-of-all-work, Patty, to whom they probably paid between five and ten guineas a year, and the impoverished Prices, in their Portsmouth back street, have two sluttish maids. Mrs Dashwood and her daughters, whose income is reduced to £500 a year, can still afford two maids and a general manservant; going up the scale, Mr Bennet as a family man with about £2,000 a year might expect to employ eight female servants and eight menservants; while Bingley, Darcy and Rushworth probably employed two dozen or more. The chief female servants were the house-keeper and the cook, with whatever assortment of ladies'-,

141

nursery-, house-, laundry-, dairy-, still-room- and kitchen-maids the employer's family circumstances might warrant. For the height of luxury the menservants would include a French chef—Mrs Bennet thinks hopefully that Darcy could afford to employ two or three—but more usually the cook was female and the menservants would be the butler, valet, coachman, footmen, grooms and gardeners.

The landowner would expect to employ his tenants, and in turn the tenants expected that the landowner would find work for them somewhere in the estate's economy. It seems to Catherine Morland, when she visits Northanger Abbey, that General Tilney has a whole parish at work within his kitchen gardens alone; in the early nineteenth century it became fashionable to employ a Scottish head gardener, as being better educated and more efficient than his English equivalent, so no doubt General Tilney in future years will boast of engaging a Scotsman to manage these gardens. On a lesser scale, Emma reminds her father that it was thanks to him that Hannah, the daughter of the Hartfield coachman James, has been engaged as housemaid by the newly married Mrs Weston. In addition to getting their uniforms, board, lodging and wages, servants could expect to receive their employers' cast-off clothing and also to see something of the world beyond their own village when accompanying the family on holiday trips to London or the seacoast. Thrifty servants might well save enough to enable them to set up in business on their own account, as innkeepers or shopkeepers; and it was a kindness on the part of local squires and their ladies to see that the village children learnt to read and write, as a first step towards such domestic service.

SHOPS AND SHOPPING

A small town or village would have very few retail outlets, as we see from the description given of Emma's Highbury, which seems to have no more than one butcher and one baker to supply the necessary basic foods to all, and Mrs Ford's premises, the 'principal woollen-draper, linen-draper, and haberdasher's shop united, the shop first in size and fashion in the place', to supply clothing for the local gentry—there is by implication some other shop, smaller and plainer, that provides for the coarse workaday clothes of the servants and labourers. A greengrocer would not be necessary, as the residents would either grow their own fruit and vegetables or else buy them from the nearest farm—Mr Knightley, in fact, gives the Bates family a sack of cooking apples every year from his Donwell Abbey orchards—and poultry, eggs, milk and butter would likewise be locally produced and sold direct. The bakery—run by Mr and Mrs Wallis and their family—perhaps sold some dry grocery goods over and above what was needed for their own shop's production.

Gloves, hats, stockings and ribbons could be bought ready-made, and we know that Mrs Ford's emporium stocks such items, but shoes and clothes were made to measure, not yet available off the peg. When Jane Austen, or one of her characters, talks of buying a gown, this means buying a suitable length of material that would then be handed over to a dressmaker for her to work on;

143

the style of the gown would be decided in discussions between the dressmaker and her client—Harriet Smith has a 'pattern-gown' which she wants simply to be copied in her latest purchase of plain muslin—and the fashion-plates printed in ladies' magazines illustrated the latest smart London styles which the local dressmaker would then adapt to suit her individual customers. The dressmaker—sometimes referred to by older ladies as a 'mantua-maker', after a garment popular in past years—would visit ladies at home, perhaps staying with them for some days in order to work on clothes for several members of the family at the same time. There were also travelling pedlars who drove their carts round rural neighbourhoods to sell fabric and haberdashery on the spot to customers who might have difficulty in reaching the nearest town, and in her early letters Jane Austen mentions buying items from one of these itinerant salesmen.

The larger country towns could of course support more, and more specialized, shops and tradesmen—during Jane Austen's childhood at Steventon the family's nearest shopping centre was Overton, which could muster five grocers and two butchers, four tailors and no less than seven shoemakers, as well as two breeches-makers, two staymakers, one hair-dresser, and a clockmaker, apart from such other necessary rural trades as millers, maltsters, carpenters and blacksmiths. Country shopkeepers would have to obtain their retail goods from wholesale dealers in the large cities, and either the owner or a senior assistant would make regular visits for this purpose—when Jane Austen was shopping in Basingstoke for a change, she found that Mrs Ryder's shop had 'scarcely any netting silk; but Miss Wood as usual is going to Town [that is, London] very soon, & will lay in a fresh stock'.

Although London and the other big provincial cities had every kind of market, shop and warehouse, whether for foods, fabrics or domestic goods, it was nevertheless still the custom for individual pedlars to wander the residential streets with a basket or cart, crying their wares for doorstep sales: 'Sweet China oranges, sweet China!—Milk below, maids!—Strawberries, scarlet strawberries!—Hot spice gingerbread, smoking hot!—Round and sound, fivepence a pound, Duke cherries!—Turnips and carrots, ho!—New mackerel, new mackerel!—Two bunches a penny, primroses!' When Anne Elliot accompanies Lady Russell unwillingly to Bath in mid-winter, her nerves are irritated by the noises of the city streets: '. . . the dash of other carriages, the heavy rumble of carts and drays, the bawling of newsmen, muffin-men and milkmen. . . .'

A SENSE OF PLACE

All Jane Austen's novels are set in the southern half of England, and in most of them the action takes place in counties or towns of which she had personal experience—the main exception being the location of *Mansfield Park* in Northamptonshire, a midland county she had never visited, and which she knew only by hearsay from her brother Henry. *Northanger Abbey* and *Persuasion* both have scenes set in Bath, and the streets and buildings mentioned in these two books nearly all survive to this day, so the keen reader can have the pleasure of following precisely in the footsteps of Catherine Morland and Anne Elliot. Part of the action of *Persuasion* is in Lyme Regis, and here again, though the town has changed in some respects, it is still possible to walk on the Cobb and guess at the place where Louisa Musgrove has her accident. The central section of *Sense and Sensibility* is set in London, and in this case the streets mentioned survive, though the houses are usually either altered or else entirely rebuilt. In the course of travelling from Kent to London in her chaise and four, Lady Catherine de Bourgh always changes horses at the Bell in Bromley; and when leaving Bath for Northanger Abbey, General Tilney rests his carriage horses at Petty France; and as many of Jane Austen's contemporary readers would know, these were perfectly genuine inns and staging-posts. The Bell has been rebuilt, but Petty France survives, though there are no longer any horses stabled in its yards. Apart from these urban episodes, the novels as a whole are set in the mansions and manor houses of country villages, about which Jane unobtrusively tells us as much as we need to know to understand the action, without wasting time or words on purple passages describing the landscape or the interior of every room of the house. But the passing of two centuries has caused so many changes in everyday living that some explanation of the conditions in which the characters of Jane's novels exist has now become necessary.

STATELY HOMES

The eighteenth century was marked by an extraordinary advance in wealth, luxury and refinement of taste, and many landowners enthusiastically pulled down the small-roomed, low-lying, rambling and higgledy-piggledy Tudor and Jacobean manor houses inherited from their ancestors, and built instead elegant symmetrical mansions in classical style and sited on rising ground, which thereby commanded extensive views over artistically landscaped gardens and parklands. Some of the peers had enormous landholdings, and country palaces such as Blenheim, Chatsworth, Knole or Castle Howard rivalled anything the Royal Family possessed. Until about the middle of the seventeenth century it had been the normal practice for the sovereign and attendant courtiers to travel round the country and stay for weeks on end with the wealthiest of the kingdom's subjects; this served the triple purpose of enabling the sovereign to judge the loyalty—or lack of it—of such subjects, to levy direct taxation

147

in the shape of free board and lodging for the entire Court for the period of the visit, and to ensure that the cost to the host of such entertainment would effectively prevent him from becoming too rich and powerful and so a potential rival to the monarchy. The greatest of the medieval manor houses consequently had to be built large enough to entertain visiting royalty; for example, at Knole the fifteenth-century house is said to contain 7 courtyards, 52 staircases, and 365 rooms. Later in the seventeenth century the sovereign's personal powers were gradually taken over by Parliamentary government, and royal progresses were no longer so significant.

Country mansions could therefore now be built on a smaller scale, but the principle of having a suite of state apartments was maintained. These would consist, in general terms, of an entrance hall off which opened saloons, dining rooms and withdrawing rooms, and probably a music room and a library; a fine staircase led upwards from the hall to the first floor, where the main bedrooms were situated. There might well also be specific rooms set aside for use during the winter or the summer months. Even if royalty were no longer expected to call, the state rooms were always large and lavishly decorated, intended to display the owner's wealth when he entertained all his friends and neighbours. It was accepted that these huge rooms, while beautiful to behold, would be exceedingly impractical—echoing, draughty, impossible to light or heat adequately—and the owner and his family would have their own suites of smaller rooms for the purposes of everyday living.

Newly built mansions of the early eighteenth century were almost invariably designed in the Palladian style. This took its name from a Venetian architect, Andrea Palladio, who had studied Roman ruins in Italy and in his work made a conscious attempt to recreate the art, architecture and civilization of ancient Rome. The style became very popular in England, especially for country mansions and public buildings, though in practice it provided uncomfortable living conditions in a climate lacking the Italian sun and warmth. The most famous English architect working in this style was William Kent (1685–1748), who also designed furniture to complement the interiors of his buildings. His successor was Robert Adam (1728–92), who was the fashionable architect in Britain between 1760 and 1780; he rejected the rigid rules imposed by Palladianism and created more delicate buildings with a wide variety of architectural ornament. Like Kent, he would design the whole house, complete with decoration and furniture. Lady Catherine de Bourgh's Rosings Park, and Sir Thomas Bertram's Mansfield Park, both described as 'modern', may be Adam-style houses. By the end of the eighteenth century, however, Adam's work was considered fussy and frivolous, and the next trend, early in the nineteenth century, was a revival of classical Greek (as opposed to Roman) styles, in both architecture and furniture. As a reaction against the smooth elegance of the neo-Greek, there grew up an Egyptian-influenced style of furniture, sparked off by public interest in Napoleon's campaign in Egypt and Nelson's victory at the Battle of Aboukir Bay; and towards

149

the end of Jane Austen's life the pendulum had swung again, this time towards the mock-medieval or supposedly Gothic style, with pointed arches, false battlements, spires and crockets being added to domestic buildings and furniture alike. The *cottage orné* which Sir Edward Denham contemplates building at Sanditon would at the very least have 'Gothick' windows and doors.

COST OF LIVING

A very substantial annual income was obviously needed to support this lifestyle, and the greater part of this usually came from farming the landowner's estate. It was therefore in the landowner's interest to keep abreast of scientific agricultural developments and do all he could to improve the output of his farms and the breed of his cattle. Mr Coke of Holkham in Norfolk became a legend in his lifetime for transforming his estate into a model of agricultural practice that was admired throughout England and beyond. Even the lesser gentry could follow this good example so far as they were able, and Mr Digweed at Steventon spent £250 on constructing a large and more efficient threshing-mill on his Manor Farm. At the other end of the scale, both socially and financially, the Duke of Devonshire's estates at Chatsworth in Derbyshire provided him with £100,000 a year, to which he could add profits from mining interests elsewhere in Derbyshire and also rents from properties in London.

It is difficult to equate these values with those of today, but a rough guide would be to multiply by fifty—allowing the Duke of Devonshire the equivalent of something more than £5 million a year. In Jane Austen's fictional world, Mr Rushworth, with his £12,000 (roughly equivalent to £600,000) a year, is too rich a catch for Maria Bertram to reject. Until the change to decimalization in 1971, the pound (£) was divided into twenty shillings (abbreviated to *s*., from the Latin *solidus*), and each shilling was made up of twelve pence (abbreviated to *d*., from the Latin *denarius*)—that is, there were 240 pence to the pound sterling. In Jane Austen's time there was no actual coin for a pound value until the gold sovereign was minted in July 1817, and a golden guinea (value 21 shillings) was the coin in normal use. There was also a golden half-guinea (value ten shillings and sixpence), and a golden third-guinea (value seven shillings) was briefly in circulation from 1797 to 1813. Silver coins were the shilling, sixpence, fourpence (called a groat), threepence, twopence (half-groat), penny and halfpenny. The 'Bank of England dollar' was an overstamped Spanish coin, valued at 5*s*., and used to offset the shortage of silver coinage at the time; also as a result of the lack of raw silver, at the end of the eighteenth century the twopence, penny and halfpenny were minted in copper.

Towards the end of Jane's life, she mentions the new silver coinage that was issued early in 1817. She also notes, in *Persuasion*, the silver three-shilling piece that was minted only between 1811 and 1816; while in *Sense and Sensibility* the newly wed Lucy Ferrars borrows all her sister's money, leaving Nancy Steele without so much as seven shillings (a third-guinea) to her name; and in *Mansfield Park* the schoolboy Edmund sends a half-guinea to his younger cousin William Price. At

151

a time when a country curate might be expected to keep himself and a family on a salary of fifty-two guineas a year—one guinea a week—Edmund's present would have been a welcome addition to midshipman William's meagre pay.

FICTIONAL HOUSES

The houses in which Jane Austen places most of her characters would by modern standards be considered far and away too large for occupation by only one family, and nowadays would be more likely to be used for schools or institutions. But in her day such country mansions were the norm for the landed gentry, and this is one reason why she does not usually give much description of the houses in her novels—all her contemporary readers would know what they were like, and many of them would indeed live in exactly such mansions. On the whole, she does little more than mention here and there that a house is either particularly old or particularly new. The oldest of her houses are Northanger Abbey (though this has been modernized, to Catherine Morland's disappointment); Norland Park and Allenham Court; Sotherton Court and Thornton Lacey parsonage; Donwell Abbey and Highbury vicarage; and Uppercross Hall and Winthrop Farm. Barton Cottage, Rosings Park, Mansfield Park, Hartfield and Kellynch Lodge are all said to be 'modern', which, for Jane Austen, must mean built in the second half of the eighteenth century; and Mr Parker's new development of Sanditon is precisely dated to 1816. Most of the other houses have no specific comments made about them, and are therefore likely to be of seventeenth-century date, in Jane's eyes neither ancient nor modern.

The parsonages which are mentioned in some of the novels vary from that at Delaford, said merely to be small and old, via Mr Elton's vicarage at Highbury, which is also said to be old and not very good, to the imposing one at Thornton Lacey—'a solid-walled, roomy, mansion-like-looking house'— which dates apparently to the sixteenth century, and where Edmund Bertram and Fanny start their married life. The rectory of Mansfield itself is smaller but newer than Thornton Lacey, probably having been rebuilt in the early eighteenth century, and does not differ appreciably from any other small manor house of the period. Mr Collins's rectory at Hunsford is only briefly described, in general terms which could apply to any number of similar parsonages in Kent: overall the house is rather small, but well built and convenient; it stands in a garden sloping to the road, entered by a small gate in the laurel hedge and green-painted wooden fence, and is approached by a short gravel walk.

There are one or two occasions when her characters have to move out of their normal homes into something smaller, and Jane makes a point of mentioning the difference—and this is when we suddenly feel the difference, too, between her century and ours. For example, Mrs Dashwood and her daughters have to leave their country mansion of Norland Park and move into Barton Cottage— which to us would mean probably a very small old house, thatched and whitewashed, with perhaps two or three tiny rooms upstairs and down—but in Jane's time such a small house would have been viewed merely as a hovel, fit to be occupied only by muddy labourers. The word 'cottage' has changed its meaning over the past two centuries: in 1809 the *Hampshire Chronicle* advertised the sale by auction of

> A Neat, Elegant, and Very Convenient Freehold Cottage Residence . . . containing a drawing-room, eating parlour, breakfast ditto, six bed-chambers, good kitchen, convenient offices, with excellent wine and beer cellars; and, in a detached building, menservants' rooms, coal and wood houses, coach house, stabling for five horses, granary, dog kennel, &c. The Cottage has southern aspect with a verandah to the sitting rooms on the ground floor, which opens to a Paddock or Pleasure Ground, skirted by the River Itchen, well stocked with Trout; the kitchen garden is fully cropped and planted . . . the Gardener will shew the House and Grounds . . .

Barton cottage appears to be not a great deal smaller than this one.

DOMESTIC INTERIORS

The interior decoration of country houses, whether real or fictional, depended upon the age of the buildings and whether their owners were rich enough to keep remodelling and modernizing them. Those with medieval foundations, such as Donwell Abbey and Northanger Abbey, would probably originally have had tapestries hanging in front of lime-plastered stone walls; later on, wooden panelling (wainscoting), full or half height, would have replaced the tapestries. In the early eighteenth century it became fashionable to have half-height wainscoting with wallpaper above it, or sometimes the whole wall was papered.

Wallpaper had originated at the beginning of the sixteenth century as a humble imitation of tapestry or other textile hangings, but it was not until the eighteenth century that printed-paper manufacturers had been able to improve and extend their range of designs sufficiently to make them acceptable to the wealthy as a new fashion for interior decoration. The papers might themselves have a printed design, or might be plain in a single colour which could then be used with decorative borders. The most expensive hand-painted wallpapers were imported from China by the East India Company's ships, and were highly fashionable during the eighteenth century. Catherine's bedroom at Northanger Abbey has wallpaper when she would have preferred something more ancient, but we are not told what this paper is like. Edward and Elinor Ferrars, once they are married and gone to Delaford, are busy choosing wallpapers from manufacturers' pattern-books, in order to redecorate their little parsonage before they move in.

Of course, not all house owners wanted to have their walls papered. Many preferred to have them painted in some pastel colour against which family portraits would show up to advantage, and which also gave scope for architectural decorations to be picked out in gilding or a contrasting colour. The walls of Mansfield Park and Rosings Park are more likely to have been painted than papered, especially as painting was the more expensive treatment.

The style of the windows in these walls would again depend upon the age of the building. The older casement windows consisted of small diamond-shaped panes of glass joined by strips of lead, the whole set within a wooden frame, which then opened outwards upon hinges. Sash windows, sliding up and down in a wooden frame fixed within the window aperture, were invented in France and came to Britain in the late seventeenth century; at first the rectangular panes of glass were small and set within thick wooden glazing bars, but as the years passed the panes grew larger and the bars thinner, until eventually plate glass was invented in the middle of the nineteenth century, which meant there need be only two panes of glass in the window, the upper and the lower sash.

At night hinged wooden shutters would be unfolded from the side of the window, and pulled across the glass to be locked in place with a metal bar. For daytime use paired curtains of light material, intended to keep out strong sunlight, might be fitted, though this was more usually done only for important rooms. During the eighteenth century it was realized that curtains could lend themselves to another display of conspicuous consumption on the part of rich owners, and every possible variation of expensive fabrics made into festoons, swags, drapes, pelmets, tassels and fringes became fashionable in turn. For less important rooms pull-down fabric blinds on spring-loaded rollers could be fitted, such as are still in use today.

At Northanger Abbey the windows to the main living rooms downstairs are a disappointment to

Catherine Morland: 'To be sure, the pointed arch was preserved—the form of them was Gothic—they might be even casements—but every pane was so large, so clear, so light! To an imagination which had hoped for the smallest divisions, and the heaviest stone-work, for painted glass, dirt and cobwebs, the difference was very distressing'—and when Catherine goes to the bedroom of the deceased Mrs Tilney, which is in the modernized part of the Abbey, she is again disappointed to find that 'the warm beams of a western sun gaily poured through two sash windows!' In *Persuasion*, when Lady Russell and Anne Elliot are driving down Pulteney Street in Bath, and Anne thinks Lady Russell must have seen Captain Wentworth walking on the pavement near by, she is disconcerted when Lady Russell merely says: '. . . I was looking after some window-curtains, which Lady Alicia and Mrs Frankland were telling me of last night . . . as being the handsomest and best hung of any in Bath . . . but I confess I can see no curtains hereabouts that answer their description.'

Marble or stone-flagged floors were left uncovered, to show their fine quality and beautiful geometric designs; wooden floors in the past had been covered by loose straw or by rush matting, but by the eighteenth century it had become fashionable to polish the floorboards of the living rooms, and leave the boards exposed except for a small square Turkey carpet in the centre of the room. During the eighteenth century carpets began to be made in England, particularly at the towns of Axminster, Kidderminster and Wilton; these carpets were loom-woven narrow strips that could easily be cut to shape, which meant that the principal living rooms could now be fitted with wall-to-wall pile carpeting. An even richer alternative was to have a carpet designed and shaped to fit a specific room. Bedrooms remained the Cinderellas of the house, and rarely had more than a U-shaped strip of carpet placed round the sides and end of the bed itself, the rest of the floor being left bare save perhaps for a small rug or two. These bedside carpets might even be home-made, worked with worsted threads in double cross stitch on very coarse canvas.

For less important rooms there was a variety of cheaper products available: the Kidderminster factories also made flat, hard-wearing stair carpeting, and the long, narrow pieces of 'Scotch' and 'Venetian' carpeting were used for passages or servants' rooms. List carpets, made from coarse strong cotton, and hair cloth (usually goats' hair), were the very cheapest form of floor covering, and as such they were used exclusively in domestic quarters. Floor cloths—canvas treated with oil and several coats of paint until it became waterproof and easily cleanable—were used specifically where spillages might occur, such as beneath the sideboard in a dining room, or the wash-stand in a bedroom. Green baize cloth was often used to cover carpets to protect them against fading, or as a crumb-cloth underneath dining tables, or even as a cheap substitute for carpet itself—hence Mrs Norris's swift action in purloining the green baize curtains from the aborted theatrical production at Mansfield Park for use in her own house.

FURNITURE
From medieval times onwards, English furniture

158

had been made from native woods—ash, beech, elm and oak—with oak providing the strongest and longest lasting pieces. Walnut, either English or imported, became fashionable in the seventeenth century; a little mahogany was imported from the Americas towards the end of that century and much more during the eighteenth century, until it became almost exclusively the wood of choice for fine furniture. All houses would have some mixture of old and new furniture, the old, as always, being relegated to the children's or servants' rooms. It was usual for new furniture to be purchased when the heir married and brought his bride to her new home; Marianne Dashwood, having visited Allenham Court in Willoughby's company and assuming that he intends to marry her, tells Elinor: '. . . there is one remarkably pretty sitting room up stairs . . . with modern furniture it would be delightful . . .'; and while Mary Crawford is considering whether to pursue Tom Bertram she tells herself that Mansfield Park needs to be 'completely new furnished'.

In the first half of the eighteenth century William Kent designed furniture—large, heavy, carved and gilded—to suit his equally heavy Palladian houses. Robert Adam's more delicate architecture required lighter furniture, and his designs were put into practice by the renowned London cabinet-maker Thomas Chippendale (*c.* 1718–79). Succeeding Chippendale as top-class cabinet-makers came George Hepplewhite (died 1786) and Thomas Sheraton (*c.* 1750–1806), whose furniture became ever more delicate and graceful; at Pemberley, the 'very pretty sitting room, lately fitted up with greater elegance and lightness than

159

the apartments below', probably contains furniture from Sheraton's designs.

At the end of the eighteenth century improved glass-making techniques led to the production of single mirror-plates up to ten feet in height, thus enabling the creation of the 'cheval' dressing-mirror, where the tall framed mirror was fitted on to a four-legged base, and could be tilted as required by means of screws or weights to give a full-length reflection. Admiral Croft tells Anne that he has removed from the Kellynch Hall dressing room all Sir Walter Elliot's large looking glasses apart from one 'great thing' that he ignores, which is very probably just such a modern cheval glass.

The item of furniture which has changed most since Jane Austen's time is the bed, with its associated bedding. For centuries the usual design for a bed had been that known as the four-poster or tester bed. This consisted of the bedstead, which was a wooden base-frame of four rails set on legs, the rails having holes drilled in them through which cords were threaded to form a loose network across the base; the headboard, usually backing on to the wall; the bedposts, rising from each corner of the bedstead; and the tester—the roof of the bed—supported by the posts. The bed-curtains, which were partly for warmth and partly for privacy, hung from the tester down to the floor, making the bed into a completely enclosed little area within the bedroom. The mattress, which might be stuffed with wool, flock, feathers or straw, was then placed on the cords of the bedstead, and covered with a layer of canvas, and the rest of the bed-furniture (bedding) was piled up on top. This usually consisted of two feather beds, sheets, blankets, another feather bed and an embroidered quilt laid over the whole. The bedstead itself was high enough for another small bed to be stored underneath, for use by a child or servant as required; and the total height of the bedstead plus bedding was such that a special item of furniture, bed-steps, had to be provided in order for the sleeper to climb in. A lighter version of the tester bed was the tent or field bed, which could be dismantled for travelling.

In the course of the eighteenth century, beds, like all other items of furniture, became lighter and more elegant. They were made in mahogany or satinwood rather than oak, and the curtains were now of silk or cotton fabrics rather than canvas, and so could be washed instead of hanging to gather the dust of decades. In 1794 Mr Austen bought two new tent beds for Jane and Cassandra, and his account with the local upholstery firm in Basingstoke shows that the beds had cotton curtains in a small blue and white check.

As well as buying new beds for his daughters, in the following year Mr Austen changed one of the bedrooms at Steventon rectory into an upstairs drawing room, or dressing room, as Jane and Cassandra liked to call it. The wallpaper was blue, the curtains blue-striped, and the fitted bookshelves in cheap wood were painted chocolate to match the carpet. His granddaughter Anna wrote in later years:

I remember the common-looking carpet with its chocolate ground that covered the floor, and some portions of the furniture. A

161

painted press, with shelves above for books, that stood with its back to the wall next the Bedroom, & opposite the fireplace, my Aunt Jane's Pianoforte—& above all, on a table between the windows, above which hung a looking-glass, 2 Tonbridge-ware work boxes of oval shape, fitted up with ivory barrels containing reels for silk, yard measures, etc. . . . But the charm of the room, with its scanty furniture and cheaply papered walls, must have been, for those old enough to understand it, the flow of native homebred wit, with all the fun & nonsense of a clever family who had but little intercourse with the outer world.

Anna's younger brother, James-Edward Austen-Leigh, also described, in his *Memoir of Jane Austen*, the scantiness of furniture, even in middle-class houses, during her lifetime:

There was a general deficiency of carpeting in sitting-rooms, bed-rooms, and passages. A pianoforte, or rather a spinnet or harpsichord, was by no means a necessary appendage. It was to be found only where there was a decided taste for music, not so common then as now [1869], or in such great houses as would probably contain a billiard-table. There would often be but one sofa in the house, and that a stiff, angular, uncomfortable article. There were no deep easy-chairs, nor other appliances for lounging; for to lie down, or even to lean back, was a luxury permitted only to old persons or invalids. . . . A small writing desk, with a smaller work box or netting-case, was all that each young lady contributed to occupy the table; for the large family work-basket, though often produced in the parlour, lived in the closet [wall-cupboard].

Another household, that of an elderly maiden lady and her companion, living in Kensington, was described by a young visitor in 1810 as being

> . . . one of those old-fashioned households now hardly remembered, where the fires were all put out, the carpets all taken up, and curtains down, upon the first of May, not to be replaced in those shivery rooms until the first of October; where the hard high-backed chairs were ranged against the wall, and a round, club-legged, darkly-polished table stood quite bare in the middle of the room. In one window was a parrot on a perch, screaming for ever, 'How d'ye do?' In the other the two old ladies with their worsted work, their large baskets, and their fat spaniel.

Jane Austen herself, when she was writing *Persuasion* in 1815, was old enough to look back on the changing fashions in furnishings during her lifetime, and described the manor house at Uppercross as having an

> . . . old-fashioned square parlour, with a small carpet and shining floor, to which the present daughters of the house were

gradually giving the proper air of confusion by a grand piano forte and a harp, flower-stands and little tables placed in every direction. Oh! could the originals of the portraits against the wainscot, could the gentlemen in brown velvet and the ladies in blue satin have seen what was going on, have been conscious of such an overthrow of all order and neatness! The portraits themselves seemed to be staring in astonishment.

SANITATION

What all these houses, great or small, lacked, were satisfactory arrangements for domestic sanitation. In medieval castles the problem had been solved by building garderobes (lavatory alcoves) high up in the thickness of the stone wall of a turret, with a chute beneath the wooden seat that dropped straight down into the surrounding moat or river; but once life became sufficiently peaceful to warrant living at ground level in houses rather than turret level in castles, this solution was no longer available. The answer, for the next few centuries, was to build a separate small 'necessary house' or privy, with a cesspit underneath it, somewhere in the grounds but not too far from the main house. This would then enable ladies to say politely that they were just going outside 'to pluck a rose'. If the weather was too bad to venture out, then the indoor alternatives were chamber pots and close-stools (a bucket inside a wooden box-seat) for bedrooms, and commodes (a false-fronted chest of drawers or bureau containing a chamber pot) for dining rooms or gentlemen's studies. Some of the country houses might be sufficiently modernized to have a little lavatory cubicle opening off a larger room, but this too would be furnished with only a pot or bucket. In all these cases, it was necessary for servants to carry the pots and buckets through the house in order to dispose of the contents into some outside cesspit, with all the resultant unpleasant smells and potential for embarrassing meetings between visitors walking upstairs as the housemaid was coming down with a brimming pot in her hand. Furthermore, the cesspits themselves would have to be emptied from time to time, especially those in towns where there was no room for a large pit. Night-soil men would come discreetly after dark to dig out the contents and take them away to be sold as manure.

The idea of a fixed pan that could be flushed by a plumbed-in water supply had first been suggested in the sixteenth century, but it was not until the second half of the eighteenth century that serious attempts were made to construct such indoor water closets and to overcome the problems of flushing, drainage and smells. The supply of water was itself the first difficulty: in London there had been early attempts to pump water from the Thames and deliver it by means of wooden water mains laid in some of the larger streets, through individual smaller pipes feeding into the basements of houses. However, this service could provide only a tiny trickle of water at strictly limited hours, and the River Thames was in any case notoriously filthy. Most houses, whether in London or in the country, would have a pump in the kitchen or backyard, fed by a well sunk into the water-table below; some larger houses might collect rainwater in a tank in the attic, which would could then be gravity-fed downwards to where it was required. The engineer Joseph Bramah invented an improved flushing system in 1778, and by 1797 claimed to have made and sold six thousand of his new model pan and fitments. From the beginning of the nineteenth century water closets were installed as a matter of course in high-class newly built houses, though it was more than a century before their installation in lower-class housing became universal. Purpose-made lavatory paper was not marketed until the end of the nineteenth century, and before that scraps of waste paper or rags were used.

Toilet tables in bedrooms provided little bowls and basins for a lady to take a strip wash, and there were also specially designed shaving tables for gentlemen; these tables could also include a pull-out bidet at low level, though still of course without fixed plumbing. Hip baths would usually be brought up to the bedrooms from the domestic quarters in the basement. All the cans of hot water necessary for these basins and baths were likewise carried in by the servants, and while the family was at breakfast the housemaid would visit each bedroom with her chamber-bucket, jug of hot water and towels, so as to empty and clean out all the various pots and basins just used.

An elementary form of portable shower bath had been invented: this consisted of a small water tank supported on three or four high metal legs, one of which was in fact a pipe up which the water was forced by a hand pump from a bucket. A hip bath or other suitable tub, in which the bather stood, was placed below the tank, and the bather then

166

pulled a cord or chain to release the water. Such shower baths were most unusual luxuries and a source of amazement to those who had never seen them before. When the 15th Regiment of Foot was stationed in Scarborough, on the Yorkshire coast, in 1810, Major Renny and his wife lodged in a house belonging to one of the local fishing-boat skippers, known as Captain Weston, and had a shower bath put up in a small dressing room which was between the bedroom and dining room.

> The door of the latter being ajar, we heard the couple coming upstairs, the Captain saying, 'What is't like, Dolly?' 'Hish't, Tummas, don'tee make a noise, they'll hear 'ee.' We listened quietly, knowing what was going to be exhibited. 'Now, Tummas, come inside and I'll show what they does.' We heard him say, 'What's this string for, Dolly?' then a great splash, a roar and a scream. . . . and you never saw such a disconcerted couple, shivering, being half drowned, and feeling so much ashamed. Thomas said Dolly did not tell him what the string was for, and she said, 'Tummas had gived it a great pull before she had time to tell 'im.' We reassured them by sympathizing with them very much, but for many days they apologized for having been 'so imperent as to look into un'.

HEATING
During the eighteenth century, the usual way to kindle a flame was to employ a tinderbox—the equivalent of a modern cigarette lighter. The box

167

contained a fire-steel and flint, which had to be struck sharply together to produce a spark, which spark then had to fall on tinder (soft old rag or dry vegetable fibre) and make it smoulder; by judicious blowing the smouldering tinder could be persuaded to make an elementary form of match, a scrap of wood dipped in brimstone, catch alight. The process could take several minutes to succeed. Chemically combustible matches tipped with phosphorus were invented in 1788, but do not seem to have become popular, perhaps because phosphorus is so dangerously volatile; another form of chemical match was invented in France in 1805, and brought to England after 1815. Safety matches as we know them were not invented until the middle of the nineteenth century.

In the main living rooms of country houses the open fireplaces were very large, and burnt mostly wood; coal was already being mined in the north-eastern counties of England, but for lack of suitable inland transport could only be sent by sea from Newcastle-on-Tyne down to London, with slow redistribution by sea or river barges thereafter, which consequently made it a scarce and very expensive fuel. These large fireplaces were notoriously smoky and inefficient, consuming much fuel while most of the heat went straight up the chimney; the ladies sitting nearest the fire might have to use hand-screens to save their faces from becoming uncomfortably hot—such hand-screens as Elinor Dashwood painted as a gift for her sister-in-law Fanny—and other people sitting further away would find themselves still uncomfortably cold.

This perennial domestic annoyance aroused the

interest of the Anglo-American Benjamin Thompson (1753–1814) of Rumford, New Hampshire, a soldier, politician and scientist, who was later given the title Count Rumford by the Elector of Bavaria as an acknowledgement of the administrative reforms he had carried out in that German principality. Count Rumford studied the mechanics of heat, and in 1797 published an influential essay on the design of grates, aimed at solving the problems of smoky chimneys and excessive fuel consumption. His ideas proved so successful in practice that 'Rumford grates' rapidly became an essential improvement for wealthy homeowners. General Tilney has had the fireplace in the common drawing-room at Northanger Abbey 'Rumfordized', much to Catherine's disappointment: 'The fire-place, where she had expected the ample width and ponderous carving of former times, was contracted to a Rumford, with slabs of plain though handsome marble . . ..' Rumford also improved the design of the cooking stove; and the General appears also to have installed Rumford stoves in his kitchens: '. . . every modern invention to facilitate the labour of the cooks had been adopted within this, their spacious theatre. . . .'

In summer, a chimney-board could be fitted in front of the fireplace to hide the black empty hole; this was a wooden panel either covered with wallpaper or fabric, or else painted with a cheerful picture. The cunning Lucy Steele uses chimney-boards as cover for eavesdropping, as her sister Nancy openly tells Elinor Dashwood: '. . . for a year or two back, when Martha Sharpe and I had so many secrets together, she never made any bones of hiding in a closet, or behind a chimney board, on purpose to hear what we said.'

LIGHTING
Candles provided the main source of domestic lighting during Jane Austen's lifetime. They were usually made either of tallow or beeswax; tallow was a mixture of molten beef and mutton fat, which was poured into metal moulds to solidify into candles of uniform sizes that were then sold by the weight—eight, ten or twelve candles to the pound. When lighted, tallow candles had an unpleasant smell of burnt fat, gave off dirty smoke and provided only a dim light, and their wicks needed constant trimming—'snuffing' was the term—if the candle were to burn slowly and steadily rather than 'guttering'—when the wick burnt its way unevenly out of the surrounding tallow and so made the candle run to waste. Tallow candles were nevertheless widely used, as they were much cheaper than beeswax.

Beeswax could not be moulded into candles, but was used either in flat sheets that were then rolled up round the wick, or else melted and poured by hand over a line of wicks hanging from a frame. Candles made from beeswax burnt without an unpleasant smell, gave a brighter and cleaner light than tallow and rarely needed snuffing, so were used in ballroom or theatre chandeliers where constant attention to the wicks would not be possible. Even so, the combined heat generated by the candles themselves and the members of the public gathered together could sometimes become so great that the candles would wilt and drop their hot wax on to the heads and finery of the guests below.

A third alternative, which became available only during the eighteenth century, was spermaceti, a hard white substance processed from the oil found in the head cavities of sperm whales. This wax-like mass could then be moulded into candles that burned with a very bright flame, but were nearly as expensive as beeswax.

It was considered very extravagant to have many candles burning at the same time, and in middle-class households it was usual for there to be only one or two placed on the table, with all the members of the family sitting round to have an equal share of the light; but in the Prices' shabby little parlour in Portsmouth Mr Price holds the solitary candle between himself and his newspaper, leaving Fanny practically in the dark. There was also of course a distinction as to which kind of candle was used for guests or visitors, wax naturally being only for those of higher social standing; this enables Mrs Elton to boast of her rich friend Mrs Bragge, who lives so lavishly as to use wax candles even in her children's schoolroom. Miss Bates is staggered at the lighting arrangements Mr Weston has provided for the ball at the Crown inn: 'I never saw any thing equal to the comfort and style— Candles every where!'

Whatever sort of candle was used, there was the added inconvenience that if the snuffing were carelessly carried out, the flame could be accidentally extinguished, as Catherine Morland succeeded in doing on her first nervous night under the roof of Northanger Abbey; and as 'the cheerful blaze of a wood fire' had died away, and she had no tinderbox handy, she had to jump terrified into bed in the dark.

Crude oil lamps were used for London street lights, but it was not until the end of the eighteenth century that a Swiss inventor, Argand, created a domestic lamp fuelled by vegetable oil, which had a round burner and tubular wick enclosed in a glass chimney, thus giving a steady and flicker-free light that was said to be the equivalent of seven candles in brightness—and, of course, correspondingly expensive. It seems strange that General Tilney, ready to be a fashion leader so far as Rumfordization of his fireplaces and kitchen stoves is concerned, has not yet installed Argand lamps at Northanger Abbey, for when Catherine stays there as his honoured guest she still only has a solitary candle to light her to bed.

PART 2

THE NOVELS

The sensation that we are visiting genuine places and joining in the lives of genuine people, whom we get to know and to like or dislike just as we might our next-door neighbours, is part of the endless fascination of Jane Austen's novels, and a tribute to her skill as an author. Such accuracy to real life was of course carefully planned, and it is evident that she worked out her plots beforehand with calendars, maps and road-books, in order that the stories should fit properly into both time and space. Another novelist might have felt that there was no need for such painstaking accuracy, but Jane clearly composed for her own amusement and satisfaction: 'An artist cannot do anything slovenly.' When her niece Anna tried to write a novel, in admiring imitation of her aunt, Jane discussed its composition with her in several long and thoughtful letters, which reveal the care she herself used in creating fictional worlds that were nevertheless entirely credible: 'They must be two days going from Dawlish to Bath; they are nearly 100 miles apart . . . And we think you had better not leave England. Let the Portmans go to Ireland, but as you know nothing of the Manners there, you had better not go with them. You will be in danger of giving false representations. Stick to Bath & the Foresters. There you will be quite at home.'

This emphasis on the desirability of a fictional

narrative being utterly true to life leads on to a question which is sometimes asked nowadays: why did Jane Austen not write about the French wars, when she lived through twenty years of international turmoil? Part of the answer is that she had no personal knowledge of actual conflict—had never travelled in war-torn Europe, nor accompanied a soldier or a sailor husband on campaign—and therefore could not have written truthfully about such matters. The other part of the answer is that she did indeed write about the French wars—from the point of view of a single young woman living in the English countryside. Without radio and television, there was no immediacy of information, and foreign news in particular took a long time to reach Hampshire. There was certainly an ongoing danger of invasion, and Steventon village had made its contingency plans; but unless an invasion actually occurred, there was no reason why daily life should not continue much as usual for most people. There was no conscription, so young men did not need to join the Army or Navy unless they chose to do so, and most of them satisfied their patriotic duty by joining the local militia—and were then perhaps posted to Hertfordshire to dazzle the eyes and hearts of the likes of younger Bennet daughters. *Persuasion* is in fact very much a wartime story—Captain Wentworth has been away fighting at sea for years, and it is only the declaration of peace in 1814 that sends sailors such as himself and Admiral Croft ashore again. Mrs Croft has been able to accompany her husband on most of his voyages, but Anne Elliot, like Jane Austen, has stayed at home in the countryside and learned what she could about Captain Wentworth's career from the paragraphs of naval information appearing belatedly in the local newspapers.

Jane's decision to limit herself to writing about what she personally knew seems to have been influenced, consciously or not, by her interest in human psychology, which encouraged her to give depth rather than breadth to her fictional creations. During one of her visits to London, in 1811, she wrote to Cassandra: 'Mary & I . . . went to the Liverpool Museum, & the British Gallery, & I had some amusement at each, tho' my preference for Men & Women, always inclines me to attend more to the company than the sight.' Many years later, her brother Frank wrote to an American admirer:

> Of the liveliness of her imagination and playfulness of her fancy, as also of the truthfulness of her description of character and deep knowledge of the human mind, there are sufficient evidence in her works; and it has been a matter of surprise to those who knew her best, how she could at a very early age and with apparently limited means of observation, have been capable of nicely discriminating and pourtraying such varieties of the human character as are introduced in her works.

Her stories are therefore quite prosaic, recounting events which could have occurred in any middle-class family of Jane's own time, and which could still occur—allowing for some changes of circumstance—in families today. They are all

175

romances, in the sense that they relate the problems encountered by young people who fall in love.

It was also Jane's deliberate decision to keep her cast list very short; once again, her letters to Anna show how she chose to work: 'You are now collecting your People delightfully, getting them exactly into such a spot as is the delight of my life;—3 or 4 Families in a Country Village is the very thing to work on'; and her novels are never sentimental but always ironic and dispassionate in their comedy, creating the characters as normal, slightly flawed human beings, who have their moral failings as well as their virtues. It is part of Jane's technique, when introducing her characters, not to give long descriptions of their physical appearance. Instead, we start by overhearing their thoughts and conversation and so begin to learn something about their nature; only later do we gradually discover what they look like. In *Mansfield Park*, it is not until Chapter 5, when the Crawfords come on the scene and we are told that they are both small, dark- haired, vivacious people, that we realize the Bertram sisters, in contrast, are tall, buxom blondes. In *Pride and Prejudice*, in fact, no complete description is ever given of Elizabeth Bennet, because most of the action is written by Jane Austen as it is seen through Elizabeth's own eyes. Similarly, there is usually no description of the house in which the heroine lives, because Jane takes us straight into a room to listen to the family's conversation, and we are given descriptions of other houses only as and when the heroine visits them—we know very little about Hartfield itself, but see Donwell Abbey and Abbey

Mill Farm through Emma's eyes. This lack of scene-setting is also quite deliberate on Jane's part, in accordance with her advice to Anna: 'You describe a sweet place, but your descriptions are often more minute than will be liked. You give too many particulars of right hand and left.'

So far as the locations of the novels are concerned, cities and towns are large public places which any person, real or fictional, might visit, and Jane had therefore no difficulty in using London, Bath and Lyme Regis as backgrounds, since to mention specific streets and inns in those places would not embarrass any current resident. But she was careful always to be rather vague about the geography of her villages and country houses, for to use the name or location of a genuine place and then describe a group of supposedly specific inhabitants would have given rise at once to the idea that she was making free with the homes and characters of living people. Highbury is said, apparently so precisely, to be nine miles from Richmond, seven from Box Hill and sixteen from London, yet if these mileages are measured out on the map of Surrey, no such focal point exists. The hunt to find 'originals' for, say, Pemberley or Northanger Abbey is a perennial amusement, spurred on by film and television producers hunting for suitable locations for their adaptations of the novels, but no such 'originals' can be identified. It is more likely that Jane Austen found inspiration by looking through popular illustrated topographical works of the period, such as William Watts's *Seats of the Nobility and Gentry*, published in 1779, which showed many handsome country houses throughout the United Kingdom, including

177

her brother Edward's inheritance of Godmersham Park in Kent. It may also be that she took elements of places familiar to her and adapted them as required for her purposes—it was a later tradition of the Austen family, for example, that Highbury was based on the small Surrey town of Leatherhead, which Jane had passed through on some of her journeys betwen Kent and Hampshire.

When her books were first published, some contemporary readers liked them for their trueness to life—'. . . these charming novels, almost unique in their style of humour . . .'—but others could not accept the idea of such veracity in works of fiction, and were puzzled and bored—' . . . too natural to be interesting'. The Prince Regent's librarian, the Reverend James Stanier Clarke, whom Jane had met at Carlton House in 1815, professed to admire her novels, but made it clear, in his subsequent correspondence with her, that he had no comprehension at all of her particular genius in choosing the subject matter which suited her. His first suggestion was that she should write a novel with himself, thinly disguised, as the hero; and a few months later, when the Prince Regent's daughter Princess Charlotte became engaged to Prince Leopold of Saxe-Cobourg, Mr Clarke recommended Jane to write an historical romance on this topical theme. In her reply, Jane clearly stated, for the benefit of both Mr Clarke and, all unwittingly, posterity, her own assessment of her literary talents:

You are very, very kind in your hints as to the sort of Composition which might recommend me at present, & I am fully

178

sensible that an Historical Romance, founded on the House of Saxe Cobourg, might be much more to the purpose of Profit or Popularity, than such pictures of domestic Life in Country Villages as I deal in—but I could no more write a Romance than an Epic Poem.—I could not sit seriously down to write a serious Romance under any other motive than to save my Life, & if it were indispensable for me to keep it up & never relax into laughing at myself or other people, I am sure I should be hung before I had finished the first Chapter.—No—I must keep to my own style & go on in my own Way; And though I may never succeed again in that, I am convinced that I should totally fail in any other.

SENSE AND SENSIBILITY

First, the title needs a little explanation for a modern reader: 'sense' has not changed its meaning, but 'sensibility' is a word not now in common use. At the end of the eighteenth century it meant having a nature that was exceptionally sensitive, emotional and susceptible, and Jane Austen uses her sister heroines, Elinor and Marianne, to personify and contrast such a nature with one of calm, rational, practical good sense. Nowadays we might express something of the contrast by calling such a story 'Head and Heart', or 'Reality and Illusion'.

It seems probable that Jane started to write a story called *Elinor and Marianne* in about 1795, and according to Austen family tradition this was originally composed as a novel-in-letters. In the novel as we now have it, the sisters are never apart for a night, so presumably the action of the plot would have unfolded through the medium of letters exchanged between Mrs Jennings and her daughters, between members of the Ferrars family, or by Elinor and Marianne each writing separately to their mother, Mrs Dashwood. However, this would be a very awkward way of telling the story, and Jane must soon have realized that straightforward narrative would suit her purpose best, and so during 1797–98 changed *Elinor and Marianne* into the novel that is *Sense and Sensibility*.

The manuscript was then laid aside, and it was

probably not until Jane had moved to Chawton Cottage in the summer of 1809 that she looked at it again with a view to publication. She made some little updating changes—the smart new foreign carriage, the barouche, in which Mrs Palmer drives about, was not known in England until after 1800; the twopenny postal service in central London, by which Marianne sends her letter to Willoughby, did not raise its charges to twopence until 1801; and Walter Scott did not become a popular poet until after 1805. Then, with her brother Henry's assistance, she offered it to a London publisher, Thomas Egerton, probably in 1810. In one of her letters in April 1811, Jane refers to her work in correcting the proofs of the text, and the book came out at the end of October 1811, in the usual three-volume format, and priced at 15s., with the anonymous wording 'By A Lady' on the title page. Some of the newspaper advertisements either carelessly or perhaps deliberately rearranged this wording, and made it appear as 'By Lady–', or 'By Lady A–', which led to confusion on the part of contemporary readers, who thought at first it had been written by one or other of two ladies in high society, Lady Boringdon or Lady Augusta Paget. It sold well and Egerton published a second edition in November 1813, increasing the price to 18s., and Jane was still receiving royalties from it in March 1817.

The story covers, overall, some five or six years, which can be calculated as being roughly from 1792 until 1797, starting with the death of old Mr Dashwood, the sisters' wealthy bachelor great-uncle, one January, followed by that of his nephew, their own father Mr Henry Dashwood, a year later,

181

and ending with the marriage of Marianne to Colonel Brandon. We go first to Norland Park in Sussex, the ancestral home of the Dashwoods since at least the sixteenth century, where the estate is worth £4,000 a year; and Jane introduces us to the recently widowed Mrs Henry Dashwood, aged about forty, and her three daughters, Elinor, Marianne and Margaret. Mrs Dashwood is an affectionate and devoted mother, but quite lacking in common sense, and it is Elinor who possesses the 'strength of understanding and coolness of judgement, which qualified her, though only nineteen, to be the counsellor of her mother, and enabled her frequently to counteract, to the advantage of them all, that eagerness of mind in Mrs Dashwood which must generally have led to imprudence'. Marianne is 'eager in every thing; her sorrows, her joys, could have no moderation. She was generous, amiable, interesting; she was everything but prudent. The resemblance between her and her mother was strikingly great.' Marianne is also quite humourless and self-centred, revelling so much in her own uncontrolled sensibility that it never occurs to her that she frequently embarrasses and hurts the feelings of those around her. At the age of sixteen she already despairs of getting married: 'Mama, the more I know of the world, the more am I convinced that I shall never see a man whom I can really love. I require so much! He must have all [the] virtues, and his person and manners must ornament his goodness with every possible charm.' Margaret is thirteen, and although a good-natured child at present, is copying Marianne's romantic ideas without as yet having any of her inclination for study.

The action of the plot is seen mainly through Elinor's eyes, and we learn only gradually that she has fair or light brown hair, a delicate complexion, regular features and a remarkably pretty figure. Marianne is much darker, a gipsyish beauty:

> Marianne was still handsomer. Her form, though not so correct as her sister's, in having the advantage of height, was more striking; and her face was so lovely, that when in the common cant of praise she was called a beautiful girl, truth was less violently outraged than usually happens. Her skin was very brown, but from its transparency, her complexion was uncommonly brilliant; her features were all good; her smile was sweet and attractive, and in her eyes, which were very dark, there was a life, a spirit, an eagerness which could hardly be seen without delight.

She loves to wander in the woods of Norland Park, especially when the leaves are falling, and as one of her favourite poets is James Thomson (1700–48), she is probably murmuring to herself some lines from his famous poem *The Seasons*, such as the descriptions of 'Autumn' and 'Winter':

> The pale descending year, yet pleasing still,
> A gentler mood inspires; for now the leaf
> Incessant rustles from the mournful grove;
> Oft startling such as, studious, walk below,
> And slowly circles through the waving air.
> But should a quicker breeze amid the boughs
> Sob, o'er the sky the leafy deluge streams;

Till choak'd, and matted with the dreary
 shower,
The forest-walks, at every rising gale,
Roll wide the wither'd waste, and whistle
 bleak . . .

. . . Then comes the father of the tempest
 forth,
Wrapt in black glooms. First joyless rains
 obscure
Drive through the mingling skies with vapour
 foul;
Dash on the mountain's brow, and shake the
 woods,
That grumbling wave below. The unsightly
 plain
Lies a brown deluge; as the low-bent clouds
Pour flood on flood, yet unexhausted still
Combine, and deepening into night shut up
The day's fair face . . .
Wide o'er the brim, with many a torrent
 swell'd,
And the mix'd ruin of its banks o'erspread,
At last the rous'd-up river pours along:
Resistless, roaring, dreadful, down it comes
From the rude mountain, and the mossy wild,
Tumbling through rocks abrupt, and sounding
 far . . .

However, when the new heir, the girls' elder half-
brother John Dashwood, brings his family to
Norland, his wife Fanny—'a little, proud-looking
woman'—is furious to see that her brother,
Edward Ferrars, is beginning to fall in love with
Elinor, and makes herself so offensive on this topic

184

to Mrs Dashwood that the latter decides to leave Norland as soon as she can. Because John, encouraged by his avaricious wife, is not prepared to give any share of the Norland estate to his stepmother and half-sisters, Mrs Dashwood and her daughters are now comparatively poor, with only £500 a year between them. Luckily, her cousin Sir John Middleton offers a home on his estate at Barton Park, near Exeter, in Devon, and the bereaved family accordingly move there very early in September, the second year of the action.

So far as is known, Jane Austen had not visited this part of the West Country when she started composing *Elinor and Marianne*, and it seems probable that on this occasion she chose the main location of her story only from hearsay. The South Devon Militia, who were recruited in the Exeter neighbourhood, were sent to serve in Hampshire, and during the winters of 1793–4 and 1794–5 were quartered in Basingstoke, where Jane would have danced with the young officers at the assembly balls held in the town hall and heard from them descriptions of their homes in that county. Another source of information would have been the Reverend Richard Buller, one of her father's old pupils, with whom the Austens kept in touch in later years; his father was the Bishop of Exeter, and he himself had the living of the village of Stoke Canon, which would seem to be very close to the location of the fictional Barton Park.

The county of Devon spans the south-western tip of England from sea to sea: on the north it has dangerous rocky cliffs dropping steeply into the Bristol Channel, and on the south it has sandy beaches stretching into the English Channel. In

185

between are the granite uplands of Dartmoor and Exmoor, rising in some places as high as 1500 feet, and covered with heather and bogs, which provide rough grazing for red deer and half-wild ponies. Between the steep hills are narrow green coombes (valleys), and in the Exeter region the mild climate encourages apple orchards and dairy farming. Hence the county was and is still renowned for its cider and for the cream provided by the sturdy little Red Devon cows, whose coats are as red as the soil beneath them. The farmhouses and cottages were usually thatched and whitewashed, often scattered about the hillsides to be safe from winter floods in the coombes. In Jane Austen's time, the little fishing ports on each side of the county traded as far afield as Greenland and Newfoundland, but this industry has now ceased.

Barton village is described by Jane Austen in some detail, because we, the readers, need to know what the Dashwoods' new home is like, and so gradually learn its geography along with the family as they settle in. It lies four miles north-east of Exeter, at the end of a long open stretch of road, and the real small town of Honiton is ten miles further on to the east. Barton valley winds between the hills, and is a pleasant fertile spot, well wooded and rich in pasture, with the manor house of Barton Park situated half a mile along the valley on the left and partly screened by a projection of one of the hills. This is a large and handsome house—so probably built in the late seventeenth or early eighteenth century—but has no billiard room. Half a mile further on, the valley comes to an end at the foot of high hills, some of which are open downland and others cultivated and woody; and

Barton Cottage lies at the foot of High-Church Down, with the village of Barton climbing up the side of the hill above and behind the cottage. There are the ruins of an old priory in the vicinity in a field called the Abbeyland, and Sir John has a farm at the edge of the down and new woodland plantations at Barton Cross. In the West Country, 'barton' is the very ancient name for the principal farm of the parish, a place where corn was grown and stored, and even today there are no less than seventeen villages or hamlets within a very limited radius northwards of Exeter which have the element 'Barton' as part of their names—Bidwell, Coombe, Court, Exwick and Hayne Barton, to mention but five.

Marianne, of course, was hoping that Barton Cottage would be ancient and romantic in appearance—irregular in its layout, with a thatched roof, green window shutters and walls covered with honeysuckle—but it is, in fact, symmetrically planned, modern and compact, with a tiled roof and casement windows. In front a neat wicket gate opens on to a small green court (grassy lawn), and a narrow passage leads directly through the house into the garden behind. On each side of the entrance is a sitting room, about sixteen feet square; and beyond are the domestic quarters and the stairs. From the front of the house there is a view over the valley towards Exeter, and the back garden has a gate which leads straight out on to the slopes of High-Church Down. The surrounding hills are steep and well wooded, the lowlands well farmed, with rich meadows and several neat farm houses scattered here and there. Upstairs there are four bedrooms, and two garrets for the servants (even on her now-limited income, Mrs Dashwood employs one manservant and two maids); Mrs Dashwood shares one bedroom with the thirteen-year-old Margaret, and the two older girls have a bedroom apiece, so there is a spare bedroom for guests. Marianne still has her handsome pianoforte, upon which she plays loud and dramatic concertos—probably some of those by the contemporary composers Dussek, Cramer or Steibelt, which were very popular at the time—and Elinor's drawings are hung on the parlour walls. As the months go by, Elinor has to admit that the stairs are dark and narrow and the kitchen smoky.

To the right of Barton valley another narrow valley winds between two steep hills, and leads to Allenham Court, an ancient manor house which reminds the Dashwoods of their own Norland. Unfortunately, the owner, Mrs Smith, is too old and infirm either to entertain guests or to leave home herself, so the sisters are unable to meet her or to explore the house and its grounds.

The nearest social centre is the old walled city of Exeter, with its cathedral, many churches and narrow medieval High Street, but now beginning to develop with modern buildings and new streets. A canal had been cut from Exeter towards the sea in 1675, and, by means of sluices and floodgates, seagoing vessels could come up the River Exe to a quay just below the city walls, thus permitting trade with Spain, Portugal and the Mediterranean. At four miles' distance, the city is a morning's excursion from Barton, and Sir John Middleton goes there regularly for the meetings of his gentlemen's dining club. Sally, one of the maidservants at Barton Park, has a brother who is postboy at the New London Inn, and this is where the newly married Robert and Lucy Ferrars stay when they are travelling through Exeter to Dawlish for their honeymoon. There the Dashwoods' manservant Thomas sees and is seen by them, and brings back Lucy's last spiteful message to Elinor. Dawlish is on the Channel coast, to the south of Exeter, and was originally a little fishing village which, in the 1790s, began to turn into a holiday resort and within a few years had become quite smart, which is presumably why the conceited Robert Ferrars thinks it a suitable honeymoon destination. Some fifty miles further westward is the great naval seaport of Plymouth, which in Jane Austen's day could accommodate a thousand sailing ships in its harbour. The Reverend Mr Pratt, Edward Ferrars's tutor, and the Steeles' uncle, lives at Longstaple, near Plymouth.

At Barton Park the Dashwoods get to know Sir John as a hearty and hospitable country squire, interested only in field sports and entertaining his neighbours; his wife, Mary, 'piqued herself upon the elegance of her table, and of all her domestic arrangements; and from this kind of vanity was her greatest enjoyment in any of their parties.' The rest of her time she spends in spoiling her four noisy little children; and the Dashwoods are disappointed to find that she is reserved and cold in manner and has nothing interesting to say for herself. Her mother, Mrs Jennings, the widow of a wealthy London tradesman, is very unlike her, being a good-humoured, merry, fat, rather vulgar, elderly woman, full of chat. Also staying at the Park is an old friend of Sir John's, Colonel Brandon; he is thirty-five, tall, silent and grave, and though he is not handsome his countenance is sensible and his address (behaviour) gentlemanlike. (Oddly enough, Jane Austen never gives him a Christian name, and it can be amusing to try to decide what name would best suit him.) Colonel Brandon has been in the Army for many years, serving in India, and it is only within the last five years that he has unexpectedly inherited the family estate of Delaford, following the death of his elder brother. It is not until halfway through the book that we learn the reason for his gravity: the lingering sadness of a failed love affair in his youth with a girl who was much like Marianne in both looks and character, and whose illegitimate daughter, Eliza Williams, he has made his responsibility.

Mrs Jennings, who prides herself on matchmaking, soon decides that Colonel Brandon is in love with Marianne, and so tells Elinor about his estate, which is worth £2,000 a year and lies in the neighbouring county of Dorset. Jane Austen lets us hear her chatter away, because in due course Marianne will indeed find herself living there:

> Delaford is a nice place, I can tell you; exactly what I call a nice old fashioned place, full of comforts and conveniences; quite shut in with great garden walls that are covered with the best fruit trees in the country: and such a mulberry tree in one corner! . . . Then, there is a dove-cote, some delightful stewponds [fishponds], and a very pretty canal; . . . it is close to the church, and only a quarter of a mile from the turnpike-

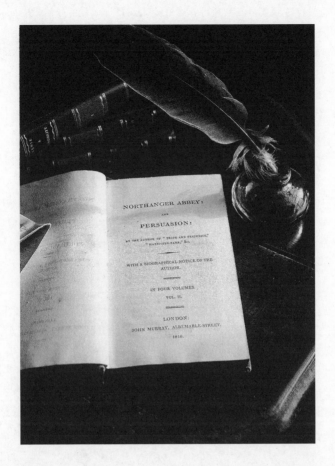

The first edition of Northanger Abbey and
Persuasion, on a small table said to have
been used by Jane Austen to support her
writing desk, at Jane Austen's House,
Chawton, Hampshire.

The dining room at Jane Austen's House. The table is laid with pieces from the Austen family's Wedgwood dinner service.

Jane Austen's House, Chawton, Hampshire: it is believed that in Jane Austen's time this room was the entrance hall. The fireplace is a modern addition.

The north front of Steventon rectory. This engraving was made for James-Edward Austen-Leigh's Memoir of Jane Austen (1870), from a drawing by one of Jane's nieces.

Godmersham Park, the home of Jane Austen's brother Edward Knight; the central block of the house was built in the 1730s, and the two wings were added in the 1770s. From Edward Hasted's The History and Topographical Survey of the County of Kent (1778–99).

The north side of Queen Square, Bath, built by John Wood the Elder in 1728–35. When they visited Bath in 1799 the Austen family party lodged in a smaller house, No. 13, on the south side of the Square, facing this imposing terrace.

An early-nineteenth-century engraving of Southampton, showing the medieval city walls as seen from the tidal inlet of Southampton Water. The Austens probably lived in the tall house above the wall. (The house has since been demolished.)

ABOVE Chawton Great House, seen from the west.

BELOW Chawton Cottage, now universally known as 'Jane Austen's House'.

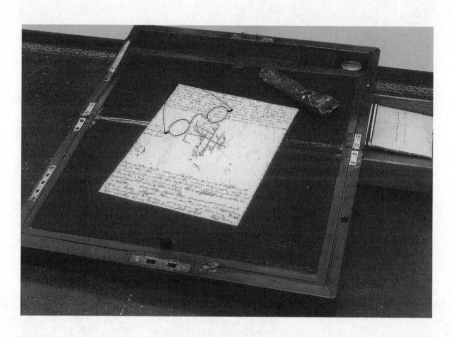

Jane Austen's writing desk, with the drawer at the side open and her spectacles lying upon one of her letters. The desk is now in the British Library, London.

road, so 'tis never dull, for if you only go and sit up in an old yew arbour behind the house, you may see all the carriages that pass along.

We also learn from Mrs Jennings later on that the house has five sitting rooms on the ground floor, and can make up fifteen beds. As the house is 'old fashioned' in the 1790s, it was probably built in the middle of the seventeenth century; and the reference to the turnpike road suggests that Delaford may be close to what is nowadays the A35/A354, the main road between Bridport, Weymouth, Dorchester and Blandford Forum. Delaford parsonage, where Edward and Elinor will eventually live, is said to be small and old, and only a stone's throw from the manor house.

The landscape of Dorset is not so rugged as that of Devon, but it has perhaps a greater diversity of scenery: the English Channel coastline has sandy beaches and shingle banks, with steep cliffs of gold or grey limestone, while inland the chalky hills provide grazing for sheep, with lush valleys of arable and pasture land in between, and sandy wastes sombre with heather and bracken. In Jane Austen's time the small coastal towns all had their fishing fleets, and Weymouth and Lyme Regis were holiday resorts as well, so when the Dashwood sisters need a change from the little village of Delaford, it will not be difficult for them to travel to the seaside.

Before this final comfortable matrimonial settlement can be achieved, however, Marianne is literally swept off her feet by John Willoughby, who appears to be the man of her dreams. He

199

picks her up and carries her home when she sprains her ankle while out walking on High-Church Down. Willoughby is the cousin and heir of the reclusive Mrs Smith of Allenham Court, who calls him down now and then from London to see her; he is twenty-five, tall and handsome, frank and vivacious in his manner, with elegance and more than common gracefulness, and on first acquaintance displays perfect good breeding. Elinor notices, however, that he is quite capable of making spiteful remarks about Colonel Brandon behind the latter's back; and he also takes Marianne to inspect Allenham Court without having the courtesy to introduce her to Mrs Smith. For the next month, during a showery October, he and Marianne are hardly ever apart for a day, and, in deliberate defiance of the manners of the time, she shows herself to be obviously and wildly in love with him. Elinor cannot understand why they do not announce their engagement. Then suddenly Willoughby disappears back to London without explanation, leaving Marianne in floods of tears.

Edward Ferrars now comes to visit the Dashwoods; about twenty-four, he is only a little younger than Willoughby, but quite unlike him, being shy, diffident and not very tall, and the best even the fond Elinor can say about him is that 'his person can hardly be called handsome, till the expression of his eyes, which are uncommonly good, and the general sweetness of his countenance, is perceived.' Poor Edward can define himself only by negatives—he does *not* want to be a soldier, a sailor, a barrister or even a smart young man about town driving a barouche. He would indeed like to become a clergyman, but his rich and disagreeable family think that this is not smart enough. So having finished his studies at Oxford, he has now nothing to do. He seems remarkably depressed during his visit, which makes Elinor wonder if she has been wrong in thinking that he loves her.

At Barton Park more guests arrive: Mrs Jennings's younger daughter, Charlotte, a plump, pretty, giggling girl, recently married to Mr Thomas Palmer, who is growing ever more morose and exasperated as he realizes too late just how silly his wife is; and also the Steele sisters from Exeter, distant cousins of Mrs Jennings. Nancy Steele is nearly thirty, 'with a very plain and not a sensible face', and proves herself to be thoroughly vulgar and foolish, thinking all the time that she has made a conquest of one of the local parsons, Dr Davies; but Lucy, who is about twenty-three, is a smart pretty blonde girl and much more intelligent than her sister, with a 'sharp quick eye'. They stay at Barton during November and December, ingratiating themselves with Lady Middleton, and Lucy makes a point of telling Elinor that she and Edward have been secretly engaged for four years, ever since he was a pupil with her uncle, Mr Pratt at Longstaple. Elinor now understands the reason for Edward's depression—even if he has now fallen in love with her and wishes to break off his engagement to Lucy, by the standards of the time he cannot do so, for such a break can be made only by the lady and not by the gentleman, and it is quite evident that Lucy has not the least intention of letting Edward go.

In Volume II (Chapter 25 in modern editions), it is now January, the third year of the action.

Mrs Jennings takes the Dashwood sisters to her own house in London to stay with her for some weeks; the Middletons and Steeles likewise come up to town to join in the social season, as do the John Dashwood family. Elinor meets Edward's mother, Mrs Ferrars—'a little, thin woman, upright, even to formality, in her figure, and serious, even to sourness, in her aspect. Her complexion was sallow; and her features small, without beauty, and naturally without expression; but a lucky contraction of the brow had rescued her countenance from the disgrace of insipidity, by giving it the strong characters of pride and ill nature'—and also his foolish conceited younger brother Robert, whose person and face were of 'strong, natural, sterling insignificance, though adorned in the first style of fashion'. Robert fancies himself as an amateur architect, and thinks he can design far more elegant country 'cottages' than can any professional, scorning the designs of the genuine well-known architect of the period, Joseph Bonomi (1739–1808).

Mrs Jennings lives in Upper Berkeley Street, near Portman Square, Marylebone, and Mrs Ferrars has her own house in Park Street, Mayfair, while the other families rent furnished houses elsewhere in the smart newly built West End for the few weeks or months of the London season. The Palmers are in Hanover Square; the John Dashwoods take a house in Harley Street for three months, and the Middletons one in Conduit Street. Willoughby, as a single man, has lodgings in Bond Street, and Colonel Brandon is further away in St James's Street, favoured by officers for its closeness to the royal palace and the War Office and Admiralty. Jane Austen would have seen these London streets for herself, in the course of her various visits in the 1780s–90s; they all survive, though there have, of course, been some changes over the ensuing two centuries, and one can still walk down them to guess at suitable houses for the characters, or go shopping in Bond Street with Mrs Palmer, 'whose eye was caught by every thing pretty, expensive, or new . . .'

The Steele sisters stay from time to time with their cousin Richard, who is probably a lawyer, and who lives much further to the east in Bartlett's Buildings, Holborn, not far from the City of London proper. In Jane Austen's time Bartlett's Buildings was also a genuine address; it had been erected in the seventeenth century as a cul-de-sac of about twenty terraced houses, with a narrow entrance closed by a gate and guarded by a night watchman, and was originally said to be a very handsome, spacious place, faced with good buildings of brick with gardens behind the houses, very well inhabited by gentry and persons of good repute. By the early nineteenth century it had become cramped, dark and dingy in comparison with the new developments in the West End, and its residents were lawyers or similar commercial people, who used the ground floor for offices and lived in the rooms above. The houses were nearly all destroyed by bombing during the Second World War, and the street itself disappeared under a huge post-war office block, which is now occupied by the *Daily Mirror* newspaper.

Of the other references Jane Austen makes to places in London, Kensington Gardens are open to the public, now as then; Drury Lane theatre has been rebuilt but is still on the same site; Gray's the jewellers, where Robert Ferrars spends so much time choosing his toothpick-case, was at No. 41 Sackville Street, but this too has been rebuilt and is no longer a shop. The menagerie at Exeter Exchange in the Strand closed in the nineteenth century, and there are now no stationers' shops in Pall Mall.

It is during this visit to London that Marianne is publicly jilted by Willoughby, because he has now engaged himself to an heiress with £50,000, and his marriage follows rapidly in February. Colonel Brandon tells Elinor more about this apparently charming young man's deceitful past—just before meeting Marianne in the previous year he had seduced and abandoned the Colonel's orphan ward, Eliza Williams. Marianne makes herself ill with grief, and Elinor, too, suffers silently on her own account from Mrs Ferrars's rudeness and Lucy Steele's spite; and in Volume III (Chapter 42) the girls are glad to leave London very early in April, travelling with Mrs Jennings to stay with Mr and Mrs Palmer at their house in Somerset before going on to Devon.

The Palmers' house is said to be at Cleveland, within a few miles of Bristol, a name which sounds like a rather thin disguise on Jane Austen's part for the genuine small town of Clevedon, which is indeed a few miles south-west of Bristol. Mr Palmer is evidently something of a *nouveau riche*, so does not have a large ancestral estate, Cleveland being only 'a spacious modern-built house, situated on a sloping lawn. It had no park, but the pleasure-grounds were tolerably extensive'—containing as they do an open shrubbery and closer wood walk, a

204

road of smooth gravel winding round a plantation and a front lawn dotted with trees. A thick screen of more trees—fir, mountain-ash, acacia, Lombardy poplars—hides the domestic quarters, which include a kitchen garden, greenhouse and poultry yard. A path through the shrubberies leads to a little folly, a Grecian temple built on a small hill at the edge of the grounds, and Marianne soon finds her way up there to imagine that she can see across country to Willoughby's own estate, Combe Magna, which is about twenty miles to the south-east of Cleveland. Too much of this wandering about in the open on cold damp spring evenings gives her a bad cold, which in her weakened state turns into something like pleurisy or pneumonia and brings her very close to death.

During the rest of this year, the complications of the story are gradually worked out: Lucy Steele flatters the foolish Robert Ferrars into marrying her, which leaves Edward at last free to become a clergyman and propose to Elinor. Colonel Brandon presents him to the living of Delaford, so Edward and Elinor marry early in the autumn, and settle happily into the redecorated parsonage, where they intend to improve the grounds by planting shrubberies and making a new sweep (carriage drive). Marianne's illness has sobered her, and she comes to realize the depth of Colonel Brandon's devotion. Their marriage takes place about a year or two later, when she is nineteen. 'Colonel Brandon was now as happy, as all those who best loved him, believed he deserved to be ... Marianne could never love by halves; and her whole heart became, in time, as much devoted to her husband, as it had once been to Willoughby.'

As Jane Austen took the trouble to add some updating touches before she published this early work, it is surprising that she did not at the same time remove one or two comments which betray the earlier date of composition; for example, Colonel Brandon's sister and her husband are said to be in the south of France, at Avignon, for the sake of her health—a journey they must have made before the outbreak of war in 1793, and a location from which, no doubt, they had to return as soon as possible thereafter. Similarly, Fanny Dashwood gives to each of the Steele sisters 'a needle book, made by some emigrant', which suggests that Jane was here thinking of the refugee French nobility who fled to England to escape the Revolution, and were largely reduced to living on the produce of their own industry.

*   *   *

Two anonymous reviews of *Sense and Sensibility* appeared in the literary journals in the spring of 1812. The writer in the *Critical Review* declared:

> It is well written; the characters are in genteel life, naturally drawn, and judiciously supported. The incidents are probable, and highly pleasing, and interesting; the conclusion such as the reader must wish it should be, and the whole is just long enough to interest without fatiguing. It reflects honour on the writer, who displays much

knowledge of character, and very happily blends a great deal of good sense with the lighter matter of the piece.

The reviewer for the *British Critic* kindly assured 'our female friends' that:

> . . . they may peruse these volumes not only with satisfaction but with real benefits, for they may learn from them, if they please, many sober and salutary maxims for the conduct of life, exemplified in a very pleasing and entertaining narrative.

Some contemporary comments by private readers have been preserved in their correspondence; the Countess of Bessborough asked Lord Granville Leveson Gower: 'Have you read "Sense and Sensibility"? it is a clever novel. They were full of it at Althorp [her parents' home], and tho' it ends stupidly I was much amus'd by it.' The Duke of York recommended it to his niece, the young Princess Charlotte of Wales, aged sixteen, and she wrote to a friend:

> 'Sense and Sencibility' I have *just finished* reading; it certainly is interesting, & you feel quite one of the company. I think Maryanne & me are very like in *disposition*, that certainly I am not so good, the same imprudence, &c, however remain very like. I must say it interested me much.

A more percipient reader, Miss Isabella FitzRoy, owned a copy of the second edition of the novel, and noticed the weaknesses in the creation of Colonel Brandon and Edward Ferrars which have puzzled literary critics ever since, and which must be put down to Jane Austen's comparative inexperience as an author at that time. She pencilled in her comments at the beginning of the third volume:

> What a pity that the characters had not been touched up a little before publication of this pretty novel—Mrs Jennings made less vulgar—and the fortunes of her daughters shd. be mentioned as their beauty—and tho' Colonel Brandon was grave why was he to be silent—the best is done to make E. Ferrars seem a mean-looking man—and Col. B. must have been good looking, or Marianne never cd. have married him.

Jane Austen told her family that Miss Steele never succeeded in catching Dr Davies, but made no further comments as to what the future might hold in store for the other characters. Fairy tales are always supposed to end with: 'And they all lived happily ever afterwards'—but Jane's novels are far too true to life for such a careless summing-up to sound credible, and this novel in particular seems to presage many ironies and difficulties. Poor Edward is so accustomed to being bullied and derided by his unpleasant family that very probably he will be quite happy to let Elinor run his life for him—though in a much kindlier way—while he grows into a vague well-meaning parson, attending to the needs of his Dorset parishioners in a conscientious if not very forceful manner. Colonel Brandon will always dote upon Marianne—but will she ever wonder if she is loved for herself alone or only for her resemblance to the girl he loved and lost twenty years before? What happens to the seduced—and therefore socially ruined—orphan Eliza and her baby by Willoughby? Colonel Brandon will no doubt continue to support them, but will Marianne ever meet them, and if so, with what sense of embarrassment? Presumably Willoughby will inherit Allenham Court when old Mrs Smith dies, and the Middletons will continue to know him and his heiress wife, Sophia, as neighbours—but how will Mrs Dashwood and Margaret, still at Barton, feel towards him? Will Elinor and Marianne and their respective husbands never go near Barton Park again? How long will Colonel Brandon live? After all, at the beginning of the book his life expectancy is assumed to be no more than fifty-five. If Marianne is left a still-young widow, could she ever marry Willoughby—if he were a widower?

PRIDE AND PREJUDICE

Pride and Prejudice, the second of Jane's adult novels to be composed, was written between October 1796 and August 1797. The action covers fifteen months, from the autumn of one year to the Christmas of the next; she probably envisaged it as happening in 1794–5. Its original title was First Impressions, and the Austen family enjoyed it so much that Mr Austen thought it worthy of publication. On 1 November 1797 he wrote to the well-known London publisher, Thomas Cadell, offering to send him the manuscript for consideration. As Mr Austen's letter was short and rather vague—he did not describe the story in any way, or state outright that it was a witty comedy of manners—it is not surprising that Cadell's clerk scrawled across the top of it: 'declined by Return of Post'. Jane was not disheartened by this initial rebuff, and, luckily for us, did not throw the manuscript away but kept it to be read and re-read in the family circle. In her letter of 8 January 1799, she says teasingly to Cassandra: 'I do not wonder at your wanting to read first impressions again, so seldom as you have gone through it, & that so long ago.' And in June of the same year, she writes again to Cassandra: 'I would not let Martha read First Impressions again upon any account, & am very glad that I did not leave it in your power.— She is very cunning, but I see through her design;—she means to publish it from Memory, & one more perusal must enable her to do it.'

The manuscript stayed with Jane for the next fifteen years, and it was not until she had succeeded in publishing *Sense and Sensibility* that she thought again of submitting this other early work for publication. It seems that she revised the text during 1811–12, as the action can be seen to fit in general terms the calendars for those years, and she also shortened it at the same time, for in her letter of 29 January 1813 to Cassandra she mentions that she has 'lop't and crop't' the manuscript. The title had to be changed, as another novel called *First Impressions* had been published in 1800, and Jane probably found the neat phrase 'Pride and Prejudice' in *Cecilia*, a novel by the successful contemporary authoress Fanny Burney, whose works Jane much admired. The manuscript was then submitted to a different London publisher, Thomas Egerton of Whitehall, who had no hesitation in accepting it and paid her £110 for the copyright. It was published anonymously ('By the Author of "Sense and Sensibility"') in three volumes at the end of January 1813, priced at 18*s.* for the set, and was an instant success, with a second edition being called for in the autumn of that year and a third edition in 1817. It is now perhaps the best known of all Jane's works—not only in the United Kingdom but all over the world, as it has been translated into thirty-five languages—and its title and opening sentence have become catchphrases in everyday life.

The opening scene is set in Hertfordshire, a county that nowadays has practically become part of Greater London, as suburban development stretches ever further northwards. In the late eighteenth century, however, it was still well-wooded countryside, with small-scale but attractive rural scenery of chalk hills above well-watered clayey valleys; it had a thriving mixed agricultural economy that produced grain, cattle and sheep, as well as market gardening to keep London supplied with vegetables. The county town, Hertford, was famous for its malting industry, which used the locally grown barley. It does not seem that Jane Austen herself ever visited the district, but her father had an elderly cousin who lived not far from Hertford and so she may have known something about the county from this family connection. For her fictional world, Jane makes the Bennet family live at Longbourn House, in the village of Longbourn which is about a mile south of the imaginary market town of Meryton and also not far from another market town, to which she does not give a name. It is not until nearly the end of the story (Chapter 46) that Longbourn is specified as lying within ten miles of the Great North Road (nowadays numbered the A1000) as it runs from London to Scotland through Barnet and Hatfield. This means that Jane could have mentally placed Meryton and the town of (Blank) somewhere in the area of either Hemel Hempstead and Watford to the west of the main road, or else Hertford and Ware to the east—and it can be deduced later on that Meryton is, in fact, Hertford and (Blank) is Ware.

If Jane did not have any personal knowledge of Hertford, she could neverthless be reasonably safe in imagining Meryton/Hertford as being something like Overton and Basingstoke in Hampshire, the two small towns nearest to Steventon and therefore the best known to Jane during her girlhood. All such country towns had the basic necessities of a town hall where meetings and assembly balls could be held, a library, an apothecary or surgeon, one or more attorneys, a butcher, a baker, a mercer and a milliner, agricultural tradesmen, and sufficient houses and inns in which militia officers and men could be quartered. In the case of Meryton, the attorney is Mr Phillips, who was once clerk to Mrs Bennet's father, Mr Gardiner senior, then succeeded to the practice and married Mrs Bennet's sister; he is now 'broad-faced stuffy uncle Phillips, breathing port wine', who compares most unfavourably with the gentlemanly officers of the visiting militia regiment.

The story begins early in September, when Jane Austen takes us straight into Longbourn House to listen to the Bennets' conversation. They are sitting in the drawing room after dinner, and Mrs Bennet is making plans for husband-hunting on her daughters' behalf with particular reference to the young Mr Bingley who is soon coming to live in the neighbourhood. 'It is a truth universally acknowledged, that a single man in possession of a good fortune, must be in want of a wife.' As we see and hear nearly all the action through Elizabeth Bennet's eyes, almost as if we were her shadow, or standing invisibly behind her, no description is ever given of Longbourn House, or of the Bennets themselves—because, of course, this is Elizabeth's home and family and she does not need to tell herself what they look like.

Mr Bennet's agricultural estate at Longbourn may have amounted to a thousand acres, which at that period was considered the average holding for a lesser landed proprietor who was the squire of his local village. The estate was worth £2,000 a year, and Mr Bennet has always spent this income up to the hilt, saving nothing. His indoor staff comprises Mrs Hill the house-keeper, the cook, two maidservants, a butler and a footman who probably acts also as Mr Bennet's valet. The outdoor staff comprises a coachman and, by definition, grooms and stableboys to help him tend both the family's saddle-horses and the horses that work on the farm and sometimes draw the family coach—as Mr Bennet comments rather sourly: 'They are wanted in the farm much oftener than I can get them.' There would be labourers to work with the livestock and in the fields and woods, and also a gamekeeper, as Mr Bennet has space for pheasant coverts on his land. 'When you have killed all your own birds, Mr Bingley,'—Mrs Bennet soon cries encouragingly—'I beg you will come here, and shoot as many as you please, on Mr Bennet's manor. I am sure he will be vastly happy to oblige you, and will save all the best of the covies for you.'

Longbourn House itself is probably a seventeenth-century small manor house, set in its own grounds; there is a shrubbery behind the house, and to one side of it a gravel walk leads to a copse or little wilderness with a 'hermitage' (a decorative rustic-style summer-house, very fashionable at the time) placed within the shelter of the trees. The carriage drive leads through a paddock to the steps at the front of the house, and from the entrance hall there is a vestibule which opens into the breakfast room; also on the ground floor and opening off the hall are Mr Bennet's library, a large drawing room and a large dining parlour for parties, when Mrs Bennet entertains some of the 'four and twenty families' in the neighbourhood with whom hospitality is exchanged. Upstairs, there is a small dining room facing west, which can be too hot for comfort in summer, and a small sitting room overlooking the drive, so the girls are able to catch a glimpse of Mr Bingley when he first comes to call and discover that 'he wore a blue coat and rode a black horse'. The Bennet parents probably have separate bedrooms by now, and Mrs Bennet certainly has her own dressing room; each of the five girls appears to have a bedroom of her own and Mary may have a separate room in which to practise her music, and there is at least one guest room in which Mr Bennet's distant cousin Mr Collins can be accommodated on his first visit to Longbourn. The indoor servants would require their respective house-keeper's room, butler's pantry, kitchen and scullery, servants' dining hall and other workrooms. The domestic offices might have been at basement level, or else behind the house in a range of lesser buildings, with the servants' bedrooms in the attics. The coachman and grooms would have their living quarters somewhere in the stable-yard.

Longbourn may have been quite similar to a genuine house of the period, which stood not far away from Bishop's Stortford in Hertfordshire and was recalled by a girl who lived there in the 1790s as being

a heavy square red brick building with little windows and dumpy chimneys; in front was

215

a small bit of shrubbery hardly hiding the road, and beyond a short double avenue of lime trees stretching across a green field. Behind was a more extensive shrubbery and flower garden, divided by a light railing from pretty meadows dotted over with fruit trees . . . on one side a walled garden and the farm offices, on the other the kitchen court, stables and stableyard, and a wide yew hedge bounded the back shrubbery on the river side. The entrance hall was a large low square dark room panelled in dark oak; the floor was the same, in a diced pattern bright rubbed; the old fashioned fire place had a hanging chimney, and a small settle on each side of the hearth, which was lined with clean blue Dutch tiles representing Bible history scenes. My mother sometimes dined in this hall when the dinner was early in the very height of summer, for the eating room looked to the south and in spite of closed venetians [slatted blinds] was often very oppressively over-heated. The drawing room was over the dining room, so that also was hot in summer; and there was a long garret under the roof. The prettiest room in the house was my mother's bedroom looking on the orchard. It had three windows in a bow, and at either hand of the fireplace, were the two light closets in two turrets, one she used as her washing closet, the other was neatly fitted up for reading in.

As for the Longbourn family themselves, Mr and Mrs Bennet have been married for twenty-three

216

years; when the story opens their eldest daughter, Jane, is aged twenty-two, Elizabeth is twenty, Mary eighteen or nineteen, Kitty seventeen and Lydia fifteen. Mrs Bennet has passed the menopause, so there is now no hope that there will ever be a son to inherit Longbourn and keep the estate safe for the Bennets under the terms of the entail. Very few people nowadays have any reason to understand the meaning of an estate's being entailed—it is, or was, a legal arrangement whereby the property could descend only to a male heir. If there was no direct male heir, as in the Bennets' case, then the next nearest male collateral descendant of the owner who had originally created the entail would inherit—in this case, Mr Bennet's distant cousin Mr Collins. Like all legal restrictive practices, over the passage of time ways had been found that made it possible for some families in certain circumstances to break an entail and re-settle an estate in a different way to include female inheritance. Unfortunately for the Bennets this was not the case. It was therefore quite true, as Mrs Bennet bitterly complains, that Mr Collins could turn herself and her daughters out of Longbourn as soon as Mr Bennet was dead.

A more energetic and prudent man than Mr Bennet would have done his best to increase his income and make savings that would provide at least a good monetary legacy for his female dependants. But Mr Bennet, 'so odd a mixture of quick parts, sarcastic humour, reserve and caprice', has become lazy and cynical, disappointed in his marriage—the pretty girl of twenty-three years ago has now shown herself to be 'a woman of mean understanding, little information, and uncertain temper'—and bored by the folly of his three younger daughters, which he makes no attempt to correct. He is fond of Jane, for her beauty and sweet nature, and Elizabeth is his favourite as she has inherited his own intelligence; otherwise, he has abdicated from his responsibilities as husband and father and spends most of the day in his library—'with a book he was regardless of time'. He has also failed to ensure that his daughters get even the limited education then thought fit for young ladies: Lady Catherine de Bourgh is quite understandably shocked when Elizabeth tells her they never had any governesses—'Five daughters brought up at home without a governess!—I never heard of such a thing . . . Without a governess you must have been neglected . . .'—and Elizabeth has to admit: 'Compared with some families, I believe we were; but such of us as wished to learn, never wanted the means. We were always encouraged to read, and had all the masters that were necessary. Those who chose to be idle, certainly might.' As things stand, the girls will have a minimal dowry of £1,000 apiece, invested in government 4 per cent stocks, and even that small sum will not come to them until after their mother's death. It is not surprising, therefore, that Mrs Bennet is so anxious to see her daughters married as soon as possible; she is not very wise in the way she goes about husband-hunting, but at least she is trying to do her best for them, which is more than can be said for their father.

The daughters whom she has to marry off are never precisely described to us; but the Meryton neighbourhood agrees that they are all pretty and that Jane indeed can be called beautiful. Mary is the plainest, and tries to make herself the intellectual and 'accomplished' one of the family as a compensation. Kitty is slight and delicate, 'weak-spirited and irritable'; we hear about her coughing at home and feeling sick when she is driving with Lydia in the coach. This weakness of nature and body leads to Lydia's domination over her. Lydia is her mother's favourite, and the most like her in looks and character. She has 'a fine complexion and good-humoured countenance', with 'high animal spirits and a sort of natural self-consequence', and boasts of being the tallest of the sisters even though she is the youngest. Of Elizabeth we only gradually learn that she is very pretty, with a figure that is 'light and pleasing', and that her face is 'rendered uncommonly intelligent by the beautiful expression of her dark eyes'. In Miss Bingley's jealous opinion: 'Her face is too thin; her complexion has no brilliancy; and her features are not at all handsome. Her nose wants character; there is nothing marked in its lines. Her teeth are tolerable, but not out of the common way . . .'

Mr Charles Bingley, on whom Mrs Bennet is pinning her hopes, arrives in Hertfordshire, with his two elder sisters and his brother-in-law, Mr Hurst; and, especially to Mrs Bennet's interest, has his own lump-sum inheritance of £100,000 and an income of between £4,000 and £5,000 a year. His riches are said to have been amassed by his father, by trade somewhere in the north of England, who had died before he could purchase an estate and enter the ranks of landed gentry. Jane Austen does not tell us anything more about Charles Bingley's origins, but as the name is a Yorkshire one we may perhaps guess that it was the woollen trade which laid the foundations of his fortune, and that Mr Bingley senior was one of the merchants who bought and sold in the great Cloth Hall in Leeds. Young Mr Bingley—he is not yet twenty-three—is presently living in London, but is being urged by his sisters to buy an estate and settle down, and as an initial step towards this he rents Netherfield Park, three miles away from Longbourn and to the north of Meryton.

The Bingley family then attends one of the monthly assembly balls in Meryton, bringing with them their friend Mr Fitzwilliam Darcy, who turns out to be an even greater matrimonial prize than Mr Bingley. Mr Darcy comes from Derbyshire, where his ancestral estate of Pemberley is said to be worth £10,000 a year; we later learn that Pemberley is in the north of the county, not far from Bakewell, so it may be that some part at least of Mr Darcy's wealth comes from mineral resources rather than agriculture. The hills of the Peak District in this part of Derbyshire provided not only limestone for buildings, but also marble and alabaster for architectural decorations or other works of sculpture and art, as well as lead, iron and coal for manufacturing purposes. Mr Darcy at the age of twenty-eight is rather older than his friend, and he inherited his great estates five years ago when his father died. Jane Austen tells us only that 'Mr Bingley was good looking and gentlemanlike; he had a pleasant countenance, and easy, unaffected manners', and that the other people present at the ball thought Mr Darcy had a 'fine, tall person, handsome features, noble mien'—until his chilly hauteur and unwillingness to join in the dancing makes them change their opinion, deciding that he has a 'most forbidding, disagreeable countenance'. Elizabeth's prejudice against him is created when she overhears him telling Bingley that he does not want to dance with her: 'She is tolerable; but not handsome enough to tempt *me* . . .' We are never in fact told why Darcy should behave in so uncivil a manner, or refuse so rudely to dance with Elizabeth—perhaps this was something that Jane Austen had to leave out when she 'lop't and crop't' the manuscript before publication.

During the next few weeks, dinner visits are exchanged, and another Meryton resident, Sir William Lucas, entertains a large party at his home, Lucas Lodge. Jane Bennet develops a bad cold while visiting Netherfield, has to stay there for a few days and is joined by Elizabeth who comes to help nurse her—a visit which confirms Elizabeth in her dislike of Darcy—and the Bingleys themselves give a ball at Netherfield. It becomes obvious that Jane Bennet and Bingley are attracted to each other, to Mrs Bennet's tactlessly outspoken delight and to the silent disapproval of Darcy and Bingley's sisters. The former is appalled by the vulgar behaviour of Mrs Bennet and her younger daughters, while Miss Bingley is in hope that her brother will marry Darcy's younger sister, Georgiana, so that she may herself stand a better chance of marrying Darcy thereafter.

The next newcomers to arrive in Hertfordshire are the officers and men of a militia regiment, who are to spend the winter quartered in Meryton and the nearby villages. Soon afterwards they are joined by George Wickham, a newly recruited

221

lieutenant, who has 'all the best part of beauty, a fine countenance, a good figure, and very pleasing address'. However, it eventually transpires, and Elizabeth admits later to her sister Jane, that Darcy is the one who really has all the goodness, while Wickham has only the appearance of it. Jane Austen cannot, of course, give a genuine name to this regiment, and so refers to them merely as 'the —shires'; but in historical fact it was the Derbyshire Militia who came to Hertfordshire in the winter of 1794–5, and whose troops were divided between the towns of Hertford and Ware and the surrounding area. This supports the suggestion that Jane took these two places, on the east side of the Great North Road, as the basis for her imaginary Meryton and town of (Blank) respectively, and shows once again how she set herself the highest standards of background accuracy in order to make her stories entirely credible. She may have seen the movements of the Derbyshires mentioned in the newspapers, or perhaps Mr Austen's cousin passed on the information to his Hampshire relations. It was probably the fact that it was the Derbyshires who came south that inspired Jane to bestow the Pemberley estate upon Mr Darcy in that county, as that would also tacitly explain why Darcy and Bingley suddenly appear in Hertfordshire. As the militia were recruited on a county basis, Darcy would probably know most of the officers of the regiment and so could suggest to Bingley that the two of them should follow their friends for society's sake, and look for houses at the same time.

A provincial newspaper, the *Cambridge*

Chronicle, reported on 3 January 1795: 'On Christmas-day the ladies and gentlemen of Hoddesdon and Broxbourne [villages a few miles south of Ware and Hertford] gave to the privates in the Derbyshire militia, who are quartered there, roast beef and plumb-pudding, and a pot of beer to each man, in consideration of their orderly behaviour in those towns, and at church.' But Lydia Bennet brings home the news that one of the privates has been flogged, so—to confuse fact with very well-researched fiction—it would seem that on another occasion one man's behaviour at least was distinctly less than orderly.

The outwardly charming Lieutenant Wickham soon begins to flirt with Elizabeth, and tells her a plausible tale of how Darcy has deprived him of a bequest due to him from the Pemberley estate under the terms of the late Mr Darcy senior's will—a tale which serves to confirm Elizabeth in her dislike of the present Mr Darcy's pride and selfishness. But all unknown to her, Darcy is changing his opinion of her, and admits to himself that she is both attractive and witty, and that he 'had never been so bewitched by any woman as he was by her. He really believed, that were it not for the inferiority of her connections, he should be in some danger.' Towards the end of the year, in order to detach her brother from Jane Bennet, Miss Bingley persuades him to return to London for the rest of the winter; and Darcy too thinks it preferable for him to leave Meryton at the same time—'He began to feel the danger of paying Elizabeth too much attention.' Jane also goes to London stay with her uncle and aunt, Mr and Mrs Gardiner (Mrs Bennet's brother and his wife), in

Gracechurch Street, in the hope of seeing Bingley again; but Miss Bingley is careful not to let her brother know of Jane's arrival there.

The next visitor to Hertfordshire is Mr Bennet's distant cousin, the Revd Mr William Collins, the entailed heir to the Longbourn estate. He has recently been presented to the rectory of Hunsford, near Westerham in Kent, and writes from there to Mr Bennet, proposing to call during November to introduce himself to his hitherto unknown relations. He turns out to be a 'tall, heavy-looking young man of five and twenty. His air was grave and stately, and his manners were very formal.' Mr Bennet soon correctly sums him up as being 'a mixture of servility and self-importance'. Mr Collins cannot stop talking about his rich patroness, Lady Catherine de Bourgh, of Rosings Park, Hunsford, and is most honoured to think that Lady Catherine is sufficiently interested in his well-being to tell him that he ought to get married; and it now transpires that the reason for his visit to Longbourn is to obey her instructions by marrying one of the Bennet daughters. There follows the comic scene of his ridiculous proposal to Elizabeth; and when he at last understands that she is refusing his offer, he immediately turns his attentions to her friend, the rather plain Charlotte, eldest daughter of Sir William Lucas. To Elizabeth's surprise and dismay, Charlotte accepts him at once, saying rather sadly: 'I am not romantic, you know. I never was. I ask only a comfortable home; and considering Mr Collins's character, connections, and situation in life, I am convinced that my chance of happiness with him is as fair, as most people can boast on entering the marriage state.' It was quite true, of course, as Jane Austen's original readers would have known, that marriage 'was the only honourable provision for well-educated young women of small fortune, and however uncertain of giving happiness, must be their pleasantest preservative from want'.

At the beginning of the second volume (Chapter 24 of modern editions), the scene now changes to Kent, when Elizabeth goes there in March of the following year, accompanied by Sir William Lucas and his younger daughter, Maria, to stay with the newly wed couple at Hunsford rectory. Hunsford is imaginary, but nearby Westerham is a genuine village, near the small town of Sevenoaks, and Jane Austen may well have passed through it on some early journey into Kent—perhaps as early as the summer of 1788, when Mr and Mrs Austen brought their two daughters to visit other branches of the Austen family in Sevenoaks and Tonbridge. This western side of the county was, and still is, famous for its large orchards of cherries, apples, plums and cobnuts, which supply the London market; and further to the east hops are grown and dried, for use in brewing beer. An enduring image of Kent in springtime is that of sheep grazing in a blossoming orchard, with a group of cowled oast-houses set amongst hop-fields.

In later years Jane came to know the eastern corner of Kent quite well, thanks to her visits to her brother, Edward, at his country house, Godmersham Park, situated between Canterbury and Ashford. Further eastwards still, the chalky hills that run across the county fall into the English Channel as the White Cliffs of Dover, from which the coast of France, only twenty-one miles away, can be seen on a fine day. Throughout the centuries this corner of England has always been in danger from European invasions, and in Jane Austen's time the Royal Navy kept a large fleet stationed off the coastal town of Deal, so that the Channel could be constantly patrolled. The county town of Maidstone had likewise built very large barracks for the accommodation of cavalry regiments who might have to be called out to resist French soldiers. Paper-making was a thriving industry, and many of Jane Austen's letters are written on paper which bears watermarks denoting Kentish manufacture, which is likely to have been purchased when she was staying at Godmersham.

The Hunsford rectory is not described in detail, for all that the reader needs to know is what sort of an establishment Charlotte has acquired by marrying Mr Collins, and how she is managing to live with him. The house is probably fairly modern, as it is said to be well-built and convenient, even though rather small; it can be seen from the road— it stands in a sloping garden entered by a small gate in the laurel hedge and green-painted wooden fence—and is approached by a short gravel walk to the front door. It might have had honeysuckles, jasmines, roses and vines trained round the windows; at that time this was the kind of planting considered most appropriate for small houses. Mr Collins has his 'book room' facing the road, and the dining parlour also faces to the front. Elizabeth 'could not help fancying that in displaying the good proportion of the room, its aspect and its furniture, he addressed himself particularly to her, as if wishing to make her feel what she had lost in refusing him'. Charlotte uses a less attractive room, at the back of the house, for her sitting room—but Elizabeth 'soon saw that her friend had an excellent reason for what she did, for Mr Collins would undoubtedly have been much less in his own apartment, had they sat in one equally lively; and she gave Charlotte credit for the arrangement.' Behind the house there is a larger, formal garden, laid out with walks and cross-walks, and there are two meadows beyond. Mr Collins attends to the cultivation of the garden himself, 'and Elizabeth admired the command of countenance with which Charlotte talked of the healthfulness of the exercise, and owned she encouraged it as much as possible. . . . When Mr Collins could be forgotten, there was really a great air of comfort throughout, and by Charlotte's evident enjoyment of it, Elizabeth supposed he must be often forgotten.'

Lady Catherine de Bourgh's Rosings Park is separated from the rectory garden only by a lane, and from his house Mr Collins can see the mansion through a gap in the trees. Here again, as the house is not important to the story, Jane Austen merely says that it is a 'handsome modern building, well situated on rising ground'—which must mean it was built in the middle or second half of the eighteenth century, perhaps designed by the famous architect, Robert Adam, at the commission of Lady Catherine's deceased husband, Sir Louis de Bourgh. Mercenary-minded Mr Collins thinks only of the expense involved, and as the party walk to their first dinner at Rosings he hastens to tell Elizabeth how much Sir Louis spent on the glazing of the many windows, and that the chimney piece in one of the drawing rooms had cost £800. This must indeed be an exceedingly grand creation, since most carved marble chimney pieces of the time did not usually cost more than £300. The hall is of 'fine proportion and finished ornaments', and this leads to an antechamber and thence to a sitting room, where Lady Catherine 'with great condescension, arose to receive them'. She is a 'tall, large woman, with strongly-marked features, which might once have been handsome. Her air was not conciliating, nor was her manner of receiving them, such as to make her visitors forget their inferior rank.' However, though Lady Catherine is a domestic tyrant and unused to anyone daring to disagree with her, her overbearing manner has its basis in benevolence, as she sincerely believes she knows what is best for everybody.

Darcy and his cousin, Colonel Fitzwilliam, come to visit Rosings while Elizabeth is staying with the Collinses, and from something the Colonel says, Elizabeth realizes that Darcy has been instrumental in breaking up the budding romance between Bingley and Jane. A few days later, to her amazement, Darcy proposes to her, but in a most tactless fashion: 'He spoke well, but there were feelings besides those of the heart to be detailed, and he was not more eloquent on the subject of tenderness than of pride. His sense of her inferiority—of its being a degradation—of the family obstacles which judgment had always opposed to inclination, were dwelt on with a warmth which seemed due to the consequence he was wounding, but was very unlikely to recommend his suit.' He does not hesitate to admit to his part in separating Bingley and Jane, but when Elizabeth taxes him also with injustice towards Wickham, the interview descends into a quarrel and she furiously rejects his proposal. The following day he gives her privately a long letter setting out the facts of Wickham's dishonest behaviour in the past, which after much re-reading and consideration Elizabeth realizes must be the true version of the matter, and that it is the Darcy family who have been injured by Wickham, not vice versa. She now grows '. . . absolutely ashamed of herself.—Of neither Darcy nor Wickham could she think, without feeling that she had been blind, partial, prejudiced, absurd.'

Later on in the year, Lydia is invited by her friend, Mrs Forster, the young wife of the colonel of the ——shire Militia, to go with them to Brighton, on the Sussex coast, where they are to join other regiments in temporary encampments on the cliffs above the town. This is also perfectly genuine contemporary background scene-setting on Jane Austen's part: Brighton offered the shortest possible overland route from the English Channel to London, and following the declaration of war with France in February 1793, soldiers from all over England took it in turns to defend this vulnerable seaside town. The summer months were spent in military drill and manoeuvres, with mock battles as practice in case of any surprise landing by the French. The Prince of Wales himself, with his favourite regiment, the 10th Light Dragoons, took part in some of these camps, and Jane Austen's brother, Henry, was there with his militia regiment, the Oxfordshires, in the summer of 1793.

In Lydia's imagination, a visit to Brighton

229

comprised every possibility of earthly happiness. She saw with the creative eye of fancy, the streets of that gay bathing place covered with officers. She saw herself the object of attention, to tens and to scores of them at present unknown. She saw all the glories of the camp; its tents stretched forth in beauteous uniformity of lines, crowded with the young and the gay, and dazzling with scarlet; and to complete the view, she saw herself seated beneath a tent, tenderly flirting with at least six officers at once.

Elizabeth, too, goes away during the late summer, taken by her uncle and aunt Gardiner on a northern tour to Derbyshire, as Mrs Gardiner wants to visit the town of Lambton in that county, where she had spent some years during her girlhood. Their route takes them through places already well known to contemporary tourists— Oxford and the urban beauty of the colleges' classical architecture, the Duke of Marlborough's palace at Blenheim, the great castle at Warwick, the picturesque red sandstone ruins of an earlier castle at Kenilworth, and, as a contrast, the rapidly growing industrial town of Birmingham, already famous for its many workshops producing all kinds of metal ware. A French visitor in 1784 commented:

. . . Birmingham is one of the most curious towns in England. If any one should wish to see in one comprehensive view, the most numerous and the most varied industries, all combined in contributing to the arts of

230

utility, of pleasure, and of luxury, it is hither he must come . . . the vast works where steam pumps are made . . . the manufactories in constant activity making sheet copper for sheathing ships' bottoms . . . plate tin and plate iron . . . the extensive hardware manufacture which employs to so much advantage more than thirty thousand hands . . . all ironmongery is made here in greater perfection with more economy and with greater abundance, than anywhere else.

They travel on into Derbyshire, through the natural beauty of the rocky and oak-wooded landscapes at Dove Dale and Matlock, and arrive at the small town of Bakewell. The imaginary Lambton is not far from Bakewell (perhaps Jane Austen envisaged it as being somewhere near the genuine little town of Tideswell), and Mrs Gardiner points out that it would be possible to make a short detour and visit Pemberley before arriving at Lambton. Once Elizabeth has reassured herself from local information that Mr Darcy and his sister are not presently at home, she agrees to her aunt's plan.

Pemberley House and grounds are now described in some detail by Jane Austen, at the beginning of the third and final volume of the novel (Chapter 43). Although we do not yet know it, this is where Elizabeth will eventually find herself living, so it is important that we can envisage the joys that await her. The park is very large—the Gardiners are later told it is ten miles in circumference—and from the lodge-gate there is a half-mile drive through woodland to the top of a hill, from which Pemberley House itself can be seen on the opposite side of the valley. It is 'a large, handsome, stone building, standing well on rising ground, and backed by a ridge of high woody hills;—and in front, a stream of some natural importance was swelled into greater, but without any artificial appearance. Its banks were neither formal, nor falsely adorned.' The house-keeper, Mrs Reynolds, gives them a tour of the principal rooms of the house: first, from the hall into the dining parlour, 'a large well proportioned room, handsomely fitted up', looking across the stream and winding valley to the hill down which they had come. The other rooms are 'lofty and handsome', and the furniture rich but neither gaudy nor uselessly fine, with less splendour and more real elegance than that of Rosings—perhaps therefore in the plainer style of the early eighteenth century. The large library contains the books collected by many generations of the family. On the cool northern side of the hall there is a saloon suitable for summer use, with windows opening to the ground and a view of beautiful oaks and chestnuts in the parkland leading up to the hills behind the house. Another of the smaller rooms had been used by Mr Darcy senior as his study, with his favourite family miniatures on the wall over the mantlepiece; and adjacent to it is Georgiana's music room, with a new piano just given to her by her brother—this is probably a grand piano, made by the London firm of Broadwood.

The great staircase has a spacious lobby at the top, off which is a 'very pretty sitting-room, lately fitted up with greater elegance and lightness than the apartments below', also for Georgiana's use and to be a surprise for her when she returns home from London. At this first floor level are two or three of the principal bedrooms, and a long gallery, now used to display many family portraits. Among these portraits Elizabeth finds 'a striking resemblance of Mr Darcy, with such a smile over the face, as she remembered to have sometimes seen, when he looked at her.' In the course of the inspection of the house, Mrs Reynolds talks much of Mr Darcy's virtues: '. . . he was always the sweetest-tempered, most generous-hearted boy in the world . . . the best landlord, and the best master . . . that ever lived', to which Elizabeth listens with the greatest interest. As they go outside again for a tour of the grounds, Mr Gardiner looks back to 'conjecture' as to the date of the house. It is therefore certainly not modern, and the existence of a great staircase and long picture gallery suggests that this part of the building at least is Elizabethan or Jacobean; no doubt like many other English country mansions Pemberley has been added to and re-modelled over the centuries.

As the party starts to walk away towards the grounds, Elizabeth is aghast to see Darcy suddenly appear from the region of the stable-yards behind the house, and it transpires that he has returned home earlier than expected. After an equal display of embarrassment on his part, he joins them in their walk, and shows himself more truly polite and anxious to please than Elizabeth has ever seen him. He invites her to dine at Pemberley, but before this engagement can be fulfilled, Elizabeth receives a desperate letter from Jane, at home in Meryton, announcing that Lydia has eloped from

Brighton with Wickham. The Gardiners cut short their tour to take Elizabeth home at once, but not before she has suffered the further dreadful embarrassment of having to tell Darcy what has happened.

Over the next few weeks, as we subsequently learn, Darcy works hard behind the scenes to help the Bennet family, for Elizabeth's sake; he arranges for Wickham to marry Lydia, and encourages Bingley to return to Hertfordshire and renew his courtship of Jane. When Darcy visits Longbourn again, in a sunny October, he and Elizabeth find time to be alone together. Now apologies and explanations can be given, Darcy can renew his proposal, and Elizabeth can this time accept him, 'with gratitude and pleasure'. Jane and Elizabeth have a double wedding before the year is out, so Elizabeth is mistress of Pemberley in time to welcome the Gardiners there for Christmas.

*   *   *

Jane Austen herself was delighted with her creation, referring to the novel as 'my own darling Child', and as soon as she had received her author's pre-publication copy on 27 January 1813, she and her mother started reading it aloud to their neighbour, Miss Benn, who had come to dine with them that evening. Jane wrote to Cassandra, on 29 January: ' . . . [Miss Benn] really does seem to admire Elizabeth. I must confess that *I* think her as delightful a creature as ever appeared in print, & how I shall be able to tolerate those who do not like *her* at least, I do not know.' The book received good notices, the writer in the *Critical Review*

234

particularly praising Elizabeth's 'archness and sweetness of manner', and agreeing that her 'sense and conduct are of a superior order to those of the common heroines of novels. From her independence of character, which is kept within the proper line of decorum, and her well-timed sprightliness, she teaches the man of Family-Pride to know himself.' The reviewer in the *British Critic* was equally approving: '. . . we have perused these volumes with much satisfaction and amusement, and entertain very little doubt that their successful circulation will induce the author to similar exertions.'

Perhaps thanks to these favourable reviews, *Pride and Prejudice* became the fashionable novel for the spring of 1813; the playwright R. B. Sheridan, author of the popular comedies *The School for Scandal* and *The Rivals*, advised a fellow guest at a dinner party to buy it immediately, for it was one of the cleverest things he had ever read. Some people believed that both *Pride and Prejudice* and *Sense and Sensibility* had been written by the vivacious young Lady Boringdon, wife of the 2nd Lord Boringdon (later the Earl and Countess of Morley) of Saltram, near Plymouth, and declared that Mr Darcy was a perfect pen-portrait of Lord Boringdon; but another gentleman considered it was much too clever to have been written by a woman.

A number of high-society readers mentioned it in their correspondence, nearly all of them recommending their friends to read such an amusing and well-written work, though a dissenting note was struck by Lady Davy: ' "Pride and Prejudice" I do not very much like. Want of interest is the fault I can least excuse in works of mere amusement, and however natural the picture of vulgar minds and manners is there given, it is unrelieved by the agreeable contrast of more dignified and refined characters occasionally captivating attention.' The future best-selling author Mary Russell Mitford (1787–1855), then a pompous and pedantic young woman very much in Mary Bennet's style, wrote in 1814, by which time Jane's authorship was beginning to be known:

> The want of elegance is almost the only want in Miss Austen. I have not read her 'Mansfield Park'; but it is impossible not to feel in every line of 'Pride and Prejudice', in every word of Elizabeth, the entire want of taste which could produce so pert, so worldly a heroine as the beloved of such a man as Darcy. Wickham is equally bad. Oh! they were just fit for each other, and I cannot forgive that delightful Darcy for parting them. Darcy should have married Jane. He is of all the admirable characters the best designed and the best sustained.

Even after publication, Jane was looking out for portraits that might embody the mental images she had formed of her characters. In May 1813 she was staying in London with her brother Henry, at his smart house in Sloane Street, Chelsea, and from there wrote to Cassandra:

> Henry & I went to the Exhibition [held by the Society of Painters in Oil and Water Colours] in Spring Gardens. It is not

thought a good collection, but I was very well pleased—particularly (pray tell Fanny) with a small portrait of Mrs. Bingley, excessively like her. I went in hopes of seeing one of her Sister, but there was no Mrs. Darcy;—perhaps however, I may find her in the Great Exhibition [held by the British Academy, at Somerset House] which we shall go to, if we have time;—I have no chance of her in the collection of Sir Joshua Reynolds's Paintings which is now shewing in Pall Mall [the British Institution had organized a memorial exhibition of 130 of his pictures], & which we are also to visit.— Mrs. Bingley's is exactly herself, size, shaped face, features & sweetness; there never was a greater likeness. She is dressed in a white gown, with green ornaments, which convinces me of what I had always supposed, that green was a favourite colour with her. I dare say Mrs. D. will be in Yellow.

Later in the day, Jane finished the letter: 'We have been both to the Exhibition & Sir J. Reynolds',— and I am disappointed, for there was nothing like Mrs. D. at either.—I can only imagine that Mr. D. prizes any Picture of her too much to like it should be exposed to the public eye.—I can imagine he wd. have that sort of feeling—that mixture of Love, Pride & Delicacy.'

Jane Austen not only carried her characters in her mind's eye, but took an enduring interest in their later lives; she told her family that Kitty Bennet was satisfactorily married to a clergyman near Pemberley, while Mary obtained nothing higher than one of her uncle Phillips's clerks, and was content to be considered a star in the society of Meryton. She did not, however, enlarge upon the summing-up with which she finished the story in the last chapter, and which still leaves scope for the reader to wonder whether Miss Bingley ever succeeded in catching a husband for herself, when and whom the shy, scholarly Georgiana married, how long it was before the Collinses dared to return to Hunsford and face their share of Lady Catherine's wrath—and even to hope that Mrs Bennet's 'poor nerves' might possibly overcome her, leaving Mr Bennet free to marry a more congenial second wife and produce a son who would oust Mr Collins from the entailed inheritance of Longbourn.

This, the third of Jane Austen's early novels, was written in 1798–9, with the action meant to be contemporary, and was originally called *Susan*. In 1802 Jane checked through it, and added a slight updating reference to the popular novel *Belinda*, by Maria Edgeworth, which had been published in 1801; and then, with her brother Henry's assistance, sold the manuscript and its copyright for £10 to a London publisher, Benjamin Crosby & Co., in the spring of 1803. Crosby advertised it that year—'In the Press: Susan, a Novel in 2 volumes'— but never, in fact, brought it out. In 1809 Jane wrote to the firm, reminding them of this six-year delay, and suggesting she could either provide them with a spare copy of the manuscript if the original had been lost, or else that she would wish to publish it elsewhere. This brought a rude response, threatening to take legal action to stop any other publisher buying the work, and offering to return her manuscript for the £10 original payment. This sum was evidently beyond Jane's limited means, and so she had to let the matter rest.

In about 1815 or 1816, when Jane had published four novels successfully and had her royalty monies in hand, she asked Henry to contact Crosby on her behalf, and he bought *Susan* back, telling Crosby only after the transaction was finalized that this manuscript, unvalued by him, was by the author of *Pride and Prejudice*. Jane went through the text again, changing the heroine's name to 'Catherine', because another novel called *Susan* had been published in 1809. She evidently thought then of offering it a second time for publication and prepared an 'Advertisement' to the reader, explaining the origins of the story. However, it seems that even as she composed the 'Advertisement' Jane discouraged herself: early in 1817 she wrote to her niece Fanny Knight: 'Miss Catherine is put upon the Shelve for the present, and I do not know that she will ever come out . . .' After Jane's death in July 1817 Henry Austen took over this manuscript and that of her last completed novel, *Persuasion*, and, as they were both shorter than her other works, arranged for them to be published together in 1818 by John Murray, in four volumes, priced 24s. Jane had apparently left both stories untitled, so it was presumably Henry who called them *Northanger Abbey* and *Persuasion* respectively.

Northanger Abbey, though still amusing today, would have been amusing in a rather different way to its first readers, because it was written as a deliberate parody of the very popular 'horrid' novels of the period—what we would now call 'thrillers'—some of which Isabella Thorpe has listed in her pocket-book and recommends to Catherine Morland: *The Italian, The Castle of Wolfenbach, Clermont, Mysterious Warnings, Necromancer of the Black Forest, The Midnight Bell, Orphan of the Rhine, Horrid Mysteries*. Under Isabella's guidance, Catherine starts by reading *The Mysteries of Udolpho*, and later on she begins to imagine that General Tilney is just such a wife-murderer as the sinister Signor Montoni in that

240

story. All the heroines of this kind of novel are of high birth, angelic beauty, extreme virtue and sensibility, and although usually orphaned and invariably growing up in poverty on some lonely foreign mountainside, nevertheless are so naturally gifted as to possess all the female accomplishments without ever having any formal tuition. After many wanderings, endurance of mysterious or ghostly horrors, and abduction by wicked relations or other envious villains which leads to imprisonment in ancient desolate castles or ruined abbeys, they are finally rescued by and united with disguised heroes of equally noble birth and virtue. The Austens were amused and not deluded by such novels, and read them together in the long winter evenings, much as nowadays we might watch some mildly foolish soap opera on television by way of relaxation. Mrs Austen's comments, in 1806, on the first sight of the old-fashioned rooms at Stoneleigh Abbey—'the State Bed chamber with a high dark crimson Velvet Bed, an *alarming* apartment just fit for an Heroine'—shows how well-versed she was in the popular fiction of the time. However, by 1816 these 'horrid' novels had proliferated to such an extent as to become commonplace and were beginning to go out of fashion in consequence, which is evidently why Jane had concerns that her parody of them might also seem outdated.

The story spans about ten years, introducing us to Catherine Morland in her childhood, but the main part of the action happens during February, March and April 1798, when she is seventeen. Her marriage to Henry Tilney takes place when she is eighteen, 'within a twelve month from the first day of their meeting'.

We start with a sketch of Catherine's entirely unromantic family and her unheroic childhood: her father, the Reverend Mr Richard Morland, is the incumbent of Fullerton in Wiltshire, a village eight or nine miles from the cathedral city of Salisbury, and so probably isolated among the bare, windy, grey-green chalk downlands of Salisbury Plain. (There is a genuine hamlet of Fullerton in Hampshire, on the River Test between Winchester and Andover, but as this is some way from the Austens' home ground of Steventon, it is probable that Jane had not heard of it—if she had known such a place existed, it is unlikely she would have used the name.) Mr Morland has 'a considerable independence besides two good livings', so he is neither neglected nor poor; he has never been handsome and he is not in the least addicted to locking up his daughters. Mrs Morland has useful plain sense, a good temper and a good constitution; so after having three sons she does not die at Catherine's birth but lives on to have another six children, thus bringing the family total to ten, three girls and seven boys. 'A family of ten children will be always called a fine family, where there are heads and arms and legs enough for the number; but the Morlands had little other right to the word, for they were in general very plain, and Catherine, for many years of her life, as plain as any. She had a thin awkward figure, a sallow skin without much colour, dark lank hair, and strong features.'

With so many brothers, it is not surprising that the ten-year-old Catherine is noisy and wild, hates confinement and cleanliness, loves rolling down the green slope at the back of the house, and enjoys boys' pastimes—cricket, baseball, riding on horseback and running about the country. 'She never could learn or understand any thing before she was taught; and sometimes not even then, for she was often inattentive, and occasionally stupid.' She has no talent for drawing, and cannot bear to learn music—'The day which dismissed the music-master was one of the happiest of Catherine's life.' Her parents succeed eventually in teaching her writing, arithmetic and a little French, but it does not appear that they ever engaged a governess or sent her to school. Had she been a fashionable literary heroine, of course, she would have played with dolls, kept docile little pets such as dormice and canaries, and her most energetic occupation would have been watering a rosebush or writing poetry while sitting decorously under a tree on a fine evening.

As she enters her teens, Catherine improves in both body and mind: '. . . her complexion improved, her features were softened by plumpness and colour, her eyes gained more animation, and her figure more consequence. Her love of dirt gave way to an inclination for finery, and she grew clean as she grew smart . . .' She starts to read more: '. . . though she could not write sonnets, she brought herself to read them; and though there seemed no chance of her throwing a whole party into raptures by a prelude on the pianoforte, of her own composition, she could listen to other people's performance with very little fatigue. Her greatest deficiency was in the pencil—she had no notion of drawing—not enough even to attempt a sketch of her lover's profile, that she might be detected in the design.' By the time she is fifteen, her parents can say placidly: 'Catherine grows quite a good-looking girl,—she is almost pretty today'—and it seems that she has dark hair and grey eyes, and is of medium height. Unfortunately there is no mysterious lover awaiting her in the Fullerton neighbourhood: 'There was not one family among their acquaintance who had reared and supported a boy accidentally found at their door—not one young man whose origin was unknown. Her father had no ward, and the squire of the parish no children.' The squire is the middle-aged Mr Allen; he and his wife are the nearest neighbours to the Morlands, their house being a quarter of a mile from the parsonage, and Catherine is much in the habit of running over there to call upon them. Mr Allen's doctor recommends him to go to Bath, for the benefit of his gouty constitution, and the Allens kindly invite Catherine to accompany them there at the beginning of February.

Although the story is called *Northanger Abbey*, in fact most of the action takes place in Bath, a city well known to Jane and her family, and we can still follow in Catherine's footsteps to visit or at least see most of the places in the city that she does. The Allens have taken comfortable lodgings in Great Pulteney Street, a wide and handsome avenue just recently constructed on the eastern side of the River Avon, outside the old city walls, and on Sundays they attend services at (probably) the Octagon Chapel in Milsom Street, with a stroll in the Royal Crescent to follow. Perhaps rather surprisingly, it seems that neither the Allens nor Catherine actually bathe in the hot mineral waters at any of the separate baths making up the great

244

complex next to the Pump Room.

Catherine goes to the Upper Rooms, in Bennett Street, for her first, unsuccessful, entrance into society, when she cannot find a dancing partner and the ballroom is so crowded that she cannot even see those who are lucky enough to be dancing; these assembly rooms suffered severe damage during the Second World War, but have now been restored to their former glory as a social centre, and the Museum of Costume displays its fine collections in the basements underneath. In the Pump Yard, next door to Bath Abbey, was the Pump Room, where, in Catherine's day, all new arrivals signed their names in the visitors' book and drank glasses of the spa water; it is now somewhat altered but still there, as is its 'great clock'—a ten-foot-high long-case timepiece by the master craftsman Thomas Tompion, presented by him to the city of Bath in 1709. The theatre that Catherine attended was in Orchard Street, and the building survives, though it is no longer used as a theatre. Unfortunately, the older Lower Rooms, down by the river, where she first dances with Henry Tilney, were burnt down in 1820, and the site is part of the Parade Gardens.

Catherine now meets, almost simultaneously, two very different families—the Thorpes and the Tilneys. Mrs Thorpe, an old school friend of Mrs Allen, is a lawyer's widow living with her children at Putney, then a separate village on the south-west fringe of London, and has brought her three daughters, Isabella, Anne and Maria, with her to Bath, where they are lodging in Edgar's Buildings in the centre of the city. Isabella is twenty-one, the tallest of the three, and a very

245

pretty blonde, with an assured manner of sophistication and fashionable, slangy chatter that quite overwhelms the innocent and naive Catherine. John Thorpe, Isabella's elder brother, an Oxford undergraduate, joins his family in Bath and brings with him James Morland, Catherine's eldest brother, who is at the same Oxford college. James is planning to enter the Church, like his father, once his studies are finished; he is an honest, quiet young man, with a brotherly resemblance to Catherine in both looks and character; but like her he is dazzled by the flashy Isabella and commits himself to a formal proposal of marriage. John Thorpe is a stout young man of middling height, with a plain face and ungraceful form, whose only idea of conversation is to boast about himself and his sporting abilities, by which course of action he thinks he is making himself irresistible to Catherine. In the terms of the parody which Jane Austen is composing, Isabella is the dangerous false friend who attempts to lead the heroine astray, and John is the villain who abducts her in order to force his suit upon her—though this abduction consists only of persuading Catherine, against her will, to drive out with him in his gig where she cannot get away from his non-stop boasting.

Not long after arriving in Bath, Catherine goes to a ball at the Lower Rooms, where Mr King, the Master of Ceremonies (and a genuine personage of the time), introduces her to the Reverend Mr Henry Tilney, who comes from a very respectable family in Gloucestershire. Henry is just recently ordained, and is about twenty-five, rather tall, with dark eyes and dark hair; he has a pleasing countenance with very intelligent and lively eyes, and, if not quite handsome, is very near it. His conversation is very amusing, and although Catherine does not always understand his witticisms, she much appreciates his company and attention. His sister, Eleanor, is a fashionable and pleasing-looking young woman, with a good figure, a pretty face, a very agreeable countenance and an air of real elegance that Catherine can now recognize as being quite different from Isabella's cheap smartness. The Tilneys are lodging in the highly fashionable Milsom Street, and Catherine meets General Tilney, their father, a tall and handsome man of commanding aspect, past the bloom but not past the vigour of life. His elder son, Captain Frederick Tilney of the 12th Light Dragoons, presently stationed at Northampton, comes to join his family for a few days; he is likewise tall, dark and handsome, and very fashionable-looking, in Isabella Thorpe's opinion. (The 12th Light Dragoons was, in fact, a genuine regiment of the standing Army, which makes it rather strange that Jane Austen should use its name in this novel, when she had been at such pains not to identify the Derbyshire Militia in *Pride and Prejudice*. Perhaps she felt able to do so because the regiment had never been stationed at Northampton in the 1790s; at the time Jane was writing it was serving in Portugal, and did not return to England until 1802.) Catherine is shocked to see how quickly Isabella starts flirting with Captain Tilney, despite her engagement to James Morland.

Catherine is also puzzled by the excessively complimentary manner General Tilney adopts towards her, and notices that Henry and Eleanor seem uncomfortable and constrained in his company; however, when he asks her to extend her holiday trip by visiting them at their home of Northanger Abbey before she returns to Fullerton, she is thrilled at the idea of staying at such a romantic place as an ancient abbey, and also very happy at the idea of seeing more of Henry, even though she hardly yet realizes that she is falling in love with him. What neither Catherine, nor we the readers, know at this stage of the story is that the boastful John Thorpe has falsely bragged to the General that the Morlands are a very rich family, that his sister is engaged to the eldest son and that he, John, intends to marry Catherine. The General, having no reason to disbelieve these statements, at once decides to remove Catherine from John Thorpe's orbit by inviting her to Northanger and so make sure that she marries his son Henry instead—hence his embarrassingly flattering attentions to her, in effect courting her on Henry's behalf.

About the middle of March the Tilneys and Catherine leave for Northanger, which is thirty miles northwards of Bath. They stop for a halfway break at the genuine location of Petty France, a hamlet on the main road (now the A46) going towards Tetbury and Nailsworth, and which consisted of little more than a large posting inn— the Georgian equivalent of a motel. The inn at Petty France still exists as a roadside hotel—a wide, low building, with a vast stable block in a courtyard to the rear, where the spare horses once waited to be hired. When the party sets off again, Jane Austen is careful not to tell us which way they

248

take when the road forks a few miles further on; but as she later says that Catherine's return journey from Northanger to Fullerton, via Salisbury, is a distance of seventy miles, they must have travelled on the Nailsworth road and then turned off again in a westerly direction, because to achieve this mileage she must have mentally located Northanger somewhere near Dursley, in the Vale of Berkeley, and not far from the River Severn.

Jane's mother, born Cassandra Leigh, came from a family of landed gentry who had been settled in Gloucestershire for more than two hundred years, and in the summer of 1794 Jane had stayed with some of her Leigh cousins at Adlestrop, in that county, so she would have known a little of its geography. On the eastern side were the limestone Cotswold Hills, which stretched from Bath to Chipping Campden; stone walls divided the sweeping sheep pastures whose flocks had made the fifteenth-century woollen merchants so rich that each small town had a fine church built from the profits of the trade. In the centre of the county was the rich agricultural valley of the River Severn; and on the western side of the Severn was the oakwood Forest of Dean, which contained coalmines and ironworks. The county town of Gloucester had an ancient cathedral, and was a prosperous inland port, with a quay, wharf and custom house built on the banks of the Severn. The Vale of Berkeley, on the east side of the river, had flat grassland crisscrossed by narrow lanes with humpback bridges over little watercourses, providing wintering grounds for wild geese.

Eleanor has told Catherine something of the

history of Northanger: that it had been a richly endowed convent at the time of the Reformation, was acquired by an ancestor of the Tilneys at the Dissolution of the Monasteries in the mid-sixteenth century, and that the present house still included a large part of the ancient buildings—which encourages Catherine to think that she will soon be able to see 'its massy walls of grey stone, rising amidst a grove of ancient oaks, with the last beams of the sun playing in beautiful splendour on its high Gothic windows'. However, the Abbey cannot in fact be seen from the main road, and almost before she is aware of it, they have driven through the gates of the modern lodges, along a smooth level road of fine gravel, and right up to the porch of the house, without seeing so much as an antique chimney.

Following the Dissolution, there were many redundant monastic buildings that were snapped up by wealthy squires and converted into their private residences; Jane may well have read about such mansions in the topographical literature of the time, or may perhaps have visited Lacock Abbey in Wiltshire when she was travelling to Bath for her family holiday in the autumn of 1797. In Hampshire, too, she might have seen Mottisfont Abbey and Titchfield Abbey; none of them is identical to the description of Northanger which she provides, but as such conversions were always governed by the specific quadrangular shape of a monastic church and its associated buildings, the resultant houses were naturally very similar in their basic layout.

Jane's description of Northanger, both inside and out, is more detailed than that of any other house in the novels—such description is given partly because we need to see it through Catherine's eyes, and understand her disappointment that it is not the kind of ruinous, mysterious medieval abbey she had been hoping for; and partly because we see it also through General Tilney's calculating eyes, as he displays his lavish lifestyle to impress this supposed heiress.

First we go with Catherine into her bedroom on the east side of the house, on the evening of her arrival at Northanger, and find that it is not uncomfortably large and gloomy, nor hung with decaying tapestries and funereally dark velvet bed-curtains. Instead, the walls are papered and the floor carpeted, and the furniture, though not of the latest fashion, is handsome and comfortable. While Catherine is dressing for dinner, the first unusual thing that catches her eye is 'a large high chest, standing back in a deep recess on one side of the fireplace . . . it was of cedar, curiously inlaid with some darker wood, and raised, about a foot from the ground, on a carved stand of the same. The lock was silver, though tarnished from age; at each end were the imperfect remains of handles also of silver, broken perhaps prematurely by some strange violence; and, on the centre of the lid, was a mysterious cypher, in the same metal. . . .' She struggles to open the heavy lid, only to find that the chest contains nothing but a properly folded, white cotton counterpane.

Later in the evening, while she is at dinner, the housemaid comes in to set a cheerful wood fire blazing in the grate, to close the shutters that keep out the cold spring winds, and to draw the long curtains across the shuttered windows and window-seats below them. As Catherine is preparing for bed, she sees another interesting piece of furniture, 'a high, old-fashioned black cabinet, which, though in a situation conspicuous enough, had never caught her notice before . . . She took her candle and looked closely at the cabinet. It was not absolutely ebony and gold; but it was Japan, black and yellow Japan of the handsomest kind . . .' and after fumbling with the locks in her excitement, she finds a roll of paper inside—but before she can read the contents she accidentally extinguishes her candle and, as the fire has by now died down, can do no more than get into bed in the dark. In the morning, to her embarrassment, she sees that the papers are only some domestic bills left behind by the servant of a previous guest, and so puts them back again, reproaching herself for her own foolishness. Although the bills are commonplace to Catherine, for modern readers they point up the passage of time: five are washing-bills (laundry lists) for shirts, stockings, cravats and waistcoats; two others are the servant's lists of expenses on behalf of his master—the receipt of letters, hair-powder, shoe-strings and breeches-ball; the last one is a farrier's (veterinary surgeon's) bill for treating the chestnut mare. Shoe-strings (shoelaces) were just becoming fashionable as an alternative form of fastening for men's shoes instead of metal buckles; and breeches-ball was a dry-cleaning compound, a mixture of lightly abrasive powders and the natural detergent ox-gall, for removing greasy marks and dirt from leather breeches.

The next day, General Tilney takes Catherine on a tour of the Abbey. It lies low in a valley,

252

sheltered from the north and east winds by rising woods of oak—knolls of old trees and luxuriant plantations—and the whole building encloses a large court (that is, the original cloister of the monastic buildings). The best view of the house is from the south-east, where 'two sides of the quadrangle, rich in Gothic ornaments, stood forward for admiration' (these are the original nave, chancel, north transept and chapter house; on the third, north, side of the cloister would have been the monks' refectory and dormitory). The stones of the south transept were probably reused to make the 'old porch' which is now at the new entrance to the house, cut across the nave, in the centre of the south front.

From here the General leads the way across a small portion of the park to the kitchen garden. 'The number of acres contained in this garden was such as Catherine could not listen to without dismay, being more than double the extent of all Mr Allen's, as well as her father's, including church-yard and orchard. The walls seemed countless in number, endless in length; a village of hot-houses seemed to arise among them, and a whole parish to be at work within the inclosure.' Beyond the kitchen garden is the 'Hermitage Walk', a narrow winding path through a thick grove of old Scotch firs, which leads to a tea-house (summer-house) elsewhere in the park.

Back in the house, the General takes Catherine through the six or seven main rooms that lie round three sides of the quadrangle and that all look outwards across the grounds. They are the dining parlour, a noble room fitted up in a style of luxury and expense; the large and lofty hall, which includes a broad staircase of shining oak; the common drawing room, with modern furniture and a Rumfordized fireplace; one useless ante-chamber; the real drawing room, magnificent both in size and furniture—satin and costly gilding—and used only with company of consequence; and the library, an apartment of equal magnificence. They return down the inner side of the quadrangle, where there are some rooms of less importance, including a breakfast parlour and supper room, a billiard room, the General's study and 'a dark little room, owning Henry's authority, and strewed with his litter of books, guns, and great-coats'. As they walk along 'a high arched passage, paved with stone', Catherine is told that 'she was treading what had once been a cloister, having traces of cells pointed out'—which is much more to her taste. However, the General's knowledge of monastic architecture was evidently limited, for these traces would have been not of cells but of carrels (study cubicles for the monks) such as can be seen in the cloister at Gloucester Cathedral to this day. The dining parlour has 'quick communication to the kitchen—the ancient kitchen of the convent, rich in the massy walls and smoke of former days, and in the stoves and hot closets of the present' and beyond this room, the western wing, or fourth side of the quadrangle, has all been rebuilt by the General's father, to provide domestic quarters and a stable-yard behind. 'Catherine could have raved at the hand which had swept away what must have been beyond the value of all the rest, for the purposes of mere domestic economy.'

They return to the hall, and ascend the broad

staircase, with the General pointing out 'the beauty of its wood, and ornaments of rich carving'; after many flights and landing-places, this ends in a gallery on the first floor. The gallery runs all round the house, on the one side with a range of doors leading into the bedrooms and on the other lit by windows which look into the quadrangle. Eleanor's bedroom and Catherine's bedroom are in the east wing; the south wing contains the accommodation for the most important guests—three large bedrooms and dressing rooms, most completely and handsomely fitted up; and this south gallery ends with folding doors that lead into the third or west gallery, where Eleanor says that her deceased mother's bedroom remains as it was before her death nine years ago. The General does not want to continue the tour of the house any further, and they all return downstairs.

As Catherine has now persuaded herself that, in the best tradition of the 'horrid' novels, if the General has not actually murdered his wife, then 'for jealousy perhaps, or wanton cruelty' he keeps her locked up somewhere in this large house, and that 'Mrs Tilney yet lived, shut up for causes unknown, and receiving from the pitiless hands of her husband a nightly supply of coarse food', she finds an opportunity to tiptoe back to Mrs Tilney's bedroom in the hope of finding a clue 'in the shape of some fragmented journal, continued to the last gasp'. On entering the room,

> she beheld what fixed her to the spot and agitated every feature. She saw a large, well-proportioned apartment, an handsome dimity bed, arranged as unoccupied with an

255

housemaid's care, a bright Bath stove, mahogany wardrobes and neatly-painted chairs, on which the warm beams of a western sun gaily poured through two sash windows! Catherine had expected to have her feelings worked, and worked they were. Astonishment and doubt first seized them; and a shortly succeeding ray of common sense added some bitter emotions of shame.

To complete her shame, Henry unexpectedly comes up the small winding staircase next to this bedroom, and gives her a kind but firm scolding for harbouring such foolish ideas.

A few days later the General takes Eleanor and Catherine to dine with Henry at his parsonage at Woodston, the family living to which his father has presented him. Here again, Jane Austen gives us a good description of the village and house, because this is where Catherine will soon be living. It is nearly twenty miles south-east of Northanger—fourteen miles down the main road, and then five miles further down a lane—and so we may surmise that it is somewhere near Tetbury. The countryside is flat, but not unpleasant, and the village is large and populous; in her heart Catherine

preferred it to any place she had ever been at, and looked with great admiration at every neat house above the rank of a cottage, and at all the little chandler's shops which they passed. At the further end of the village, and tolerably disengaged from the rest of it, stood the Parsonage, a new-built substantial stone house, with its semicircular sweep and green gates; and, as they drove up to the door, Henry, with the friends of his solitude, a large Newfoundland puppy and two or three terriers, was ready to receive and make much of them.

The General has told Catherine that 'the house stands among fine meadows facing the south-east, with an excellent kitchen-garden in the same aspect; the walls surrounding which I built and stocked myself about ten years ago, for the benefit of my son'; and for the ornamental part of the premises, Henry is planting a shrubbery round two sides of a meadow, with a green bench in the corner. Inside, there is a comfortable dining parlour, a study for Henry and a drawing room as yet unfurnished. 'It was a prettily-shaped room, the windows reaching to the ground', and to Catherine's delight it looks over green meadows towards a little cottage among apple trees. The General asks her to choose the colour of the wallpaper and curtains for the room, but this pointed request embarrasses her, because she still does not know what Henry's feelings towards her are.

However, only ten days later, the General returns from a trip to London, and uncivilly turns Catherine out of the house, without any explanation, sending her off at seven o'clock the next morning to make a long journey back to Fullerton on her own. One can envisage that Catherine travelled from the Dursley area via the main coaching routes of Tetbury, Malmesbury, Chippenham, Devizes, Salisbury. She arrives home

257

nearly twelve hours later, which confirms a distance of about seventy miles, necessitating several changes of horses and an overall travelling time of six miles an hour. Henry follows her as soon as he can, to ask her to marry him and to explain the reason for his father's behaviour—John Thorpe is at the bottom of it—and they are married the next year—'the bells rang and every body smiled'.

*   *   *

In March 1818, the reviewer in the *British Critic* appreciated the accuracy of Jane's plots and character drawing, but thought that she was not composing but merely reporting from life:

In imagination, of all kinds, she appears to have been extremely deficient; not only her stories are utterly and entirely devoid of invention, but her characters, her incidents, her sentiments, are obviously all drawn exclusively from experience. The sentiments which she puts into the mouths of her actors, are the sentiments, which we are every day in the habit of hearing . . . she seems to have no other object in view, than simply to paint some of those scenes which she has herself seen, and which every one, indeed, may witness daily . . . Her heroes and heroines, make love and are married, just as her readers make love, and were or will be, married; no unexpected ill fortune occurs to prevent, nor any unexpected good fortune to bring about the events on which her novels hinge. She seems to be describing such people as meet together every night, in every respectable house in London; and to relate such incidents as have probably happened, one time or other, to half the families in the United Kingdom . . . our authoress gives no definitions; but she makes her *dramatis personae* talk; and the sentiments which she places in their mouths, the little phrases which she makes them use, strike so familiarly upon our memory as soon as we hear them repeated, that we instantly recognize among some of our acquaintance, the sort of persons she intends to signify, as accurately as if we had heard their voices.

However, the anonymous critic goes on to praise *Northanger Abbey* as being 'one of the very best of Miss Austen's productions, and will every way repay the time and trouble of perusing it'— although even then qualifying his praise by disapproving of General Tilney—'. . . it is not a very probable character, and is not pourtrayed with our authoress's usual taste and judgment.' Very little other contemporary comment on *Northanger Abbey* and its companion novel is known, and part of the edition ended up being remaindered in 1820.

Jane did not tell her family any little scraps of sequel information about the characters; which leaves us room to hope that the unpleasant John Thorpe overturns his gig and breaks his neck; and that Isabella, having jilted James Morland in the mistaken belief that she has succeeded in

259

captivating Captain Tilney, will end up married to some local shopkeeper in Putney.

THE WATSONS

It may have been the acceptance for publication of *Susan* in 1803 that encouraged Jane to start work on another novel in that year or perhaps a little later. She wrote a roughly scribbled first draft of about seventeen and a half thousand words without chapter divisions, but then abandoned the text and never returned to it. She did preserve the fragmentary manuscript, however, which was inherited by Cassandra at Jane's death and later passed down by her to their niece, Caroline Austen. The fragment was first published in 1871 in the Reverend James Edward Austen-Leigh's *Memoir of Jane Austen*, and as Jane herself had left it untitled, it was his decision to call it *The Watsons*.

The Watsons are a large and rather unhappy family, living in the Surrey village of Stanton, which is on the outskirts of some small town. In one part of the manuscript Jane refers to the 'town of D—', and elsewhere to the 'town of R—', so it seems probable she had either Dorking or Reigate in mind—possibly her fictional location was to include elements from both of these genuine towns. The Reverend Mr Watson, the head of the family, is a melancholy, ailing, impoverished widower, barely able to fulfil his clerical duties, and quite unable to exercise any control over his quarrelling unmarried daughters. The eldest son, Robert, aged about thirty, has become a brusque, money-grubbing attorney and lives in Croydon with his conceited wife, Jane, and their spoilt little daughter, Augusta; the youngest son, Sam, about twenty-two, is a surgeon in Guildford, having just finished his apprenticeship there to Mr Curtis. Still at home is the eldest daughter, Elizabeth, aged twenty-eight and so by contemporary standards verging on middle age. She is worn and weary with the difficulties of running the household on a very small income, tending her father, and trying to keep the peace between her next two sisters, Penelope and Margaret, aged twenty-six and twenty-four and each becoming steadily more desperate to catch a husband. The Watson daughters are all well aware that as soon as their father dies, they will have to vacate the parsonage in favour of the next incumbent; without any private income for themselves, marriage is the only hope they have of acquiring their own homes and avoiding a rapid descent into crippling poverty. Elizabeth had once thought that a Mr Purvis was starting to court her, but Penelope tried to get him for herself and only succeeded in frightening him away altogether. A smart young man, Tom Musgrave, has amused himself flirting with all three sisters in turn, and Margaret is still hoping that he will eventually propose to her.

The youngest daughter of the family, Emma, now nineteen, was semi-adopted by a widowed aunt fourteen years ago and taken to live in Shropshire; but her aunt has suddenly married again and her new husband does not want Emma to continue living with them, so she has been unceremoniously returned to this poverty-stricken home where she is now an unwanted stranger. She is a very pretty girl, as Elizabeth kindly tells her; and as the story opens, in mid-October, Elizabeth is driving Emma

262

into the town one afternoon, so that she can stay with the Edwards family there overnight in order to attend the first assembly ball of the winter season, and so stand a chance of meeting an appropriate suitor. We first see the two sisters sitting in the old chair (a small, cheap, open carriage) behind their plodding old mare, as she splashes along the dirty lane from Stanton towards the turnpike road that leads to the town. Mr Tomlinson, the banker, possesses a fine newly erected house at the end of the High Street, with a shrubbery and carriage drive, which in consequence he likes to think is out in the country. In the town, Mr Edwards' house is the best in the High Street, higher than most of its neighbours, with two windows on each side of the door, the windows guarded by posts and chain, the door approached by a flight of stone steps. Mr Edwards keeps several servants, including a footman in livery with a powdered head, as Elizabeth admiringly tells Emma. Mrs Edwards is a very friendly woman, although she has a reserved air and a great deal of formal civility. She has two satin gowns to go through the winter's entertaining, and this evening is wearing a new cap from the local milliner. The Edwards' daughter, Mary, still has her hair in curl-papers when Emma arrives.

Later in the evening, the party set off for the White Hart Inn, where the assembly balls are held.

At a little before eight, the Tomlinsons' carriage was heard to go by, which was the constant signal for Mrs. Edwards to order hers to the door; and in a very few minutes,

263

the party were transported from the quiet warmth of a snug parlour, to the bustle, noise and draughts of air of the broad entrance passage of an inn. Mrs. Edwards carefully guarding her own dress, while she attended with yet greater solicitude to the proper security of her young charges' shoulders and throats, led the way up the wide staircase, while no sound of a ball but the first scrape of one violin, blessed the ears of her followers . . . passing along a short gallery to the assembly-room, brilliant in lights before them . . . Mrs. Edward's satin gown swept along the clean floor of the ball-room, to the fireplace at the upper end, where one party only were formally seated, while three or four officers were lounging together, passing in and out from the adjoining card-room. . . . The cold and empty appearance of the room and the demure air of the small cluster of females at one end of it began soon to give way; the inspiriting sound of other carriages was heard, and continual accessions of portly chaperons, and strings of smartly dressed girls were received, with now and then a fresh gentleman straggler, who if not enough in love to station himself near any fair creature seemed glad to escape into the card-room.

The guests now start to notice this pretty stranger and she is soon asked to dance. 'Emma Watson was not more than of the middle height—well made and plump, with an air of healthy vigour. Her skin was very brown, but clear, smooth and glowing; which with a lively eye, a sweet smile, and an open countenance, gave beauty to attract, and expression to make that beauty improve on acquaintance.' The most important guests of the evening are the party from Osborne Castle, the country mansion in the nearby parish of Wickstead, which consists of the Dowager Lady Osborne, her son the present Lord Osborne, her daughter Miss Osborne, and the daughter's friend Miss Carr, the Reverend Mr Howard, clergyman of the parish, with his widowed sister Mrs Blake, and her young son Charles. Tom Musgrave, the constant flirt, attaches himself to the Castle party in his capacity of social-climbing toady to the clumsy and boorish young Lord Osborne. Emma dances with Mr Howard and likes him, but is annoyed by Lord Osborne's oafish manners and Tom Musgrave's impudent persistence in forcing his company upon her.

In the days following the ball, Robert and Jane come to Stanton, bringing Margaret home with them, and Emma sees that 'Margaret was not without beauty; she had a slight, pretty figure . . . but the sharp and anxious expression of her face made her beauty in general little felt. On meeting her long-absent sister, as on every occasion of shew, her manner was all affection and her voice all gentleness; continual smiles and a very slow articulation being her constant resource when determined on pleasing.' Once the novelty of Emma's acquaintance has worn off, Margaret soon shows herself to be perverse and quarrelsome, and Robert and Jane are also in their different ways unattractive characters, from whom Emma will

265

obviously not receive any affection or sympathy. Penelope is said to be busy husband-hunting in Chichester, and Sam has his professional obligations keeping him in Guildford, so at this stage of the story neither Emma nor we, the readers, meet these last two members of the family.

*   *   *

According to Cassandra's memories, which she passed on to her younger nieces, Mr Watson was soon to die, and Emma to become dependent for a home upon Robert and his selfish little wife. She was to decline an offer of marriage from Lord Osborne, and much of the interest of the tale was to arise from Lady (or Miss) Osborne's love for Mr Howard, and his counter affection for Emma, whom he was finally to marry. One of these younger nieces, in later life Mrs Hubback, tried to finish the story along these lines, in a three-volume work called *The Younger Sister* which she published in 1850; and since then other completions have also been attempted, none very convincingly.

It is not known exactly why Jane Austen abandoned the work, but it may well have been due to a combination of circumstances: her own father died early in 1805, and perhaps she found that Emma's predicament too closely mirrored her own; she may have felt that the story was becoming too sad—not much hope for these disagreeable girls, a bitter re-run of *Pride and Prejudice*; or perhaps she was simply too busy over the next few years moving from Bath to Southampton and then to Chawton to have time to concentrate on literary composition. As she liked the name Emma, she evidently felt it would be a pity to abandon it along with the uncompleted tale, and so used it for a different heroine ten years later.

MANSFIELD PARK

Mansfield Park is the first of Jane Austen's three later novels, written after a fallow period of some six years, and the first product of her truly adult abilities. It seems that she started planning it early in 1811, and commenced writing in 1812, once she had finished work on *Sense and Sensibility* and *Pride and Prejudice*. By January 1813, references in her letters to Cassandra show that she was about halfway through the composition; in July 1813 she was writing to her brother Frank asking his permission to use the genuine names of some of the ships on which he had served. It was probably finished and offered to Egerton late in 1813, and was published by him on 9 May 1814, priced 18*s*. for the three volumes. It sold fairly well, but Egerton did not want to produce a second edition; instead, her brother Henry offered it on Jane's behalf to another London publisher, John Murray of Albemarle Street, who reprinted it in 1816.

Mansfield Park is set in Northamptonshire, a county Jane had never visited, and in her letters of January 1813 she asked Cassandra and Martha for their help with enquiries about the background: 'If you cd. discover whether Northamptonshire is a Country of Hedgerows, I shd. be glad. . . .' Perhaps she wanted to check that what she had already written about hedgerows in Chapter 22 was correct. It may have been Henry who gave her the idea of choosing Northamptonshire for the location—one of his banking partners, James

Tilson, was a relation of the baronet family of Langham, whose family estate was at Cottesbrooke, not far from the supposed site of Mansfield, and Henry knew Sir James Langham through this business connection. Cottesbrooke Hall itself is too old a house to be an appropriate model for the 'modern-built' (that is, 1750–1780) Mansfield Park, and it seems that Jane mentally removed Godmersham from Kent to Northamptonshire, and used this as the basis for the Bertrams' home.

The book opens with a quick retrospective glance to about 1780, explaining how the marriages of the three Ward sisters in that decade have brought them to their present situations in life: Lady Bertram, tranquil and indolent—and no doubt correspondingly fat—the mother of four and the wife of a rich baronet, Sir Thomas Bertram of Mansfield Park; her elder sister, Mrs Norris, spiteful and fidgety, the miserly childless widow of the previous rector of Mansfield; and the youngest of the three, Mrs Price, thin, harassed, overwhelmed with children and living in poverty in Portsmouth with her husband, Lieutenant Price of the Royal Marines, who is now disabled for active service. The timespan overall is from about 1801 to 1811, starting with the arrival of Lady Bertram's niece Fanny Price at Mansfield as an unhappy little ten-year-old, and the main action of the story takes place over the four years 1807–10, with the marriage of Fanny and Edmund Bertram following at some unspecified time in 1811.

In Jane Austen's time, Northamptonshire was known for its 'spires and squires'—that is, its many fine churches and country houses, built of either grey limestone or else golden-brown ironstone—and was celebrated for its large acreage of excellent grazing land, upon which cows and sheep flourished alongside the local breed of large black horses. The county town of Northampton, sixty-six miles from London, was famous for its great horse-fairs, held eight times a year and reckoned to exceed all others in the kingdom, and had also developed its own particular industry in the manufacture of boots and shoes. The wide open and gently rolling grazing lands of Northamptonshire and the adjoining county of Leicestershire were ideal also for foxhunting, giving plenty of room for galloping and jumping.

The action of the story nearly all takes place within a limited radius of Mansfield Park, but there are several houses which we, the readers, visit along with the characters, and so we come to know something of the surrounding parts of Northamptonshire. The village of Mansfield is said to be seventy miles from London, which places it on the north side of Northampton, and there are fine views from Mansfield Common. Mansfield Park is a handsome, spacious modern-built house, well placed at the top of a hill, and by walking fifty yards from the hall door, Fanny can look down the park and command a view of the parsonage and all its demesnes, gently rising beyond the village road. The parsonage is half a mile away, but the great clock in the Park's stable-yard strikes loudly enough to be heard at that distance. Mansfield village itself lies further down the hill, and when Mrs Norris becomes a widow and leaves the parsonage, she goes to the White House, the 'smallest habitation which could rank as genteel among the buildings of Mansfield parish'. It has half an acre of garden, and apparently three bedrooms, sufficient to accommodate a maidservant as well as Mrs Norris herself, plus a spare room which she claims she will keep so that her friends can visit her. Later on, however, we learn that the spare room has become a locked store room. Mrs Norris spends as much time as possible at the Park, sponging off her brother-in-law's estate.

The parsonage is marked by an oak tree just outside it in the lane, under which Fanny tries to shelter on a wet day. The house is elegant and moderate-sized, commodious and well fitted up; it is approached by a carriage sweep, with the coach-house and stable-yard close by, and Mrs Norris had planted an apricot tree against the stable wall a few years before. The present rector, the Revd Dr Grant, thinks the fruit from this apricot tree tasteless and does not hesitate to tell Mrs Norris so. Since taking up residence there he has made a number of changes: he has extended the garden wall and made a plantation to shut out the view of the churchyard, and has also created a shrubbery, planted with laurels and other evergreens, out of a hedgerow running along the upper end of a field which has a farmyard on the other side. Mrs Grant has a choice collection of plants and poultry in her part of the garden. Inside, the small hall leads to a drawing room filled by Mrs Grant with pretty furniture.

Mansfield Park is situated in a park five miles in circumference, 'so well placed and well screened as to deserve to be in any collection of engravings of gentlemen's seats in the kingdom'. Close to the house are the usual shrubbery and flower garden for the benefit of the ladies: Lady Bertram sits in the alcove in the garden on a hot day—'Sitting and calling to Pug, and trying to keep him from the flower-beds, was almost too much for me'—while Fanny cuts the roses and takes them to the White House upon Mrs Norris's orders. The grandeur of the house and its furnishings had astonished and frightened little Fanny when she first arrived there—'the rooms were too large for her to move in with ease; whatever she touched she expected to injure'—and we learn gradually that in addition to the usual dining room and breakfast room, there is a great staircase, a very long drawing room, a ballroom and a billiard room, with a plasterwork ceiling in high relief, that has a door leading through into Sir Thomas's study.

Upstairs, Fanny's bedroom is the cold little white attic, near the housemaids' room and the old nurseries; and underneath the white attic is the old school room, renamed the East Room now that the Bertram children have grown up, and which Fanny has tacitly been allowed to use as her study. The East Room contains her pot plants, books and her writing desk, and the work-boxes and netting-boxes given to her over the years. Jane Austen then gives us a surprisingly detailed description of the room: its plain furniture

> had suffered all the ill-usage of children—
> and its greatest elegancies and ornaments
> were a faded footstool of Julia's work, too ill
> done for the drawing-room, three
> transparencies, made in a rage for
> transparencies, for the three lower panes of

one window, where Tintern Abbey held its station between a cave in Italy, and a moonlight lake in Cumberland; a collection of family profiles thought unworthy of being anywhere else, over the mantle-piece, and by their side and pinned against the wall, a small sketch of a ship sent four years ago from the Mediterranean by William, with H.M.S. Antwerp at the bottom, in letters as tall as the main-mast.

We may speculate that the East Room could perhaps be based on memories of the schoolroom at Godmersham. Although Jane visited many country houses, as a guest she would not have been taken into any such strictly domestic apartments— whereas it is known from her letters that during her visits to Godmersham she spent a good deal of time playing with her brother's young children and helping teach them their lessons.

We hear some of the names of the staff necessary to run the estate: Sir Thomas employs both a steward and a bailiff, and a full-time carpenter, 'my friend Christopher Jackson', whose ten-year-old son, Dick, is scolded away from the servants' hall by Mrs Norris; rheumatic old Wilcox is the coachman, and Stephen and Charles are the postillions, senior to John who is merely a groom. Indoors, Baddely is the butler, who builds up a 'noble fire' in the ballroom, only to see Mrs Norris 'fresh arranging and injuring' it; there is an unspecified number of footmen, one of whom can play the violin, and is called up from the servants' hall one September evening so that the young Bertrams can have an impromptu dance. Mrs

Chapman is lady's maid to Lady Bertram, Ellis is lady's maid to Lady Bertram's daughters Maria and Julia, and the upper housemaid is also supposed to help Fanny dress if need be. Mrs Norris pesters the unfortunate anonymous housekeeper with troublesome directions, and she also insults the footmen with injunctions to hurry up.

We are never told exactly what Sir Thomas Bertram's annual income amounts to, but to support this lifestyle it would probably have to be about £10,000 a year. Some of it comes from the farming of the Mansfield estate, but the remainder comes from plantations in Antigua, where the profitable production of crops was dependent upon the use of slave labour. In real life, the Anti-Slavery Committee, led by William Wilberforce and other evangelical Christians, had been campaigning since 1787 for an end to the slave trade within British possessions, and Parliament passed a bill abolishing the slave trade in March 1807 that would come into full effect in May 1808. The cutting-off of a constant supply of an unpaid workforce of new slaves would have serious repercussions for the plantation owners within a few years. Mrs Norris is quick to realize: 'Sir Thomas's means will be rather straitened, if the Antigua estate is to make such poor returns.' It is not therefore surprising that in September 1807 'Sir Thomas found it expedient to go to Antigua himself, for the better arrangement of his affairs'; he takes his elder son Tom with him 'in the hope of detaching him from some bad connections at home'.

At the time Jane Austen was writing many English families had similar investments in the

West Indies, because ever since the early seventeenth century younger sons had gone out there to try to make their fortunes by developing plantations and exporting the resultant crops back to the United Kingdom; the Civil War in the middle of the century increased the flow, when defeated Royalists fled to the West Indies to escape Cromwell's new puritan republic at home. Jane could have endowed Sir Thomas Bertram with other estates elsewhere in the United Kingdom; but this would have been unsatisfactory in plot terms, because he could then have written in advance to announce his homecoming on a particular day. She had to send him far away from Mansfield Park in order to make his return an unpredictable event. The West Indies was obviously the logical answer for her purpose, and a destination that would have been accepted as reasonable by her contemporary readers.

Tom returns from Antigua in September 1808, now twenty-six and as frivolous and extravagant as ever, but Sir Thomas stays out there for another year, due to the continuing 'very great uncertainty in which every thing was then involved'. In the meantime, Fanny, though still the Cinderella of the Mansfield Park family, has grown into a slender, delicately pretty blonde teenager, with a sweet smile and soft light eyes, silently cherishing her childhood devotion to her cousin Edmund Bertram and just as silently enduring Mrs Norris's spiteful bullying. Edmund has decided to become a clergyman and, at the age of twenty-four, will soon be ordained; Maria Bertram engages herself, at twenty-one, to the stupid young Mr James Rushworth, who has recently inherited the nearby estate of Sotherton Court and with it £12,000 a year; Julia Bertram is twenty and on the lookout for a husband too. Henry and Mary Crawford, the younger half-brother and sister of Mrs Grant and both likewise in their twenties, come to stay at Mansfield Parsonage in July 1809, when Fanny is just eighteen. Now Jane Austen obliquely describes the physical appearance of the main characters:

> Miss Crawford's beauty did her no disservice with the Miss Bertrams. They were too handsome themselves to dislike any woman for being so too, and were almost as much charmed as their brothers, with her lively dark eye, clear brown complexion, and general prettiness. Had she been tall, full-formed, and fair, it might have been more of a trial; but as it was, there could be no comparison, and she was most allowably a sweet pretty girl, while they were the finest young women in the country.

Henry, though only of middle height and not strictly handsome, dark-haired like his sister, nevertheless has 'so much countenance [expressive features, animation], and his teeth were so good, and he was so well made . . . that he was, in fact, the most agreeable young man the sisters had ever known, and they were equally delighted with him.' He has an estate at Everingham, in Norfolk, worth £4,000 a year, which he had inherited while still a schoolboy at Westminster, and 'improved' as soon as he came of age. This experience encourages him to advise Mr Rushworth as to how the grounds of

Sotherton, which date from the end of the seventeenth century and consequently now appear old-fashioned and dull, could likewise be improved; and in the middle of July there is a family party of Bertrams and Crawfords to call upon Mr Rushworth and his mother at Sotherton and discuss the question on the spot.

Jane Austen tells us quite a lot about Sotherton Court, partly because we see it through Fanny's eyes as she goes on this unexpected pleasure-trip— Aunt Norris, of course, has done her best to prevent Fanny from being included—and partly because the afternoon spent here is crucial to the development of the plot. The village of Sotherton is ten miles from Mansfield, and the journey there includes a stretch of rough stony lane so narrow that Wilcox, the coachman, fears the hedges will scratch the varnish on the carriages, while the long ascent of Sandcroft Hill has still to be overcome. At the top of the hill the woodlands of the Sotherton estate begin, and Maria Bertram can point out the improvement to this stretch of road which Mr Rushworth has already carried out. The village begins with some tumbledown cottages, the church has a remarkably handsome spire, and is not so close to the Great House as to make its bell-ringing an annoyance there; the parsonage is a tidy-looking house, and Maria understands that the clergyman and his wife are very decent people; the Rushworths have also built an alms house, and the estate steward, a very respectable man, lives near the lodge gates.

Through the lodge gates, there is a drive through the wooded park for nearly a mile, winding downhill to the low-lying house—which dates to

277

the sixteenth century, and is a large, regular, brick building, heavy but respectable-looking, and with many good rooms—and there are spacious stone steps at the principal entrance on the east side of the house. Inside, the party is greeted by old Mrs Rushworth and her son, and she gives them a tour of the house:

> . . . a number of rooms, all lofty, and many large, and amply furnished in the taste of fifty years back [that is, about 1760], with shining floors, solid mahogany, rich damask, marble, gilding and carving, each handsome in its way. Of pictures there were abundance, and some few good, but the larger part were family portraits, no longer any thing to any body but Mrs Rushworth, who had been at great pains to learn all that the house-keeper could teach, and was now almost equally well qualified to shew the house.

The house is big enough to have a private chapel, an ecclesiastical luxury which presumably was granted to past Rushworths because the parish church is about two miles away in the village. The chapel is entered from both ground and first-floor levels; and Fanny, rather like Catherine Morland, is disappointed to find that it is not ancient, but only a spacious oblong room, fitted up for the purpose of devotion, with nothing more striking or more solemn than a profusion of mahogany and crimson velvet cushions appearing over the ledge of the family gallery above. Mrs Rushworth says the mahogany pews and panelling were installed at

278

the end of the seventeenth century; before that the pews were only wainscot and the cushions purple cloth. As mahogany was not imported in any quantities until the early eighteenth century, this reference to its use at an earlier date could be taken to indicate that the Rushworths of that time were sufficiently rich to be able to purchase this rare new luxury wood. While the party are in the chapel Mary Crawford, who has already noted that Edmund is tall, fair and handsome, learns to her annoyance that he intends soon to be ordained.

The low-lying site of the house means that there is not much prospect from any of the rooms, and all those on the west front look across a lawn to the beginning of the avenue of oak trees which ascends for half a mile to the edge of the park, and which starts immediately beyond some tall iron palisades and gates. The party leave the house by a door at the south end, temptingly open on to a flight of steps leading upwards to turf and ornamental shrubs. They find a lawn bounded on each side by a high wall, a bowling green beyond the lawn, and beyond the bowling green a long terrace walk, backed by iron palisades, and commanding a view over them into the tops of the trees of the adjoining wilderness. The terrace walk, in turn, has a door in the palisades; and to escape the heat of the July sun on the terrace, Edmund, Mary Crawford and Fanny go down a considerable flight of steps into the wilderness—which is, in fact, a planted wood of about two acres, set out with larch, laurel and beech, and regularly divided by walks and cross-walks, with benches at intervals. At the edge of the wilderness is a ha-ha to keep out any animals grazing in the park beyond, with iron gates to allow access for human wanderers. The three of them sit on one of the benches, and Mary attacks Edmund on the subject of ordination, trying to mock him out of his choice of profession; the two presently go off to walk together in the wilderness, leaving Fanny alone on the bench.

Fanny is then joined by Maria, escorted by Mr Rushworth and Henry Crawford, and she has to listen with embarrassment as Maria snubs Rushworth and flirts with Henry. While Rushworth goes off to get the key for the iron gates, Henry and Maria manage to slip round the edge of the spiked railings instead, and they scramble across the ha-ha together and into the parkland beyond— as we later realize, this is Jane Austen's careful symbolism prefiguring their actual elopement at the end of the book. The unfortunate Rushworth returns, hot and cross—he is probably one of those large, bulky people whose faces shine greasily upon the slightest degree of warmth—to find that his fiancée and Henry Crawford have disappeared from sight. The afternoon ends with all the young people at odds with each other—Fanny miserable to see how Edmund is falling under Mary Crawford's spell, Mary cross at Edmund's determination to enter the Church, Rushworth jealous of Henry Crawford, Maria already regretting her engagement to Rushworth, and Julia, who considers that Henry ought to be her admirer, jealous of Maria's flirtation with him.

Tom Bertram now returns home from a seaside holiday at Weymouth, bringing with him his friend John Yates, who has a passion for amateur dramatics; and after much selfish argument, the young people finally decide they will act *Lovers'*

280

Vows, a genuine popular play of the early nineteenth century. This play has been so long forgotten that the significance of its choice for performance in the Bertram household is something we modern readers do not understand, but Jane's contemporary readers would at once have realized that trouble was bound to follow. The play was originally German, written by Kotzebue, later translated and adapted by the English actress Mrs Inchbald, and first performed at Covent Garden Theatre in London on 11 October 1798. We do not know when or where Jane Austen saw it, but it remained popular for some years, and the script was kept constantly in print. The action is set in Germany, where some twenty years previously Agatha Friburg, an innocent village maiden, was seduced under the promise of marriage by Baron Wildenhaim and then left to bring up their son, Frederick, alone; Agatha tells Frederick this in the opening scene, thus informing the audience as well. The Baron subsequently went to France and married there, and has now returned to his native estate in Germany as a widower, with one youthful daughter, Amelia. The Baron is considering marrying Amelia off to the rich Count Cassel, but she loves her tutor, the Reverend Mr Anhalt; and in a long dialogue with him persuades him to admit that he loves her too. Meanwhile, Frederick and the Baron, as yet ignorant of their relationship, come to blows and the Baron puts him in the dungeons of the castle. In the final scene, the repentant Baron acknowledges Frederick as his heir, marries Agatha, and permits Amelia to marry Anhalt. Although the play ends with morality restored, some critics of the time considered it still too risqué, so it is hardly surprising that Fanny is shocked when she reads the text: 'Agatha and Amelia appeared to her in their different ways so totally improper for home representation—the situation of one, and the language of the other, so unfit to be expressed by any woman of modesty . . .' Maria Bertram is cast as Agatha, and Henry Crawford as Frederick, which gives them much scope for affecting scenes together, as Agatha either clasps her son to her bosom or else faints into his arms. Edmund is Anhalt and Mary Crawford Amelia, and Fanny has to listen to them rehearsing their big scene: 'The whole subject of it was love—a marriage of love was to be described by the gentleman, and very little short of a declaration of love be made by the lady.' Unfortunately for Mr Yates, who was enjoying himself ranting away in the part of the remorseful Baron Wildenhaim, Sir Thomas Bertram returns home unexpectedly and puts an instant stop to the proceedings.

Some people wonder why, since the young Austens themselves performed plays at home in Steventon, Jane should apparently disapprove of the amateur dramatics at Mansfield Park; but such critics here confuse reality and fiction. The point Jane is making in the novel is not that amateur dramatics are themselves wrong in principle, but that the Bertrams know their father would disapprove and are therefore disobeying him in his absence, as well as choosing a play which, as Fanny realizes, is unsuitable for performance in a domestic circle, and which only exacerbates the jealousies and quarrels already existing among the young people. As Jane intended, the sexual tensions created at this time between Maria and Henry Crawford, and Edmund and Mary Crawford, as they rehearse their parts all too enthusiastically, make the production of *Lovers' Vows* the turning point for the eventual collapse of the Bertram family group.

Sir Thomas seems to have been lucky, in that he returns home no more the worse for wear than being grown thinner and having the burnt, fagged, worn look of fatigue and a hot climate. The West Indies were notoriously unhealthy for Europeans, with yellow fever the greatest risk, the progress of which could be so rapid that it was not unusual for the doctor, the coffin-maker and the undertaker to be sent for at the same time. Other local diseases were the incurable 'black scurvy' (either leprosy or syphilis) and some unnamed infection which covered the body with itching boils. Fanny says that she loves to hear her uncle talk of his travels and Sir Thomas is no doubt happy to tell his family about the exotic fruits of the West Indies—the tamarinds, mangoes, yams, shaddocks and pineapples—and probably also talks of the mosquitoes, spiders, cockroaches, wall-scorpions, centipedes and vicious wasps that hide in the wooden houses, as well as the land-crabs which appear after dark from their burrows. The town of St John's, even though the capital of Antigua, was no more than a succession of irregular wooden houses on brick foundations, the streets all dust and desolation, and grass-grown in the rainy season. He probably does not tell his family any such stories as those recounted in real life by a young British officer stationed in the Caribbean who was shocked to discover that:

> Our opposite neighbour on the Ridge at
> Antigua at a distance of a short mile was a
> Mr Dow, an employee in the dockyard.
> Besides a family of five handsome
> daughters—whites—he had generally under
> the same roof as many black daughters, who
> were let out as mistresses to the officers as
> chance offered, and the mutual intimacy
> between this double brood was not
> considered extraordinary by the residents.

Maria has been hoping that Henry Crawford will
now formally ask her father's permission to marry
her, in which case she would have had no
hesitation in breaking her engagement to Mr
Rushworth; however, to her rage and dismay,
Henry does no such thing, but promptly leaves
Mansfield for Bath. Maria goes ahead with her
loveless marriage in November—'In all the
important preparations of the mind she was
complete; being prepared for matrimony by an
hatred of home, restraint, and tranquillity; by the
misery of disappointed affection, and contempt of
the man she was to marry'—and Julia accompanies
the newly weds on a trip to Brighton. Tom too has
gone off, to the races at Newmarket, so Fanny is
the unhappy and sole observer of Edmund's
growing infatuation with Mary Crawford, who
hopes she will eventually persuade him to give up
his intention to take Holy Orders and marry her on
her own terms.
  Henry presently returns to Mansfield early in
December to enjoy the fox-hunting season, and, by

284

way of callous amusement, decides to flirt with Fanny, telling his sister:

> My plan is to make Fanny Price in love with me. . . . No, I will not do her any harm, dear little soul! I only want her to look kindly on me, to give me smiles as well as blushes, to keep a chair for me by herself wherever we are, and be all animation when I take it and talk to her; to think as I think, be interested in all my possessions and pleasures, try to keep me longer at Mansfield, and feel when I go away that she shall be never happy again. I want nothing more.

However, Fanny is soon distracted from anything Henry can say to her by the arrival on leave of her beloved elder brother, William, now a midshipman in the Royal Navy, and whom she has not seen for the last seven years.

At the end of the eighteenth century naval officers started their career at an age when nowadays they would still be in primary school: a boy could join a ship at the age of ten and be classed as a volunteer, something like a modern officer cadet. At fourteen he became a midshipman, and had to serve for at least six years before he could apply for promotion to lieutenant, the most junior of the commissioned officer ranks. There were several lieutenants aboard any ship, and a young man would hope to become first lieutenant as those senior to him either died or were promoted. 'A bloody war and a sickly season!' was the ruthless toast among the junior lieutenants at ward-room dinners, and William 'was not very merciful to the first lieutenant'. From the first lieutenant's rank, further years of good service, as well as luck in battle, might bring promotion to commander and then to post-captain, after which promotion to admiral followed automatically as a matter of seniority. One of the biggest hurdles was to make the initial transition from midshipman to lieutenant, and, in order to ingratiate himself with Fanny, Henry Crawford applies to his uncle, a retired admiral, to use his influence to expedite William's promotion.

During the course of William's visit, the topic of Edmund's impending ordination is mentioned again, and Mary Crawford learns, to her annoyance, that he will soon leave Mansfield Park to live in his parsonage at Thornton Lacey, several miles away. Edmund and Henry Crawford discuss the question of how much 'improvement' the parsonage and its grounds might need, and we, the readers, hear a good description of the house in consequence; we need to know this, because at the end of the book this is where Edmund and Fanny start their married life together. Thornton Lacey itself is a little village between gently rising hills, approached past an old farmhouse sheltered by yew trees, and with a small stream running beside the lane. On one side of the lane the large and handsome church stands on a small hill, and on the other side is the ancient parsonage, which Henry admires as being 'a solid-walled, roomy, mansion-like-looking house, such as one might suppose a respectable old country family had lived in from generation to generation, through two centuries at least, and were now spending from two to three thousand a year in'. In his opinion, as there is no squire's mansion in the parish, the parsonage instead can be made into the dominant house in the landscape—'receive such an air as to make its owner be set down as the great land-holder of the parish, by every creature travelling the road'. Henry recommends, accordingly, that the farmyard in front should be cleared away entirely, and trees planted to shut out the view of the blacksmith's shop. The parsonage at present faces north, so this aspect must be changed, with the entrance and principal rooms made to face east, where the view is pretty, and approached through the present garden. A new garden should be made at the rear of the house, sloping towards the south-east; and the several meadows beyond, which are finely sprinkled with timber, must all be thrown into one, and the stream must also be improved in some way. The more rational and less extravagant Edmund plans to do no more than remove the farmyard, which will then give a tolerable approach to the house: 'I must be satisfied with rather less ornament and beauty.'

Sir Thomas kindly arranges to hold a Christmas ball at the Park so that William can enjoy himself dancing before his leave comes to an end, and this event, like the trip to Sotherton, leads to further emotional complications between the four main characters. Mary Crawford and Edmund are mutually vexed with each other, because she tells him she will never dance with him again if he proceeds with his plans for ordination. Henry Crawford now believes himself to be sincerely in love with Fanny, and tells Mary so: 'Fanny's beauty of face and figure, Fanny's graces of manner and goodness of heart were the exhaustless theme.'

However, as Fanny has seen the way in which he deliberately flirted with the Bertram sisters, and the unhappiness this caused both of them, she distrusts and dislikes the sudden pressure of his courtship, and is utterly dismayed when he proposes to her a few days later. Sir Thomas cannot understand why Fanny persists in refusing this apparently excellent matrimonial settlement, and decides that she should pay a visit to her parents' poor home in Portsmouth:

> . . . a little abstinence from the elegancies and luxuries of Mansfield Park, would bring her mind into a sober state, and incline her to a juster estimate of the value of that home of greater permanence, and equal comfort, of which she had the offer.

In February 1810, therefore, William takes Fanny back to Portsmouth with him when he returns to Hampshire to take up his new appointment as second lieutenant of the sloop HMS *Thrush*—the result of Admiral Crawford's string-pulling at Henry's request. It takes them two days to make the journey, travelling from Northampton to Oxford and spending the night at Newbury, and then reaching Portsmouth just before dusk on the second day. At that time Portsmouth was not only a great naval base, with a harbour deep enough to take the largest ships then built, but also had a resident military garrison to protect the town and dockyard from invasion by either sea or land. The town had stone walls around it, and on the landward side there was, in addition, a complicated tangle of defensive moats, walls, ramparts and bastions, broken by one narrow entrance, the Landport Gate, itself approached only by a drawbridge over the moat: 'They passed the Drawbridge, and entered the town . . . they were rattled into a narrow street, leading from the High Street, and drawn up before the door of a small house now inhabited by Mr Price.'

The landward fortifications to the town have long since been swept away, and although the Landport Gate still stands in its original location, it is no longer used as an entrance to Portsmouth. As ever when dealing with genuine places, Jane Austen is careful not to say exactly where the Prices live, but it might have been in either Highbury Street or Peacock Lane, both of which are turnings directly off the High Street, one to the west and the other to the east. The High Street still exists, as do these two smaller streets; but this area of Portsmouth was so badly bombed during the Second World War and so drastically rebuilt thereafter that the houses are now very different from those which Fanny would have seen as she entered the town. Further down the High Street, towards the sea, the other places where she goes later on—the Garrison Chapel, the ramparts and the dockyard—are still there, and it is possible to follow in her footsteps even though these locations have also been somewhat modernized.

The best idea of the kind of house in which the Price family lives can be gained from looking at the old terraces still surviving in St Thomas Street, which runs parallel to the High Street; the houses here, though now neat and well maintained, are probably very similar in size to the one in which Jane mentally placed Fanny's slovenly family. As we enter with Fanny, we find it has a narrow entrance passage, off which opens a small parlour that seems to be the family's one and only living room. The carpet is ragged, the walls have greasy marks where her father leans his head back from his arm-chair, the table is cut and notched by her three youngest brothers, and on it stands the tea-board, never thoroughly cleaned by Rebecca or Sally, the two maidservants who look like trollops. Somewhere beyond the parlour is the kitchen, from which the maids shout out their excuses for not doing their work properly. Fanny has to share a bedroom with her younger sister, Susan, and this too is small, cold and scantily furnished. Once William has sailed off on HMS *Thrush*, Fanny is stranded in this dirty little den, in the midst of closeness and noise, bad air and bad smells, and half-starved as well, since she often cannot face 'Rebecca's puddings, and Rebecca's hashes, brought to table as they all were, with such accompaniments of half-cleaned plates, and not half-cleaned knives and forks'. Mrs Price is always so ineffectually busy at home that she hardly ever goes out, except for a visit to the Garrison Chapel for morning service on Sundays and a walk on the ramparts above the sea afterwards; and, as the town is full of soldiers and sailors, if Fanny and Susan walked out unescorted they would run the risk of being taken for prostitutes and addressed accordingly.

A few weeks later Henry Crawford comes to Portsmouth in pursuit of Fanny, and she is amazed to find how much improved in character he seems to be—'he was much more gentle, obliging, and attentive to other people's feelings than he had ever been at Mansfield'. He takes her and Susan for a walk to the dockyard, where they can sit down from time to time to rest upon some timbers in the yard, or on board a vessel in the stocks which they all went to look at. Fanny knows that Edmund has gone to London with the intention of proposing to Mary Crawford, but does not dare to ask Henry if such a meeting has yet taken place.

Over the next few weeks the story rapidly comes to its climax: instead of going to Norfolk to attend to business on his Everingham estate, as Henry promised Fanny that he would, he changes his mind and stays in London. Here he meets Maria again, bored and miserable in her marriage to the stupid Mr Rushworth, and cannot resist renewing his flirtation with her, with the result that she forces an elopement upon him. Julia, afraid of being recalled to Mansfield, likewise runs away to Gretna Green with Mr Yates; Tom has an accident at Newmarket and is brought home dangerously ill; and when Edmund does finally see Mary Crawford he is so shocked by her callous, worldly attitude to these social and moral calamities that he realizes that he has never understood her before, but has been loving a creature of his own imagination. Fanny returns to Mansfield in May and is now welcomed by Sir Thomas and Lady Bertram as the only daughter upon whose honesty and affection they can rely. The story ends with Jane Austen politely telling us:

I purposely abstain from dates on this occasion, that every one may be at liberty to fix their own, aware that the cure of unconquerable passions, and the transfer of unchanging attachments, must vary much as to time in different people. I only intreat every body to believe that exactly at the time when it was quite natural that it should be so, and not a week earlier, Edmund did cease to care about Miss Crawford, and became as anxious to marry Fanny, as Fanny herself could desire.

*   *   *

In the summer of 1813 Jane's brother Edward Knight brought his family for a holiday at Chawton Great House, and one of his daughters, the nine-year-old Louisa, listened to her aunts' conversation and remembered many years later that she had heard Cassandra trying to persuade Jane to alter the end of the story and let Henry Crawford marry Fanny Price. Louisa recalled that they argued the question, but that Jane stood firm and would not allow the change. However, this discussion may have been responsible for the paragraphs in the last chapter where Jane admits that the ending might have been different:

> Henry Crawford, ruined by early independence and bad domestic example, indulged in the freaks of a cold-blooded vanity a little too long. Once it had, by an opening undesigned and unmerited, led him into the way of happiness. Could he have been satisfied with the conquest of one amiable woman's affections, could he have found sufficient exultation in overcoming the reluctance, in working himself into the

esteem and tenderness of Fanny Price, there would have been every probability of success and felicity for him. . . . Would he have persevered, and uprightly, Fanny must have been his reward—and a reward very voluntarily bestowed—within a reasonable period from Edmund's marrying Mary.

And yet, had the ending been different, would Edmund and Fanny have been any happier if they had married the Crawfords? Mary would never have been content to settle down in rural Northamptonshire as the wife of a serious, conscientious clergyman, and would always have been nagging Edmund to give it all up and live in London instead. As for Henry, with his actor's instincts for taking on different roles, he might have played the part of a devoted husband to Fanny for a few months, but thereafter would soon have grown tired of her virtue and piety, just as she would have been unable to cope with his smart, heartless society friends of whom we hear Mary Crawford talking. A more sentimental author might have pretended that Edmund and Fanny could have redeemed or converted the Crawfords to their own more virtuous lifestyles; but it would have been quite unnatural for two such worldly people to change their ways so completely at short notice, and Jane Austen's studies of human character are nothing if not natural and unsentimental.

Jane did not, in fact, tell her family anything more about the later life of the Bertrams, beyond saying that Edmund was one of her favourite characters; but it is tempting to think that Tom's

293

accident and ensuing illness did shorten his life, and that Mansfield Park came to be inhabited by Sir Edmund and his family.

For some unknown reason *Mansfield Park* was never reviewed, but Jane Austen kept her own list of 'Opinions' gathered from family and friends. Her brother Henry liked it very much, as she mentioned in three letters to Cassandra in the spring of 1814:

> He took to Lady B. & Mrs N. most kindly, & gives great praise to the drawing of the Characters. He understands them all, likes Fanny & I think foresees how it will all be. . . . I beleive *now* he has changed his mind as to foreseeing the end; he said yesterday at least, that he defied anybody to say whether H.C. would be reformed, or would forget Fanny in a fortnight. . . . Henry has finished Mansfield Park, & his approbation has not lessened. He found the last half of the last volume *extremely interesting*.

Her brother Frank and his wife Mary wrote: 'We certainly do not think it as a *whole*, equal to P. & P.—but it has many & great beauties. Fanny is a delightful Character! and Aunt Norris is a great favourite of mine. The Characters are natural & well supported, & many of the Dialogues excellent .—You need not fear the publication being considered as discreditable to the talents of its Author.' Her schoolboy nephew James-Edward (son of James) also liked it very much, and when the question of a second edition was discussed wished she would add another volume: 'The Novel has but one fault; it is too quickly read . . .'

Opinions amongst the Austens varied quite widely, some of them taking Fanny's part, others thinking her insipid and dull. Of their immediate neighbours, Mrs Bramston of Oakley Hall was '—much pleased with it; particularly with the character of Fanny, as being so very natural. Thought Lady Bertram like herself.—Preferred it to either of the others—but imagined *that* might be her want of Taste—as she does not understand Wit.' Her sister-in-law, the eccentric Miss Augusta Bramston, did not attempt a civil response, but 'owned that she thought S.&S.—and P.&P. downright nonsense, but expected to like MP. better, & having finished the 1st vol.—flattered herself she had got through the worst.'

Other contemporary readers, unknown to Jane, mentioned the book to each other in their letters; a Scottish lady, Mrs Grant of Laggan, herself an author, wrote: 'I am glad you approve so much of Mansfield Park, it being a great favourite with me, on account of its just delineation of manners and excellent moral, which is rather insinuated than obtruded throughout—the safest and best way, I think.' The Dowager Lady Vernon told a friend: 'I now recommend you "Mansfield Park" if you meet with it. It is not much of a novel, more the history of a family party in the country, very natural, and the characters well drawn'; and Lady Anne Romilly asked: 'Have you read Mansfield Park? It has been pretty generally admired here [in London], and I think all novels must be that are true to life which this is, with a good strong vein of principle running thro' the whole. It has not however that elevation of virtue, something

295

beyond nature, that gives the greatest charm to a novel, but still it is real natural every day life, and will amuse an idle hour in spite of its faults.'

EMMA

Jane Austen started composing *Emma* on 21 January 1814, even while she was still correcting the proofs of *Mansfield Park*, and finished it on 29 March 1815. The story covers fourteen months, from the September of one year to the November of the next, and it seems likely that she envisaged it as taking place in 1813–14. In the late summer of 1815 Jane went to London, taking the manuscript with her, so her brother Henry could, as before, negotiate with publishers on her behalf; and this time the book was published on commission by John Murray of Albemarle Street. It actually appeared at the end of December 1815, but as there had been delays in the printing, the title page ('by the Author of "Pride and Prejudice", &c. &c.') was dated 1816. It came out in the usual three-volume format, priced at 21*s.* for the set, and Jane sent a specially bound and dedicated pre-publication copy to Carlton House for the Prince Regent.

The author Mary Russell Mitford, although initially thinking that *Pride and Prejudice* was lacking in elegance and taste, by now had changed her mind and, in 1816, spoke warmly in praise of Jane's novels: 'By the way, how delightful is her "Emma"! the best, I think, of all her charming works.' In later years she commented:

Even in books I like a confined locality, and so do the critics when they talk of the unities. Nothing is so tiresome as to be whirled half over Europe at the chariot wheels of a hero, to go to sleep at Vienna, and awaken at Madrid; it produces a real fatigue, a weariness of spirit. On the other hand, nothing is so delightful as to sit down in a country village in one of Miss Austen's delicious novels, quite sure before we leave it to become intimate with every spot and every person it contains . . .

She may well have had *Emma* in her mind as she wrote this, because it is the most static of all the stories, with the heroine at no time travelling more than seven miles away from her home in Highbury.

The Austens had cousins who lived in Surrey, the Reverend and Mrs Samuel Cooke, of Great Bookham, near Leatherhead, whom Jane visited from time to time; and it was no doubt the knowledge she had thus gained of Surrey that prompted her to set her next novel in that county. According to Austen family tradition, the fictional Highbury is based on Leatherhead, though, as always, no place or house can be precisely identified. In the summer of 1814, Jane stayed at Great Bookham for a fortnight, and probably went with the Cookes for a trip to the nearby Box Hill, just as Emma does. Surrey is a county of very differing scenery: in the north it borders in part on the river Thames; in the west are sandy commons where nothing but pine trees, heather and fern will grow; and, in the middle, the long chalk ridge of the North Downs, varying in height from 400 to 900 feet above sea level, runs through on an east to west line from Hampshire into Kent, with the beauty spot of Box Hill, between Mickleham and Dorking, standing out at over 600 feet in height. The steep southern escarpment of the North Downs is largely covered with tough, hardy trees and shrubs such as yew, box (hence the name of Box Hill, where this tree grows in particular abundance), beech and juniper. Below the North Downs are woodlands and fertile valleys watered by a number of small rivers which flow north into the Thames, and which can therefore support mixed agriculture. The ancient town of Kingston-upon-Thames, where several of the early Saxon kings had been crowned and which stands ten miles upriver from London, was in Jane's time one of the three principal towns in the county, while Richmond-upon-Thames had become a smart riverside resort early in the eighteenth century, since it was close enough to London for Georgian gentry to go there for the weekend.

According to an Austen family tradition, Jane said that for this book she was going to create a heroine 'whom no one but myself will much like'; and after introducing Emma Woodhouse as being 'handsome, clever, and rich, with a comfortable home and happy disposition', she sounds the warning note that 'the real evils indeed of Emma's situation were the power of having rather too much her own way, and a disposition to think a little too well of herself; these were the disadvantages which threatened alloy to her many enjoyments.' As in her other novels, the action is seen through the eyes of the heroine; the ironic difference here is that only at the end of the book do we realize that Emma's vision is distorted, and that in consequence we have been led astray and reached the same wrong conclusions as she has. The plot has been developed by Jane as a detective story without a murder, and the book needs to be read twice before we can see that the clues to the secret engagement between Frank Churchill and Jane Fairfax have been there all the time, but because Emma did not notice them, neither did we.

Highbury is a large and populous village, nearly a town. Our visit there begins, late in September, at Hartfield, Emma's home, where she and her elderly father, Mr Henry Woodhouse, are settling down to a lonely evening together, following the marriage that morning of Emma's beloved governess and companion, Miss Taylor, to the cheerful widower Mr Weston. The Woodhouses are a younger branch of a very ancient family, and have lived at Highbury for several generations, though Hartfield itself is a modern and well-built house—presumably, therefore, it dates to the 17760s or 1770s; perhaps it was built by Emma's father when he inherited the property. The house has its own name, and its small but neat and pretty grounds—a large tree with a circular bench round it stands on the lawn, with a shrubbery of laurel bushes behind and a carriage drive to the iron gates in front—separate it from the road to the village, but it is really part of Highbury. There is little agricultural land attached to Hartfield, apparently just enough for Mr Woodhouse to graze his carriage horses and keep some pigs—'Hartfield pork is not like any other pork'—and all the rest of Highbury, together with the neighbouring parish of Donwell, belongs to Mr Knightley of Donwell Abbey. Mr Woodhouse, however, is a wealthy man thanks to his private means, and Emma will have a dowry of £30,000 when she marries. We are never told the origin of these private means—did an earlier Woodhouse perhaps sell off the Hartfield estate to an earlier Knightley?—but it seems probable that Mr Woodhouse has an income of about £3,000 a year from his invested funds.

As Hartfield is Emma's home, she has no need to describe it to herself; and therefore all that we, her unseen visitors, learn about it is that it is a comfortable family house of the period, with several living rooms and enough spare bedrooms to accommodate Emma's elder sister Isabella, her husband Mr John Knightley and their five children when they come to stay from time to time. Mr Woodhouse does not keep a large staff of servants: indoors there seems to be only Serle the cook-house-keeper, a butler and some maidservants, and outdoors are James the coachman and grooms or stableboys to assist him. Mr Woodhouse is much influenced by James, and is always afraid of giving him offence by asking for the carriage and horses to be used for short journeys: 'But James will not like to put the horses to for such a little way;—and where are the poor horses to be while we are paying our visit?' Serle has to put up with the demands of Mr Woodhouse's hypochondriac's diet: his favourite dish is a 'nice basin of gruel', and when his elderly friends, Mrs and Miss Bates and Mrs Goddard, come to play cards with him, their supper may be a selection from a fricassee of sweetbreads and asparagus, minced chicken, scalloped oysters and soft-boiled eggs, followed by an apple tart and custard ('Ours are all apple tarts. You need not be afraid of unwholesome preserves

301

here'), or baked apples and biscuits. Surprisingly, although Mr Woodhouse thinks roast pork indigestible, he is happy to eat fried pork steaks, or a salted leg of pork which has been boiled with turnips, carrots and parsnips.

Mr Woodhouse is a small, thin, feeble man, probably in his late sixties or early seventies, and 'having been a valetudinarian all his life, without activity of mind or body, he was a much older man in ways than in years; and though everywhere beloved for the friendliness of his heart and his amiable temper, his talents could not have recommended him at any time. . . . He was a nervous man, easily depressed; fond of every body that he was used to, and hating to part with them; hating change of every kind'—and from his habit of gentle selfishness was never able to suppose that other people could feel differently from himself. He had married late in life and his wife had died young, leaving him with their two daughters, Isabella and Emma, then aged about twelve and five respectively. Jane Austen does not tell us the cause of Mrs Woodhouse's death—could she perhaps have caught a chill which turned to pneumonia, and is this why Mr Woodhouse is now so terrified of colds and draughts? Nor does she attempt to explain how Mr Woodhouse could ever have brought himself to contemplate so drastic, strenuous and potentially unhealthy a change in his lifestyle as matrimony and paternity must involve. As it is, Emma is nearly twenty-one, and kept captive at Hartfield like a fairy-tale princess, not by an ogre but by her daughterly duty and affection for this clinging and helpless old father. She has never been so far as the seaside, and in general goes only seldom from home, where she has to spend her time studying, drawing, playing the piano—though she is always too impatient to become really accomplished in any of these subjects—and keeping her father amused. It does not seem that she has even been to London to visit Isabella and her family in Brunswick Square, because sixteen miles there and back would mean four or five hours' travelling time, so she would have to leave her father alone for a night, something neither of them could contemplate.

Emma herself is quite the reverse of her father, in body and mind, for she is full of energy and hardly knows what it is to be indisposed. The newly married Mrs Weston, her fond ex-governess, who has been scarcely less than a mother to her, thinks she is quite beautiful: 'Such an eye!—the true hazel eye—and so brilliant! regular features, open countenance, with a complexion!—oh! what a bloom of full health, and such a pretty height and size. . . . She is loveliness itself.' Mr Knightley agrees: 'I think her all you describe. I love to look at her . . . .' It is her restless energy and intelligence, fed by the degree of self-will and conceit of which Jane Austen has warned us, and coupled with the boredom of her lonely home life, that drives Emma into busying herself with her neighbours' affairs in a most reprehensible manner that nearly leads to lasting unhappiness for all those with whom she interferes.

Isabella takes after her father, being small and slight in build, and having the same excessive concern for her own health and that of her children; now in her late twenties, she is a pretty, elegant little woman of gentle quiet manners and a disposition remarkably amiable and affectionate. Her husband, Mr John Knightley, the younger brother of the owner of Donwell, is in his early thirties, and is a tall, gentlemanly and very clever man, a barrister doing well in his profession. He married Isabella about seven years ago, and they already have five children, ranging from Henry, aged six, through John, Bella and George, to Emma aged eight months. They live in Brunswick Square, which was built during the 1790s on what was then open land on the northern outskirts of London, so Isabella can proudly assure her father: 'Our part of London is so very superior to most others! . . . We are so very airy!' The garden in the centre of the square still exists today, as do a few of the original houses, and despite modern traffic there is something left of the airiness to which she lays claim.

A mile or so south of Hartfield, in the next parish, lies Donwell Abbey, originally a small monastery that was converted to a house in the sixteenth century, and now the home of Mr George Knightley. We see it through Emma's eyes—this time observing quite accurately—and need to have this information because she will eventually live here: 'The house was larger than Hartfield, and totally unlike it, covering a good deal of ground, rambling and irregular, with many comfortable and one or two handsome rooms.' In the house Mr Knightley is able to show, for his guests' amusement, books of engravings, and cabinets containing family collections of small *objets d'art* such as medals, cameos, corals and shells. The building lies in a low and sheltered situation, nearly at the foot of a considerable slope; there are ample gardens stretching down to meadows washed by a stream, and an 'abundance of timber in rows and avenues, which neither fashion nor extravagance had rooted up'—that is, the gardens are still planted in the formal manner of earlier centuries, and have not been 'improved' by the destruction of these avenues, and nor have any of the Knightley family been so short of money as to necessitate selling these purely decorative trees. The kitchen gardens at Donwell are famous locally for their strawberry beds, and there are also orchards. The remains of the old monastic fishponds strike a note of historic interest. A broad short avenue of lime trees provides a shady walk to the low stone wall with high pillars which terminates the pleasure grounds, and from here the view is very pretty:

> . . . at half a mile distant was a bank of considerable abruptness and grandeur, well clothed with wood; and at the bottom of this bank, favourably placed and sheltered, rose the Abbey-Mill Farm, with meadows in front, and the river making a close and handsome curve around it. It was a sweet view—sweet to the eye and the mind— English verdure, English culture, English comfort, seen under a sun bright, without being oppressive.

Mr Knightley, the owner of this pleasant estate, is 'a sensible man about seven or eight-and-thirty'; he is very much the practical landowner, and having little spare money and a great deal of health, activity and independence, does not bother to keep unnecessary carriage-horses but walks or rides everywhere. He is tall, strong and upright, and no doubt of a healthily weather-beaten appearance, thanks to his outdoor life. Part of the estate he manages for himself as a sheep farm, with the help of William Larkins, his faithful bailiff—they check the weekly accounts together—and for the large Abbey-Mill Farm he has excellent tenants in the Martin family. His income is probably around £4,000 a year, and as a bachelor he has no need for a large domestic staff; we hear only, indeed, of Mrs Hodges the house-keeper, and Harry the clumsy footman, who may perhaps do double duty as a farmworker when he is not needed to wait upon guests. Mr Knightley is a magistrate, and thereby involved in the civic affairs of both Donwell and Highbury parishes; and in the evenings his limited spare time is spent in his library, or in walking up to Hartfield to call on the Woodhouses after dinner. He is a devoted uncle to his brother John's children, playing with them and tossing them up to the ceiling in a way that terrifies Mr Woodhouse to watch; and he is one of the few people who can see faults in Emma Woodhouse, and the only one who ever tells her of them.

At the Abbey-Mill Farm the Martin family consists of a widowed mother and her three children—her son Robert, who holds the tenancy, and his two younger sisters, who have just recently finished their education at Mrs Goddard's school in Highbury. Emma has to admit to herself, grudgingly—at the beginning of the story—that Robert Martin is a neatly dressed and sensible-looking young man, while Mr Knightley has no hesitation in calling him a gentleman-farmer, and relying upon his good sense just as much as he relies upon that of William Larkins. Robert rides to Kingston-on-Thames every Saturday to attend the market there, and is keen to improve his professional knowledge by reading the latest agricultural reports. From the road, the Abbey-Mill farmhouse is approached by a white gate which opens on to a broad, neat gravel walk leading between espalier apple trees to the front door. There are two good-sized parlours, and on occasion the shepherd's son is brought in to the parlour at night to sing for the enjoyment of the family assembled there. Robert Martin runs a fine flock of sheep and gets very good prices for the wool, and although the Martins have not yet risen sufficiently in the social scale to employ a manservant, they have several domestic maidservants, the senior of whom has been with them for twenty-five years, and Mrs Martin is considering taking on a pageboy in a year or two. They have a small dairy herd of eight cows, an orchard and a poultry yard, from which Mrs Martin sends a fine goose to Mrs Goddard. The summerhouse in the garden is large enough to hold twelve people, and on summer evenings the family have merry games and go for moonlight walks.

We, the readers, can quite easily fall into step beside Mr Knightley as he walks northwards up Donwell Lane—which in summer is never dusty and is therefore suitable even for ladies' lightly shod feet—towards Hartfield and Highbury. The hamlet of Langley is close by, and the footpath to it cuts through some of Donwell Abbey's home meadows—hence Mr Knightley would prefer to reroute the path if it will not inconvenience the Highbury people too much. Hartfield is at the south end of Highbury's broad, though irregular, main street—'that airy, cheerful, happy-looking Highbury'—and in this main or High Street are the shops and houses belonging to the various residents whom we hear mention of or meet. Mr Woodhouse's great friend Mr Perry, the apothecary, with his wife and children and perhaps an apprentice or two to work in his dispensary, must have a respectable house with a large brass door-plate, appropriate to his status as a successful professional man—he will soon be able to afford to set up a carriage, as his wife wishes. The Coles' house will certainly also be noticeable at this end of the village. The Coles have lived in Highbury for ten years, and have been growing steadily richer thanks to the increasing profits of their shop or business in London, so are now nearly as well off as the Woodhouses. They keep their own carriage and horses and in addition Mrs Cole has a donkey upon which she can patter about the lanes of Highbury without getting her feet either dusty or muddy. They have recently made a new approach to the house, built on a new dining room, increased the number of their servants and purchased a Broadwood grand pianoforte for the drawing room, in the hope that their little girls may eventually learn to play it. Emma is in two minds about the Coles, admitting to herself that they are friendly, liberal and unpretending, but being somewhat disparaging because they are of low origin, in trade, and only moderately genteel. At first she intends to refuse their dinner invitation in February, but the more sensible Westons persuade her to accept.

Getting nearer the centre of the village, we pass the house where Mr Weston grew up and lived until he could afford to buy the Randalls estate, and where some cousins of his still live; and then comes the post office. John Saunders, the village watchmaker, probably has his little premises about here; and there may be a small shop that sells cheap hard-wearing fabrics suitable for the labourers and servants of the village. The butcher's shop is also in one of these older central cottages, and he walks up and down the High Street with his tray on his head to deliver the joints of meat as ordered. It is, no doubt, in front of his shop that Emma sees two curs quarrelling over a dirty bone, while a tidy old woman travels homeward with a full basket.

At the crossroads in the centre, by the church, Broadway Lane leads off on one side to the farmhouse belonging to Farmer Mitchell, where, four years before, Mr Weston darted away with so much gallantry to borrow two umbrellas for Emma and Miss Taylor when it started to mizzle, an event which started Emma on her career as a matchmaker. On the other side, Vicarage Lane is a sharp turning off the High Street—a corner which Mr Woodhouse thinks is so very dangerous for carriages—and here there are several small poor cottages, in one of which Frank Churchill's old nursemaid probably lives, and after which comes the vicarage, now the home of the newly arrived parson, the Reverend Philip Elton. The living of Highbury is not very valuable, but Mr Elton is a Londoner and has some independent means; the vicarage is old and not very good, almost as close to the road as it could be, but Mr Elton has put palings round the front garden and smartened up the house, fitting it up comfortably and hanging yellow curtains in the front windows, these last being much admired by Miss Nash, one of the teachers at Mrs Goddard's school. Miss Nash's sister is married to a linen-draper, so no doubt Miss Nash has learnt from her to appreciate the cost of such curtains. As a bachelor, Mr Elton has only a house-keeper, Mrs Wright, and one or two other servants, so he is always delighted to be invited by Emma to dine at Hartfield.

Further down Vicarage Lane is a wretched ramshackle cottage in which lives a poor family, whom Emma and her friend Harriet Smith visit in mid-December, treading with difficulty the narrow slippery path through the cottage garden.

> Emma was very compassionate; and the distresses of the poor were as sure of relief from her personal attention and kindness, her counsel and her patience, as from her purse. She understood their ways, could allow for their ignorance and their temptations, had no romantic expectations of extraordinary virtue from those, for whom education had done so little; entered into their troubles with ready sympathy, and always gave her assistance with as much intelligence as good-will.

In this instance, as a first step, she tells one of the children to call at Hartfield to be given a pitcher full of nourishing broth or stew; and presently discusses with Mr Elton what could be done and should be done in the longer term to help them.

Returning to the crossroads and turning north up the High Street, on the east side is the bakery, run by Mr and Mrs Wallis and their family; the old cottage has a little bow window round which a string of dawdling children stand eyeing the gingerbread on display within. Some people say that Mrs Wallis can be uncivil and give a very rude answer, but Miss Bates, who goes to the shop to get her Donwell apples twice-baked, has never known anything but the greatest attention from them, despite the fact that the Bates household buys so little bread even at the best of times. Further away is the larger house where the Cox family, two brothers and two sisters, live above their business premises; Mr William Cox is a pert young lawyer, in Emma's opinion, and his sisters are the most vulgar girls in Highbury.

Nearly at the top of the High Street lives the Bates family—Mrs Bates, the widow of a previous vicar of Highbury, a very old lady and rather deaf, almost past everything but tea and quadrille, and her middle-aged daughter Miss Hetty Bates, short, neat, brisk-moving and a great talker upon little matters. They have only a very limited income, and so lodge in a small old house which belongs to people in business, perhaps corn-dealers or maltsters; the owners have modernized the ground floor by refronting it in brick and inserting new sash windows, but the first floor still has casement windows and probably is of half-timbered construction with lath and plaster panels. The staircase is narrow and dark, with an awkward step at the turning, and leads up to the low-ceilinged first floor, where the Bates ladies rent three or four

311

small rooms. They have a very moderate-sized living room whose window overlooks the High Street, an adjoining room where Mrs Bates sleeps—and perhaps Miss Bates has to share it with her—and a separate bedroom for Jane Fairfax, the orphaned granddaughter of Mrs Bates, when she comes to visit them; Patty, their one little maidservant, works in the kitchen on the ground floor at the back. Miss Bates is a happy soul, despite being neither young, handsome, rich nor married, and is very popular in Highbury: 'She loved every body, was interested in every body's happiness, quick-sighted to every body's merits; thought herself a most fortunate creature, and surrounded with blessings in such an excellent mother and so many good neighbours and friends, and a home that wanted for nothing.' At present she is anxious about old John Abdy, the father of the head ostler at the Crown. Old John was the parish clerk for the late Reverend Mr Bates for twenty-seven years, but is now bedridden with rheumatic gout in his joints; and, even though young John has a good job, he needs to apply to Mr Elton for parish relief on his father's behalf. Miss Bates plans to call upon old John as soon as she can.

From the crossroads, on the west side, is Mrs Ford's shop, the principal woollen-draper's, linen-draper's and haberdasher's, the shop first in size and fashion in the place, where Harriet Smith cannot decide between plain or figured muslin and is tempted by beautiful blue ribbon even though she really needs yellow. Close to Mrs Ford's shop there lives a dressmaker who makes up Harriet's muslins into gowns for her. This dressmaker, no

312

doubt, generally finds good business at Mrs Goddard's girls' school up the road. The school must occupy a large house, because, in addition to Mrs Goddard herself (the owner and headmistress), there are three teachers, the Misses Nash, Prince and Richardson, and a visiting writing-master, forty little girls, and several older girls classed as parlour-boarders—the two Misses Abbot, Miss Bickerton, the two Misses Martin who have just left school, besides Harriet, whose future at present seems uncertain—not to mention all the cooks and maidservants necessary to maintain such an establishment. Jane Austen approves of Mrs Goddard, as she runs

> . . . a real, honest, old-fashioned boarding-school, where a reasonable quantity of accomplishments were sold at a reasonable price, and where girls might be sent to be out of the way and scramble themselves into a little education, without any danger of coming back prodigies . . . she had an ample house and garden, gave the children plenty of wholesome food, let them run about a great deal in the summer, and in winter dressed their chilblains with her own hands.

Mrs Goddard is a plain, motherly kind of woman, who has worked hard to build up her business, and can now relax in her neat parlour hung round with fancy-work, or come out in the evening to play cards with Mr Woodhouse.

At the top of the High Street, and opposite the Bates' lodgings, is the Crown inn, run by Mrs Stokes; it is a small and rather shabby old

313

establishment, though still the main inn of the village. A chaise and couple of pair of post-horses are kept here for hire, under the care of Mrs Stokes's head ostler, John Abdy, more for the convenience of the neighbourhood than from any great need for transport to and from Highbury. A large room tacked on at the side of the inn many years ago was intended for a ballroom, and has occasionally been used as such, but no dances have been held there for a long time and the room is now mainly used to accommodate the gentlemen's weekly whist club meetings, or the regular parish meetings. It has two superior sashed windows, but the wallpaper is dirty and the wainscot yellow and forlorn; nevertheless, when the Westons succeed in organizing a ball here, Mr Weston manages to get it cleaned and decorated, making Miss Bates cry out: 'Oh! Mr Weston, you must really have had Aladdin's lamp. Good Mrs Stokes would not know her own room again.' There is a small card room next to the ballroom, but for their supper the dancers have to go through a long awkward passage to a room at the other end of the building. Other respectable residents in the neighbourhood whom we meet briefly at this dance are the Otway family with their four adult children, and the Reverend Dr. Hughes with his wife and his son Richard.

At this northern end of the High Street the road divides. One branch goes to Kingston-upon-Thames, passing by Mr Weston's property, Randalls, which is a small estate separated from Highbury by a bleak part of the common field. The house is probably of the late seventeenth century, a symmetrical little red-brick box; its dining room only holds ten people in comfort and the drawing room is no larger, while upstairs there are just four bedrooms. Mr Woodhouse has arranged with Mrs Weston that Hannah, the daughter of the Hartfield coachman James, should be employed as a maidservant at Randalls. Further away from Highbury, but within Mr Perry's professional territory as apothecary, is Clayton Park, probably where the Gilbert family live—the unobjectionable country family whom the Coles invite to their dinner party, and who also attend the ball at the Crown later in the year.

The other branch of the northern road leads to Richmond-upon-Thames, and about half a mile beyond Highbury, making a sudden turn and deeply shaded by elms on each side, it becomes for a considerable stretch secluded, which enables a gipsy gang to lurk here in order to threaten unwary pedestrians, such as Miss Bickerton and Harriet— who is luckily saved by the unexpected appearance of Frank Churchill on his way to Richmond-upon-Thames.

At the beginning of the story, the three Highbury residents who come most often to Hartfield to play cards with Mr Woodhouse after dinner are Mrs and Miss Bates and Mrs Goddard, the schoolmistress, and these long dull evenings are exactly what Emma has been dreading, now that she no longer has Mrs Weston as her companion. However, one evening Mrs Goddard brings along one of her parlour boarders, the seventeen-year-old Harriet Smith, who is 'a very pretty girl, and her beauty happened to be of a sort which Emma particularly admired. She was short, plump and fair, with a fine bloom, blue eyes, light hair, regular features, and a look of great sweetness.' Harriet is accepted as being illegitimate, and her unacknowledged father has paid for her to live with Mrs Goddard for several years past—and before the end of the evening Emma decides that her father must be a gentleman and therefore that it would be a very kind undertaking on her part to patronize and improve Harriet and make her into a lady fit for good society.

With this aim in mind, Emma now starts meddling in Harriet's life in an unpardonably overbearing way; first of all, she persuades her to reject a proposal of marriage from the young farmer Robert Martin, and then she tries to matchmake her with the vicar, Mr Elton. He has only been in Highbury for about twelve months, but is adored by all the teachers and parlour boarders at Mrs Goddard's school and his person is much admired in general, though Emma notes 'a want of elegance of feature' in his broad, handsome face. Emma frequently invites Mr Elton to Hartfield so that she can throw the two of them together; but instead of becoming interested in Harriet, Mr Elton is conceited enough to think that Emma herself is displaying a preference for him, and at Christmas seizes an opportunity to propose to her. This is Emma's first awful embarrassment in the course of the story, as she has to offend Mr Elton by rejecting him, and then explain to a weeping Harriet how wrong she has been in her encouraging guesses and fantasies.

Soon after Christmas Jane Fairfax pays a visit to Mrs and Miss Bates, her grandmother and aunt. Orphaned as a child, she has been semi-adopted by Colonel and Mrs Campbell, and brought up by them in London as a companion to their only daughter. Now that Miss Campbell has married and gone to Ireland, to live at Ballycraig, near Dublin, with her husband, Mr Dixon, Jane Fairfax has to set about earning her own living as a governess, but the Campbells want her to stay with her relations for a few months before taking up any such position. She and Emma are very similar in age, and have known each other slightly ever since childhood, but have never become good friends; Mr Knightley says this is because Emma sees in Jane the really accomplished young woman that she wanted to be thought herself, and Emma's conscience cannot quite acquit her as to the truth of his statement. Jane has grown up into a very elegant young woman, dark-haired, with deep grey eyes, dark eyelashes and eyebrows, and a pale but very clear and delicate complexion; she is tall and graceful, but rather slender, with a slight appearance of ill health that is a constant source of worry to her doting aunt, bearing in mind the fact that her mother died of tuberculosis. Emma now tries conscientiously to get to know Jane better, but feels constantly rebuffed by her non-committal conversation and unwillingness to express any opinion or provide any information about herself; as a result, Emma guesses—correctly—that Jane has something to hide, and guesses again— incorrectly—that she must be in love with Mr Dixon, her foster-sister's husband.

In February another newcomer appears in Highbury—Frank Churchill, Mr Weston's son by a first marriage. In a situation that parallels that of Jane Fairfax, Frank was adopted by his uncle and aunt and brought up on their estate at Enscombe

317

in Yorkshire. After much anticipation by the village gossips over the past few months, now at last he comes to meet his new stepmother. To Emma's delight he turns out to be:

> . . . a *very* good looking young man; height, air, address, all were unexceptionable, and his countenance had a great deal of the spirit and liveliness of his father's; he looked quick and sensible. She felt immediately that she should like him; and there was a well-bred ease of manner, and a readiness to talk, which convinced her that he came intending to be acquainted with her, and that acquainted they soon must be.

Frank and Emma rapidly become very friendly. She passes on to him her unkind and quite unwarranted suspicions about Jane Fairfax and is most gratified when he professes to admire her perspicacity in discovering this secret. Emma cannot understand why Mr Knightley does not share her enthusiasm for Frank's society; nor does she know, of course, that Frank and Jane Fairfax have been secretly engaged since they met at the seaside in Weymouth the previous autumn, and that he is only paying attention to Emma as a means of distracting Highbury's inquisitive eyes from his interest in Jane. The engagement has to be secret because Frank fears his ailing and capricious aunt will disapprove and persuade his uncle to disinherit him.

The third new arrival in Highbury is Mr Elton's wife—Miss Augusta Hawkins of Bristol, whom he met in Bath and married very rapidly thereafter, as she has a dowry of nearly £10,000. Mrs Elton's father had been a petty tradesman, and until her marriage she lived with her uncle, an attorney's clerk, in the heart of Bristol—origins which would raise misgivings in any contemporary mind. At that date Bristol was renowned as a squalid, overcrowded sea-port and commercial centre closely linked with the slave trade. It was greasy and smelly with the smoke from its refineries where imported West Indian molasses was converted into lump sugar, and from the kilns where a special deep-blue glass was produced, known as 'Bristol Blue'. The richer merchants were beginning to move out of the city and build themselves houses in Clifton, a separate village to the north-west of Bristol and situated on the airy hillside above the narrow Avon valley into which the docks, factories and tall medieval houses were crammed; and it is in Clifton that Maple Grove, the home of Mrs Elton's sister Selina and her husband, Mr and Mrs Suckling, is located, with, according to Mrs Elton's boasts, an 'immense plantation' around it. Mrs Elton turns out to be a vain woman, flashily dressed—we hear of lace and pearls, extra trimming for a white and silver poplin dress, and a purple and gold ridicule (handbag)—extremely well satisfied with herself, and thinking much of her own importance, with manners both pert and familiar. 'She had a little beauty and a little accomplishment, but so little judgment that she thought herself coming with superior knowledge of the world, to enliven and improve a country neighbourhood.' She and Emma soon come to dislike each other, and as Harriet is Emma's friend, the Eltons dislike her as well.

Mrs Elton turns her attentions to Jane Fairfax, and patronizes her in a most tiresome way, which Jane seems content to endure, much to Emma's amazement.

For the next few months, as spring turns to summer, cross-purposes flourish between the main characters. Mr and Mrs Weston hope for a match between Emma and Frank Churchill, and indeed he flirts constantly with her, but, although she is flattered by his attentions, she does not fall in love with him; instead, after he has rescued Harriet from the gipsies, Emma thinks that this is a promising start for a romance between those two. In the meantime, Frank and Emma together lose no opportunity of teasing the silent Jane Fairfax on the subject of her supposed love for Mr Dixon— including an alphabet-game with significant anagrams—while the Highbury gossips think that Mr Knightley is beginning to fall in love with Jane, and he thinks that Emma is seriously in love with Frank. When the ball at the Crown takes place, Mr Elton rudely snubs Harriet in public by refusing to dance with her, and Mr Knightley rescues her from her embarrassment by dancing with her himself; it is at this ball that Emma for the first time realizes that Mr Knightley is a good-looking and physically attractive man, not just the elder-brother figure he has for so long seemed to be. Two hot midsummer parties—a picnic at Donwell Abbey and a trip to Box Hill the following day—bring matters to a head, when Frank Churchill's excessive flirtation with Emma goads Jane Fairfax into quarrelling with him and accepting Mrs Elton's offer to find her employment as a governess in Bristol. Emma is publicly rude to Miss Bates and is thoroughly scolded for this by Mr Knightley; and her shame and distress are compounded when Harriet tells her that, so far from wanting to marry Frank Churchill, she has now set her sights on Mr Knightley and believes he returns her affection. This at last makes Emma realize that Mr Knightley is part of her own life, and that she cannot bear to think of him marrying anyone but her.

The tangle of misunderstandings is resolved when Frank Churchill's aunt dies suddenly, and he is able to confess to his uncle the secret of his engagement to Jane Fairfax. Mr Churchill, no longer under his wife's domination, is perfectly happy to consent to Frank's marriage to this penniless girl. Mr Knightley and Emma bring to light their own long-standing affection for each other, and Harriet now cannot resist a renewed proposal from the persevering Robert Martin. Harriet and Robert are married in September; Jane and Frank will be married in November as soon as a three months' mourning period for the late Mrs Churchill has been observed; and Mr Knightley and Emma are married in October, once Mr Woodhouse's selfish objections have been overcome on the understanding that Mr Knightley will move into Hartfield rather than Emma leave to go to Donwell.

> The wedding was very much like other weddings, where the parties have no taste for finery or parade; and Mrs Elton, from the particulars detailed by her husband, thought it all extremely shabby, and very inferior to her own.—'Very little white satin, very few lace veils; a most pitiful business!—

Selina would stare when she heard of it.'
But, in spite of these deficiencies, the
wishes, the hopes, the confidence, the
predictions of the small band of true friends
who witnessed the ceremony, were fully
answered in the perfect happiness of the
union.

*   *   *

Although Emma's love story is entirely
homegrown, the start of Frank and Jane's romance
is at the smart seaside resort of Weymouth, on
the Dorset coast. An early nineteenth-century
guidebook explained Weymouth's recent history:

This charming place is partly indebted for
its celebrity to the late Duke of Gloucester,
who here passed the winter of 1780. Finding
his health greatly improved, His Royal
Highness erected *Gloucester Lodge*, which
was purchased by the King. Their Majesties
accordingly repaired thither in 1789, and
the late Princess Charlotte of Wales
afterwards resided in the same mansion. . . .
Being sheltered by the surrounding hills,
possessing a pure salubrious air, a fine
beach of sand, and a calm bay, forming a
semicircle of more than two miles, it is
extremely well adapted for the purpose of
health and pleasure, and as a bathing place
it is perhaps unparalleled. Till within the
last twenty or thirty years, it was small and
meanly built; but by rapid enlargements,
and the erection of many elegant houses, it

has now become a very respectable place, with a population of 6000 souls. . . . In the time of peace, a trip to the Continent, or to the islands of Guernsey, Jersey, and Alderney, is not unfrequent; and here company may be accommodated with excellent yachts and experienced navigators.

However, one visitor was certainly not impressed by Weymouth, and told himself crossly in his diary:

. . . a sandy shore, being excellent for bathing, has first induced the neighbours to come; and since, by fashion, and the Duke of Glosters having built a house, is become the resort of the giddy and gay; where the Irish beau, the gouty peer, and the genteel shopkeeper blend in folly and fine breeding. At these places there is ever an abundance of the fair sex, being so well adapted for the elder ladies to get cards and company, and for the misses to procure flattery, lovers, and sometimes husbands. That the infirm, and the upstart, should resort to these fishing holes, may perhaps be accounted for; but that the healthy owners of parks, good houses, and good beds should quit them for confinement, dirt, and misery, appears to me to be downright madness.

*　　　*　　　*

Emma was noticed by eight reviewers in the spring and summer of 1816, John Murray evidently being far more efficient in advertising his publications than was Thomas Egerton. Several of the reviews were short and amiably dismissive: 'The story is not ill-conceived; it is not romantic but domestic . . . a strain of genuine natural humour . . . an amusing, inoffensive and well-principled novel . . . delineates with great accuracy the habits and the manners of a middle class of gentry, and of the inhabitants of a country village at one degree of rank and gentility beneath them . . .' but the others were more considered and flattering, and Sir Walter Scott wrote a complete essay on modern fiction for the *Quarterly Review*, in which he referred very favourably to *Sense and Sensibility* and *Pride and Prejudice*—though oddly enough, he did not mention *Mansfield Park*—and devoted several paragraphs to an admiring discussion of *Emma*.

The Prince Regent's Librarian, the Reverend James Stanier Clarke, acknowledged the receipt of the presentation copy, writing: 'You were very good to send me Emma—which I have in no respect deserved. It is gone to the Prince Regent. I have read only a few Pages which I very much admired—there is so much nature—and excellent description of Character in every thing you describe'; there is no evidence that the Prince really did read it, but some months later Mr Clarke wrote again: 'I have to return you the Thanks of His Royal Highness the Prince Regent for the handsome Copy you sent him of your last excellent Novel—pray dear Madam soon write again and again. Lord St. Helens and many of the Nobility who have been staying here, paid you the just tribute of their Praise.'

A rather less exalted reader, Lady Morley, wrote to her sister-in-law:

I did not say that *I did not like* Emma—I only said that I did not like it so much as Mansfield Park or Pride & Prejudice—nor more I do. Yet I think there is much of it that is admirable. Mr Woodhouse, Mrs Elton, Miss Bates & a few others are delightful; but there is such a total want of story & there is so very little to like in the heroine & so little to interest in the hero, who gives me only the idea of an elderly, sensible, good sort of man. . . . I do think that Emma's passion for match-making is by no means natural—a match-making *Miss* is a non-descript—that is a metier so much more confined to the matronly part of her sex. Then, surely, with all the sense & cleverness wch. Emma is represented to possess it is not natural that she shd. have formed such a violent friendship with such a vulgar little fool as Harriet—then, surely, her talking characters talk too much. The pages filled with Miss Bates & Mrs Elton wd. make up one of the volumes & that is more than can well be afforded. Still their conversations are certainly admirable.

The novelist Maria Edgeworth did not like it:

There was no story in it, except that Miss Emma found that the man whom she designed for Harriet's lover was an admirer of her own—& he was affronted at being refused by Emma & Harriet wore the willow—and *smooth, thin water-gruel* is

325

according to Emma's father's opinion a very good thing & it is very difficult to make a cook understand what you mean by *smooth thin water gruel*!!

Lady Anne Romilly likewise thought there was 'so little to remember in it'; but the Irish poet Thomas Moore considered it ' the very perfection of novel-writing', and novelist Susan Ferrier viewed it with a professional eye: 'I have been reading "Emma", which is excellent; there is no story whatever, and the heroine is not better than other people; but the characters are all so true to life, and the style so piquant, that it does not require the adventitious aids of mystery and adventure.'

As with *Mansfield Park*, Jane herself kept a long list of 'Opinions of *Emma*' gathered from her family and friends; amongst others, her brother Frank 'liked it extremely, observing that though there might be more Wit in P & P—& an higher Morality in MP—yet altogether, on account of its peculiar air of Nature throughout, he preferred it to either.' Her youngest brother Charles, voyaging at sea, wrote: 'Emma arrived in time to a moment. I am delighted with her, more so I think than even with my favourite Pride & Prejudice, & have read it three times in the Passage.' Mrs Austen 'thought it more entertaining than MP, but not so interesting as P & P. No characters in it equal to Ly. Catherine & Mr Collins.' Their neighbour Mrs Digweed admitted that she 'did not like it so well as the others, in fact if she had not known the Author, could hardly have got through it.'

Jane Austen told her family some few afterwords: that Mr Woodhouse survived his daughter's marriage, and kept her and Mr Knightley from settling at Donwell, about two years; and that Mr Knightley was one of her two favourite characters, the other being Edmund Bertram. The letters placed by Frank Churchill before Jane Fairfax, at the end of the irritating alphabet-game in the Hartfield drawing room, and which she swept away unread, contained the word 'pardon'; and Jane Fairfax only lived another nine or ten years after her marriage—succumbing, no doubt, to an inherited tendency to tuberculosis. One can feel sure, however, that Emma's health and energy will be channelled into producing a brood of sturdy little Knightleys, and that she will be too busy as a devoted wife and mother to make any more matches for her neighbours—apart, of course, from thinking that Mrs Weston's new baby, Anna, might very well marry one of Isabella's sons in years to come.

PERSUASION

Jane Austen began *Persuasion*, the last novel she was to complete, on 8 August 1815, but its composition must have been hindered by Henry Austen's illness in the autumn of that year and his firm's bankruptcy in the spring of 1816, which caused financial losses to several members of the Austen family. The spring of 1816 also saw the insidious onset of Jane's own terminal illness. It may be in part a consequence of these unhappy events that *Persuasion* is shorter than her other works and also of a more sombre tone. Jane first finished it on 18 July 1816, but she was not satisfied with the original version of how the lovers' reunion is brought about, as her nephew and biographer, James Edward Austen-Leigh, remembered:

> She thought it tame and flat, and was desirous of producing something better. This weighed upon her mind, the more so probably on account of the weak state of her health; so that one night she retired to rest in very low spirits. But such depression was little in accordance with her nature, and was soon shaken off. The next morning she awoke to more cheerful views and brighter inspirations; the sense of power revived; and imagination resumed its course.

The work was finally completed to her satisfaction on 6 August 1816. The manuscript of the first version of the ending is now preserved in the British Library in London.

However, Jane was never in any hurry to offer her books for publication, as her brother Henry remembered: 'For though in composition she was equally rapid and correct, yet an invincible distrust of her own judgement induced her to withhold her works from the public, till time and many perusals had satisfied her that the charm of recent composition was dissolved.' Unfortunately, this meant that both *Northanger Abbey* and *Persuasion* ended up being published posthumously, with their titles probably chosen for them by Henry. There was an Austen family tradition that Jane had referred to this last book as *The Elliots*. The two stories were published by John Murray, and appeared together in a four-volume set (two volumes for each work), priced at 24*s.*, at the very end of December 1817, with the title page actually dated 1818.

This novel, perhaps more than any of the others, is based very much on Jane Austen's personal knowledge of places and events. Since writing *Northanger Abbey*, which gives a visitor's impression of life in Bath, she had actually lived in that city for some five years, and so in this later work she was able to set her characters in precisely the correct addresses to suit their various stations in life, and to walk with them on their daily business and shopping expeditions. She had also visited Lyme Regis twice, in November 1803 and August 1804, and no doubt passed through Crewkerne *en route* between Bath and Lyme. As for *Mansfield Park*, her two sailor brothers, Frank and Charles—Frank in particular—were able to

329

provide her with correct information on naval matters and advise on the style of conversation that might be exchanged between naval officers.

The action of *Persuasion* covers nine months—from the summer of 1814 to the spring of 1815—and *Persuasion* is itself a sequel to a novel she never wrote, of the romance between the young naval officer Commander Frederick Wentworth, at a loose end in the Somerset countryside during his shore-leave in the summer of 1806, and the lonely girl ignored and neglected in her rich but unloving home: 'He was, at that time, a remarkably fine young man, with a great deal of intelligence, spirit and brilliancy; and Anne an extremely pretty girl, with gentleness, modesty, taste, and feeling. . . . It would be difficult to say which had seen highest perfection in the other, or which had been the happiest; she, in receiving his declarations and proposals, or he in having them accepted.' However, both Anne's father, Sir Walter Elliot, and her godmother, Lady Russell, disapproved, and she 'was persuaded to believe the engagement a wrong thing—indiscreet, improper, hardly capable of success, and not deserving it'—with the result that Wentworth thought Anne was weak and cowardly, considered himself ill-used by her, and disappeared back to sea angry and resentful.

Eight years have now elapsed, and the story opens again in Somerset in the summer of 1814, at Anne's home, Kellynch Hall. Somerset is a mild, moist, green county, with small limestone and sandstone hills divided by hidden narrow valleys, the hills in some areas rising above peat marshes crisscrossed with drainage ditches and lanes lined with willow trees. Even today there are still many beautiful and unspoilt stone-built villages, blue-grey or golden, with farmhouses and cottages dating back to the sixteenth century, and large stone barns resulting from centuries of rich farming. Many of the parish churches benefited from this richness and were rebuilt at the same time. Spires are rare, but the county is noted for its fine church towers. The village of Kellynch is said to be fifty miles from Bath and three miles from the next village of Uppercross, with Crewkerne being the nearest town; as ever, Jane Austen is careful not to be too precise about her locations, but both Kellynch and Uppercross—and, later in the story, Winthrop—are all probably somewhere in the rectangle between the genuine small towns of Ilminster, South Petherton, Crewkerne and Chard.

Kellynch Hall is the ancestral home of the Elliot baronets; it is probably a sixteenth-century mansion, but as the action soon moves away from this starting point there is no need for us to know much about it—we later hear from Admiral Croft that the breakfast room chimney smokes when the wind is in the north and that the door to the laundry is inconvenient, while the present holder of the title, Anne's father Sir Walter Elliot, vain and foolish as he is, has filled his dressing room with looking glasses that the Admiral has no wish to use. The only other house of any size in the village is the modern and elegant Kellynch Lodge, owned by Sir Walter and tenanted by Anne's widowed godmother Lady Russell—who is 'a benevolent, charitable, good woman, and capable of strong attachments; most correct in her conduct, strict in her notions of decorum, and with manners that were held a standard of good-breeding'. No rector or vicar of Kellynch is mentioned—despite the church being considered well worth seeing—but it may be that Sir Walter is too snobbish to acknowledge a mere country parson as a neighbour who can be invited to dine.

In real life, 1814 was a year of national rejoicing—in the spring the rapid advance of the Allied forces through France made it clear that an end to the war was in sight; in April Napoleon was forced to abdicate and exiled to the Mediterranean island of Elba; and on 30 May a peace treaty with France was signed at Paris. Between 6 and 27 June, Tsar Alexander I of Russia and King Frederick William III of Prussia, accompanied by other European politicians and generals, made a state visit to England to celebrate the victorious peace, and this state visit is referred to in two of Jane Austen's letters written in June of that year.

For the Elliot family, however, 1814 is the year when Sir Walter's extravagant way of life has brought him so deeply into debt that even he realizes that some economizing is essential.

> Vanity was the beginning and end of Sir Walter Elliot's character; vanity of person and of situation. He had been remarkably handsome in his youth; and, at fifty-four, was still a very fine man. . . . He considered the blessing of beauty as inferior only to the blessing of a baronetcy; and the Sir Walter Elliot who united these gifts, was the constant object of his warmest respect and devotion. . . . It had not been possible for him to spend less; he had done nothing but

what Sir Walter Elliot was imperiously called on to do; but blameless as he was, he was not only growing dreadfully in debt, but was hearing of it so often, that it became vain to attempt concealing it longer.

Mr Shepherd, his lawyer and agent, is called over from Crewkerne to advise on these delicate financial problems. He suggests that the Elliots should go to Bath, where it would be possible to live more cheaply, and rent out Kellynch Hall.

Sir Walter is a tall, florid, fair-haired man, who has been a widower for thirteen years, and his eldest daughter, Elizabeth, now aged twenty-nine, resembles him greatly in both looks and character. To the world she appears very handsome, with well-bred elegant manners, but in domestic life she is just as selfish and conceited as her father; and the two of them unite in considering Anne of very inferior value. Anne takes after her deceased mother in looks and nature; she 'had been a very pretty girl, but her bloom had vanished early; and as even in its height, her father had found little to admire in her (so totally different were her delicate features and mild dark eyes from his own); there could be nothing in them now that she was faded and thin, to excite his esteem'—and indeed he thinks contemptuously that she has already become quite haggard with age. Elsewhere Jane Austen tells us that Anne is slender and pensive, an 'elegant little woman of seven and twenty, with every beauty excepting bloom, and with manners as consciously right as they were invariably gentle . . . Anne, with an elegance of mind and sweetness of character, which must have placed her high with

333

any people of real understanding, was nobody with either father or sister; her word had no weight; her convenience was always to give way; she was only Anne.'

Mr Shepherd points out that the present time is very suitable for renting out country houses. 'This peace will be turning all our rich Navy Officers ashore. They will be all wanting a home'—and finds a tenant for Kellynch Hall in the shape of the recently demobilized Admiral Croft and his wife, who have cousins at Minehead in Somerset and therefore want to retire to this county. The news brings all Anne's sad memories of her broken engagement flooding back to her, because, although they have never met, she knows that Mrs Croft is the elder sister of Frederick Wentworth. It is agreed that Sir Walter and Elizabeth will go to Bath in the middle of September, and Elizabeth takes with her as companion Mr Shepherd's widowed daughter, Mrs Clay—'a clever young woman, who understood the art of pleasing; the art of pleasing, at least, at Kellynch Hall; and who had made herself so acceptable to Miss Elliot, as to have been already staying there more than once, in spite of all that Lady Russell, who thought it a friendship quite out of place, could hint of caution and reserve.' Both Lady Russell and Anne suspect that Mrs Clay has hopes of wheedling her way into Sir Walter's affections, since despite her physical imperfections, of which he is so conscious— freckles, a projecting tooth and a clumsy wrist— she is nevertheless well-looking, and has an acute mind and assiduously pleasing manners.

In the meantime, Anne goes to stay with her youngest sister Mary, at Uppercross, the neighbouring village to Kellynch. Mary is married to Charles Musgrove, the eldest son of the squire of Uppercross, whose landed property and general importance in that part of the county are second only to Sir Walter's, and Jane Austen gives us a description of the family and their home as seen through Anne's eyes as she travels there.

> Uppercross was a moderate-sized village, which a few years back had been completely in the old English style; containing only two houses superior in appearance to those of the yeomen and labourers,—the mansion of the squire . . . and the compact, tight parsonage, enclosed in its own neat garden, with a vine and a pear-tree trained round its casements; but upon the marriage of the young squire, it had received the improvement of a farm-house elevated into a cottage for his residence; and Uppercross Cottage, with its viranda, French windows, and other prettinesses, was quite as likely to catch the traveller's eye, as the more consistent and considerable aspect and premises of the Great House, about a quarter of a mile farther on.'

The young Musgroves had new furnished the Cottage at the time of their marriage, but as Anne enters, she finds her hypochondriac sister Mary 'lying on the faded sofa of the pretty little drawing room, the once elegant furniture of which had been gradually growing shabby, under the influence of four summers and two children . . .'

At the Great House, Uppercross Hall, live the

rest of the family:

> The father and mother were in the old English style, and the young people in the new. Mr and Mrs Musgrove were a very good sort of people; friendly and hospitable, not much educated, and not at all elegant. Their children had more modern minds and manners. There was a numerous family; but the only two grown up, excepting Charles, were Henrietta and Louisa, young ladies of nineteen and twenty, who had brought from a school at Exeter all the usual stock of accomplishments, and were now, like thousands of other young ladies, living to be fashionable, happy, and merry. Their dress had every advantage, their faces were rather pretty, their spirits extremely good, their manners unembarrassed and pleasant. . . . The neighbourhood was not large, but the Musgroves were visited by everybody, and had more dinner parties, and more callers, more visitors by invitation and by chance, than any other family. They were more completely popular.

Later in the year, when the younger children come home from boarding-school for the Christmas holidays, Anne finds a cheerful noisy scene in the drawing room—on one side is 'a table, occupied by some chattering girls, cutting up silk and gold paper; and on the other were tressels and trays, bending under the weight of brawn and cold pies, where riotous boys were holding high revel; the whole completed by a roaring Christmas fire, which seemed determined to be heard, in spite of all the noise of the others.'

The Musgroves, in turn, are cousins of the poorer Hayter family, who live at Winthrop, two miles away from Uppercross on the other side of the hill, and on a fine November day a party from Uppercross, including Anne, walk over there. Mary Musgrove, who has her fair share of the Elliot snobbery, resents her husband's connection with this less genteel family, and is annoyed to look down from the hilltop and see that 'Winthrop, without beauty and without dignity, was stretched before them; an indifferent house, standing low, and hemmed in by the barns and buildings of a farm-yard.' Winthrop is evidently still basically a medieval manor house, which has not yet been enlarged or rebuilt, but we are told that the eldest Hayter son intends to modernize the property when he inherits.

The Crofts move into Kellynch Hall at the Michaelmas quarter-day, 29 September, and Anne wonders in advance if there will be any family resemblance between sister and brother:

> Mrs Croft, though neither tall nor fat, had a squareness, uprightness, and vigour of form, which gave importance to her person. She had bright dark eyes, good teeth, and altogether an agreeable face; though her reddened and weather-beaten complexion, the consequence of her having been almost as much at sea as her husband, made her seem to have lived some years longer in the world than her real eight and thirty. Her manners were open, easy, and decided, like

one who had no distrust of herself, and no doubts of what to do; without any approach to coarseness, however, or any want of good humour.

Oddly enough, Jane Austen, in fact, does *not* tell us if Mrs Croft resembles her brother; and when, as Anne fears, Wentworth comes to join them at Kellynch, and we, the readers, together with the Musgrove family, are introduced to him, we still do not see his features distinctly. All that we learn, through Anne's eyes, is that 'the years which had destroyed her youth and bloom had only given him a more glowing, manly, open look, in no respect lessening his personal advantages.'

In 1806 Wentworth had tried to persuade Anne and her family that he would soon rise in the Navy to become rich and successful: 'Such confidence, powerful in its own warmth, and bewitching in the wit which often expressed it, must have been enough for Anne; but Lady Russell saw it very differently. . . . He was brilliant, he was headstrong. Lady Russell had little taste for wit; and of any thing approaching to imprudence a horror.' By 1814, just as he had envisaged eight years ago, he has been promoted to post-captain and is therefore assured of rising by seniority to the rank of Admiral, like his brother-in-law; and during his wartime service he has amassed prize-money to the value of £25,000 (something like £1.25 million in modern terms); so, now that the war has ended and he is demobilized on half-pay at the age of thirty-one, he intends to marry and settle down. Time and success have not modified his resentment of Anne's rejection, and he is barely civil towards her when they meet, but is delighted to bask in the attention of both Henrietta and Louisa Musgrove, as they listen round-eyed to his descriptions of voyages, battles and life aboard ship. He is tactless enough to tell the girls that Anne Elliot is so altered that he should not have known her again—a remark which, of course, is repeated back to her—and argues quite rudely with the Crofts 'that he would never willingly admit any ladies on board a ship of his, excepting for a ball, or a visit, which a few hours might comprehend', even though Mrs Croft points out that she has been very comfortable when living aboard her husband's ships. In real life, when an intelligent young lady visited HMS *Bellerophon* in 1817, she was struck by 'the ingenious comforts of the cabins, the light, airy, cheerful aspect of the Captain's in particular, the excessive cleanliness, every board so white, every bit of metal so brightly polished, the order, the quiet, the neatness, the most made of each small space, the real elegance of some of the arrangements'.

Captain Wentworth now hears that old friends of his, Captain Harville and family, and Captain Benwick, are staying for the winter at the seaside resort of Lyme Regis, on the Dorset coast, and the Uppercross group decide to make a trip there to meet them. Lyme is only seventeen miles from Uppercross, but as the roads are hilly this would mean three and a half hours' travelling time each way, and Mr Musgrove does not want his carriage horses to be so overworked in one day; and the plan is therefore changed to include an overnight stay at Lyme. The route from Crewkerne to Lyme is via Clapton, Three Ashes, Blackdown,

Marshwood, Uplyme and so on downhill coastwards, on what is now the modern B3165 road—and which, in real life, would have been the road taken by the Austens when they travelled there from Bath in November 1803 and again in the summer of 1804. On this fictional occasion, Henrietta and Louisa, with Anne and Mary, travel in the Musgrove family coach, while Charles Musgrove drives his own curricle with Captain Wentworth as his passenger; and by dint of finishing an early breakfast at nine in the morning, they are able to reach Lyme at about 12.30 p.m.

An early-nineteenth-century guidebook tactfully recommends Lyme as being suitable for people of limited income: '. . . a retired spot . . . lodgings and boarding at Lyme are not merely reasonable, they are even cheap; amusements for the healthy, and accommodations for the sick, are within the reach of ordinary resources. It is frequented principally by persons in the middle class of life . . . there arises no necessity for making any inconvenient sacrifices to the support of style, or to the extravagance of exterior show.' It is therefore a very suitable choice for Captain Harville, who has a wife and several children and is still convalescing from a severe wound received two years ago.

Naturally enough, over the course of two centuries Lyme has grown in size and has also lost some of its old buildings, but it is still possible to follow the route of the Musgroves' carriages as they descend the long hill into Lyme and enter the still steeper street (Broad Street) of the town itself. There were then two good inns in the little town—the Lion halfway down Broad Street, and the Three Cups further on at the bottom of the hill and facing out to sea—and as the Three Cups is recommended by the guidebook as being the principal inn, this is probably where the party secured accommodation and ordered dinner.

> The next thing to be done was unquestionably to walk directly down to the sea. They were come too late in the year for any amusement or variety which Lyme, as a public place, might offer; the rooms were shut up, the lodgers almost all gone, scarcely any family but of the residents left—and, as there is nothing to admire in the buildings themselves, the remarkable situation of the town, the principal street almost hurrying into the water, the walk to the Cobb, skirting round the pleasant little bay, which in the season is animated with bathing machines and company, the Cobb itself, its old wonders and new improvements, with the very beautiful line of cliffs stretching out to the east of the town, are what the stranger's eye will seek . . .

The Uppercross party accordingly walk round the bay to the Cobb, where the Harvilles are lodging in a small house near the foot of an old pier of unknown date; in this little house the rooms are correspondingly small, but Captain Harville is good at handicrafts and has made all sorts of improvements to the furniture and fittings in advance of winter storms. 'His lameness prevented him from taking much exercise; but a mind of usefulness and ingenuity seemed to furnish him with constant employment within. He drew, he varnished, he carpentered, he glued; he made toys for the children, he fashioned new netting-needles and pins with improvements; and if every thing else was done, sat down to his large fishing-net at one corner of the room.' Mary Musgrove is scornful to find that the Harvilles cannot afford a manservant, and are waited on at table by a mere maidservant.

The next morning the party take a last walk on the Cobb before their return journey, and it is now that the headstrong Louisa has her near-fatal accident:

> There was too much wind to make the high part of the new Cobb pleasant for the ladies, and they agreed to get down the steps to the lower, and all were contented to pass quietly and carefully down the steep flight, excepting Louisa; she must be jumped down them by Captain Wentworth. . . . He advised her against it, thought the jar too great . . . she was too precipitate by half a second, she fell on the pavement on the Lower Cobb, and was taken up lifeless!

Louisa's injury appears to be concussion, or perhaps a slight fracture of the skull, and she is taken to the Harvilles' cottage for nursing while Captain Wentworth, Anne and Henrietta return as fast as possible to Uppercross with the news.

In present-day Lyme the Lion inn (now the Royal Lion) is still in Broad Street, but the building which housed the original Three Cups was burnt down in the mid-nineteenth century. The name of the Three Cups was then transferred to a newer building—in Jane Austen's time known as

Hiscott's Boarding House—which is also in Broad Street, opposite the Royal Lion. The Assembly Rooms lingered on until the early twentieth century, being used at the last as a cinema, but were pulled down in 1927 and the site is now a car park at the end of Broad Street. The pleasant walk round the curve of the little bay to the hamlet at the base of the Cobb is still there, as is the Cobb itself, though it has been frequently repaired and rebuilt since Jane Austen's time. The last of the several original flights of steps leading from the Upper to the Lower Cobb survives—uneven blocks of stone jutting out of the wall and nicknamed locally 'Granny's Teeth'—and if this cannot be proved to be the site of Louisa's accident, at least it is now the best place to gain an impression of the event. In 1824 a great storm swept away or damaged most of the Cobb hamlet, so it is not possible to identify the cottage in which Jane Austen places the Harvilles.

In January 1815 it is time for Lady Russell to take Anne to rejoin her family in Bath, and on a wet afternoon Anne sees dimly through the carriage windows the extensive buildings, smoking in rain, and hears the noises of the city in winter—'the dash of other carriages, the heavy rumble of carts and drays, the bawling of newsmen, muffin-men and milk-men, and the ceaseless clink of pattens'—as they drive across the Old Bridge and continue northwards through the long course of streets to Camden-place, where Sir Walter Elliot has taken a furnished house, undoubtedly the best in the street. Elizabeth is delighted to show Anne the two large interconnecting drawing rooms, the style of the fitting-up and the taste of the furniture—the mirrors and china—and to boast of their social success in the city: 'Their acquaintance was exceedingly sought after. Every body was wanting to visit them. They had drawn back from many introductions, and still were perpetually having cards left by people of whom they knew nothing.' Even Sir Walter is in a sufficiently good mood to tell Anne that she is looking better—'less thin in her person, in her cheeks; her skin, her complexion, greatly improved'.

Elizabeth is also very pleased to tell Anne that their distant cousin Mr William Elliot, heir-presumptive to the baronetcy and to the Kellynch estate, is now staying in Bath and is very assiduous in his attentions towards her and Sir Walter. When he pays a call one evening, Anne recognizes him as someone she had seen in Lyme, a visitor who had looked admiringly at her as they passed by each other at the steps leading upwards from the beach. Anne had been looking remarkably well, 'her very regular, very pretty features, having the bloom and freshness of youth restored by the fine wind which had been blowing on her complexion, and by the animation of eye which it had also produced'. Mr Elliot is in his thirties, has something of the Elliot countenance, and is quite good-looking despite being very under-hung (that is, having a rather long, prominent lower jaw). Thanks to his gentlemanlike appearance and his air of elegance and fashion, Sir Walter has no objection to being seen with him anywhere.

Anne has lived in Bath before; she was at school there for three years in her teens, after her mother's death, and also spent some unhappy months with Lady Russell in the winter of 1806–7, following her broken-off engagement. We know that Lady Russell has a house in Rivers Street, a quiet and respectable terrace close to the Royal Crescent and the Circus, but Jane Austen does not give us the name of Anne's old school. However, it seems probable that it would have been the large and efficient establishment run by the Misses Lee at Belvidere House in Lansdown Road, as this was considered to be the best school in Bath, and so might very well have been Sir Walter's choice. In real life a teenager more cheerful than the bereaved Anne spent three very happy years at Belvidere House between 1797 and 1799; there were fifty pupils and two parlour boarders, as well as twenty day girls, who were instructed by the Misses Lee themselves with the assistance of two governesses and three other teachers. The girls were well fed and well taught, with every encouragement to make friends and take healthy outdoor exercise; one year the school term ended with a great ball in the Assembly Rooms, when all the girls were dressed in book-muslin frocks, with wide, long, primrose-coloured sashes and wreaths of roses of the same colour on their heads. The Prince of Wales happened to be in Bath at the time, and he also attended the ball, the girls noting that he had a green coat and white waistcoat, with his diamond star of the Garter on his breast, and wore his hair powdered and frizzled with a queue (pigtail) at the back.

Anne calls on a former governess from the establishment she attended, who tells her that one of her old school friends, a widowed Mrs Smith, has been badly crippled by rheumatic fever and is now lodging in Westgate Buildings while seeking treatment in the hot mineral water baths. Anne renews her friendship with Mrs Smith, much to her father's annoyance, as this older part of the city has become cheap and unfashionable: 'Westgate Buildings must have been rather surprised by the appearance of a carriage drawn up near its pavement!' Sir Walter's own choice of friends depends, naturally for him, upon their rank in society, and he is delighted to be able to introduce himself to some distant Irish cousins, the Dowager Viscountess Dalrymple and her daughter the Honourable Miss Carteret, who are staying in the modern and expensive Laura Place on the eastern side of the city. Anne is ashamed of her father's constant boasting about 'Our cousins in Laura-place', as, rank apart, they have no intelligence or accomplishments to render them desirable companions. The portly dowager is affable enough, with a smile and a civil answer for everybody, but Miss Carteret is plain and awkward with nothing to say for herself. Mr William Elliot introduces his friend Colonel Wallis, who lives in Marlborough Buildings; both the place and the person are quite acceptable in Sir Walter's eyes, as Colonel Wallis is a fine military figure, even though sandy-haired.

In earlier years the North and South Parades had been a smart corner of the city in which to stroll, but the guidebooks of Jane Austen's day advised that 'from the upper part of Milsom-street, through Bond-street and Union-street, to the Pump-room, now constitutes the midday promenade of the fashionable visitants; and in the height of the season, the throngs of elegant females that pass and repass these situations, form

346

a spectacle of no common interest.' Sir Walter, however, laments the fact that there are so many plain women in Bath—'as he had stood in a shop in Bond-street, he had counted eighty-seven women go by, one after another, without there being a tolerable face among them.' Bond Street in Bath, like Bond Street in London, contained many smart shops, and no doubt Jane Austen knew exactly which shop it was where Sir Walter stood—we, the readers, can but guess that it might have been William Bassnett, jeweller and goldsmith, at No. 1; Thomas Field, watchmaker, at No. 2; Harding & Frankham, hatters and hosiers, at No. 3; Samuel Faulkner's wine business or Joseph Barratt's circulating library elsewhere in the street; or possibly, if Sir Walter was escorting Elizabeth, he might have been waiting for her while she was choosing from the stock of Thomas Coward, linen-draper, haberdasher, laceman and hosier, or trying on bonnets and hats made by Madame Rosalie, the milliner at No. 8.

Early in February the Crofts come to Bath and take lodgings in Gay Street, and soon Wentworth comes to join them. Anne is daring to hope that his old affection for her is reviving, and that he may even be jealous of the way Mr William Elliot frequently visits Camden Place. When it starts to rain, and the company has to take shelter in Molland's confectioner's shop at No. 2 Milsom Street, gossip there very pointedly suggests that Mr Elliot will soon marry Anne, gossip which Captain Wentworth cannot help but overhear. At a concert in the Upper Rooms a few days later it seems again that he resents the attention which Mr Elliot is paying towards Anne, and she does not know how to convey to him the fact that Mr Elliot's courtship is of no interest to her. A few more days resolve the issue: early in March, the Musgrove family, accompanied by Captain Harville, come to Bath, and stay at the big coaching inn, the White Hart—'where the accommodations and treatment are excellent'—in Stall Street in the centre of the city. Henrietta Musgrove is now engaged to one of her Hayter cousins, and Louisa, while convalescing under the care of the Harvilles, has fallen in love with their friend Captain Benwick—so Mrs Musgrove has come to Bath to buy wedding clothes for her daughters. While all the family and friends are gathered together in the parlour of the White Hart, Anne and Captain Harville fall into a discussion as to the different ways in which men and women love, a discussion which leads Anne to make her heartfelt confession: 'All the privilege I claim for my own sex (it is not a very enviable one, you need not covet it) is that of loving longest, when existence or when hope is gone.' On hearing this, Captain Wentworth writes a secret note to her, begging her to forgive him and renew their engagement, which he presses into her hand as he leaves the room with Captain Harville. As she goes home he overtakes her, and 'soon words enough had passed between them to decide their direction towards the comparatively quiet and retired Gravel Walk, where the power of conversation would make the present hour a blessing indeed; and prepare for it all the immortality which the happiest recollections of their own future lives could bestow.'

The visitor to modern Bath can follow in Anne Elliot's footprints nearly all the way through the novel, the main difference being the disappearance of the White Hart, which was demolished in 1867 and rebuilt as the Pump Room Hotel. That, in turn, was demolished in recent years, and an office block, Arlington House, now occupies the site in Stall Street opposite the Abbey Churchyard. The Old Bridge, too, has gone, and is replaced by Churchill Bridge a few yards to the west of the original river-crossing. Camden-place is now called Camden Crescent, and the house rented by Sir Walter, as it was undoubtedly the best, must be the one with the decorative pediment in the original centre of the terrace. Lady Russell's house in Rivers Street can be guessed as No. 10, where in real life an elderly Mrs Lillingston lived, a friend of the Austen family. Milsom Street is still one of the smart shopping streets of Bath, though No. 2 is no longer the premises of Mollands, the pastry-cook and confectioner. In the Bath of Anne Elliot's time, Captain Wentworth may have bought his brand-new umbrella at Ashley's shop, No. 11 Bond Street; the gunsmith where Charles Musgrove has an appointment is evidently William Smith in New Market Row; and the printshop in Milsom Street where Admiral Croft is looking in the window may be No. 28, the premises of Archibald Sharp, landscape painter. Admiral Croft is alone, as he explains to Anne, because his wife 'has a blister on one of her heels, as large as a three shilling piece.' The three-shilling piece was a silver token, not a coin, issued only between 1811 and 1816, as a temporary measure to combat the shortage of small change while the creation of a new silver coinage was under discussion, this new coinage being introduced on 18th January 1817. The three-shilling piece had a diameter of nearly one and a half inches, which makes poor Mrs Croft's blister a very large one.

The 'Baronetage' that was Sir Walter Elliot's favourite reading matter was probably Debrett's *Baronetage of England*, published in two volumes in 1808. As he, Elizabeth and Mary are all so anxious for the correct order of precedence to be observed, it may be noted that—assuming all the various ladies were in one room together—they would walk out of the door in the following order: the Dowager Viscountess Dalrymple, as a peeress, in front of her daughter, the Hon. Miss Carteret; then Lady Russell, as the widow of a knight, before Elizabeth, Anne and Mary, the daughters of a baronet; and Mary Musgrove, as daughter of a baronet, before her mother-in-law Mrs Musgrove, the wife of an untitled country squire. 'It was Mary's complaint, that Mrs Musgrove was very apt not to give her the precedence that was her due, when they dined at the Great House with other families; and she did not see any reason why she was to be considered so much at home as to lose her place'—while Henrietta and Louisa murmur to Anne: 'Nobody doubts her right to have precedence of mamma, but it would be more becoming in her not to be always insisting on it.'

Jane Austen's first idea for the reunion of the lovers was short and unconvincing: Anne meets Admiral Croft in the street, and he invites her back to his Gay Street lodgings, where she finds

Wentworth. The Crofts have heard that Anne is to marry Mr William Elliot and return with him to live at Kellynch Hall; and when she assures Captain Wentworth that there is no truth in any part of this rumour, he immediately proposes to her. It is indeed tame and flat, as Jane herself realized, for there is no apparent reason why Captain Wentworth should think Anne still cares for him. The extension and enlargement of the scene, with the anxious lovers straining to overhear each other in the midst of the noisy family party at the White Hart, gives Anne the chance to declare her constancy in a way that encourages Wentworth to renew his proposal.

There were three reviews of *Persuasion* in the spring of 1818. The *British Critic* gave most of its space to discussing *Northanger Abbey*, saying of *Persuasion* only: 'It is in every respect a much less fortunate performance than that which we have just been considering. It is manifestly the work of the same mind, and contains parts of very great merit; among them, however, we certainly should not number its moral, which seems to be, that young people should always marry according to their own inclinations and upon their own judgment . . .' The *Gentleman's Magazine* agreed: 'The two Novels now published have no connexion with each other. The characters in both are principally taken from the middle ranks of life, and are well supported. *Northanger Abbey*, however, is decidedly preferable to the second Novel, not only in the incidents, but even in its moral tendency.' The *Edinburgh Magazine* reviewer judged that 'The first is the more lively, and the second the more pathetic. . . . There is the same good sense, happiness, and purity in both.'

Jane Austen assures us, in her closing sentences, that 'Anne was tenderness itself, and she had the full worth of it in CaptainWentworth's affection. His profession was all that could ever make her friends wish that tenderness less; the dread of a future war all that could dim her sunshine.'

SANDITON

At the end of 1816 there was a remission in Jane Austen's illness, and on 27 January 1817 she felt well enough to start work on another novel, that now known to us as *Sanditon*. Over the next few weeks she wrote about 24,000 words, divided into twelve chapters, of what was evidently going to be a long and wickedly comical tale concerning a group of seaside residents, some hopeful, some foolish, some cunning, but all interested in making money by developing their little local fishing village into a smart holiday resort. These twelve chapters introduce a long list of characters, and end with the first indication of some kind of intrigue between two of them; but, after the date of 'March 18' at the top of the last page, the rest of it is blank.

The manuscript was handed down within the Austen family for the next century, and some extracts from it were quoted in the *Memoir of Jane Austen*, a biography written by her nephew, the Reverend James Edward Austen-Leigh, in 1871. He referred to it merely as the 'last work', and did not attempt to give it a title, though another branch of the Austen family believed that Jane had thought of calling it *The Brothers*. The manuscript was first published in full in 1925, under the title *Fragment of a Novel*; but since then, by popular consent, it has been felt more appropriate to refer to it as *Sanditon*, the name of the fishing village upon whose development the interest is centred

353

and where the bulk of the action consequently takes place. Even more so than in *Emma*, Jane gives us a great deal of information about the geography of the setting, and we can envisage both the old village and the new residential development very clearly.

The story begins in June 1816, at hay-making time, and the fragment ends only a few weeks later, in July or August of the same year. Young Mr Thomas Parker, one of the principal landowners in the parish of Sanditon, on the Sussex coast, has travelled inland with his wife to Willingden, a little village on the border of Kent and Sussex, with the intention of engaging a surgeon who will attend to the health of the anticipated visitors to his new creation of seaside villas at Sanditon. The Parkers have been driving in their hired post-chaise along the turnpike road that runs from Eastbourne through Hailsham to Tonbridge (the modern A267), and from this road have turned off into a rough lane, a long ascent half rock and half sand, which leads towards the only house that can be seen from the main road—a gentleman's house, with a hayfield adjoining it. Their chaise overturns in the rough lane, Mr Parker badly sprains his ankle, and the couple are rescued by the squire, Mr Heywood, who has seen the accident from the field where he is busy with his haymakers. Despite the fact that Mr Parker hopes to find his surgeon in 'a Cottage, which was seen romantically situated among wood on a high Eminence at some little Distance', this turns out to be inhabited at one end by Mr Heywood's shepherd and at the other by three old women. Mr Parker, in fact, has made a mistake over the address, and has come to the

354

hamlet of Willingden, which Jane must have imagined as being somewhere in the vicinity of the genuine village of Heathfield, instead of going to Great Willingden, or Willingden Abbots, which is said to be seven miles away on the eastern side of the genuine town of Battle.

In real life, there is a Willingdon and Willingdon Hill just to the north of the town of Eastbourne— did Jane Austen see this on some map, as she thought about the location for her story, and did the name perhaps stick in her memory? A contemporary guidebook mentionsWillingdon as being a 'pleasant village, about two miles from East Bourne, in which is a handsome house belonging to Mr Thomas, who has a park, decoy-pond, gardens, pleasure grounds, &c.'

Thanks to Mr Parker's sprained ankle, the couple have to stay with the Heywoods for a fortnight; the latter are a thoroughly respectable family, Mr Heywood being a well-looking, hale, gentleman-like man, aged fifty-seven, who has lived in Willingden all his life. The Heywoods have been married for more than thirty years and have fourteen children, so all their time and money have to be spent on their family, and they cannot afford to repair their local roads, or to spend an occasional month at Tunbridge Wells or a winter in Bath. 'Excepting two Journeys to London in the year, to receive his Dividends, Mr Heywood went no farther than his feet or his well-tried old Horse could carry him, and Mrs Heywood's Adventurings were only now and then to visit her Neighbours, in the old Coach which had been new when they married and fresh lined on their eldest son's coming of age ten years ago.' This enforced fortnight's rest gives Mr Parker plenty of time to enthuse to his hosts about his plans for developing his lands at Sanditon into a smart residential seaside resort; and in return for the Heywoods' hospitality, Mr Parker invites their daughter, Charlotte, a tall and 'very pleasing young woman of two and twenty, the eldest of the Daughters at home', to travel back with him and his wife to Sanditon to see its delights for herself. Jane does not, in this fragment, give any description of Charlotte Heywood's appearance, but in real life she knew a Charlotte Williams, daughter of one of the Hampshire clergy, and wrote to Cassandra in 1813: 'I admire the Sagacity & Taste of Charlotte Williams. Those large dark eyes always judge well.—I will compliment her, by naming a Heroine after her.' So perhaps Charlotte Heywood shares large dark eyes as well as a Christian name with the intelligent Miss Williams of Hampshire.

The county of Sussex borders on the English Channel, and is famous for the long stretch of its steep, rounded South Downs, with their grass-covered, sheep-grazed slopes and exhilarating air, which break into tall chalk cliffs at the sea's edge and end with the jutting point of Beachy Head, near Eastbourne. Eastwards from Beachy Head the shore is more varied, with outcrops of chalk cliffs between broad sandy levels and salt marshes, terminating in Romney Marsh on the Kent side of the county. Inland there are thick woods clinging to sandstone ridges—such as the situation of Mr Heywood's Willingden—and rich, heavy clay land which affords good farming, though in Jane Austen's day the roads here were notoriously bad and sometimes impassable under winter

356

conditions.

The most famous seaside resort in Sussex was then, and is still, Brighton, originally called Brighthelmstone, which at the end of the eighteenth century was only a fishing village, but rocketed into fashion and popularity when the Prince of Wales chose it as a holiday resort and spent several decades there, building and rebuilding what had originally been a large farmhouse until he had succeeded in converting it into the exotic Brighton Pavilion. Other villages on the Sussex coast followed Brighton's example, though on a smaller scale and without the benefit of royal patronage, and by the beginning of the nineteenth century the less-wealthy visitor to Sussex could choose between Hastings, Eastbourne, Bognor, Littlehampton and Worthing for a seaside holiday. Jane herself stayed for some weeks in Worthing, in the autumn of 1805, and her memories of this holiday, plus visits to the Kentish resort of Ramsgate in earlier years, no doubt gave her the local colour for the creation of Sanditon.

According to Mr Parker, Sanditon can offer the finest, purest sea breeze on the coast, and excellent bathing, with all the benefits of fine hard sand, deep water ten yards from the shore, no mud, no weeds, and no slimy rocks, and is one complete measured mile nearer to London than is Eastbourne. A rival new resort, Brinshore, is also on the same stretch of coastline, but Mr Parker dismisses this place as a paltry hamlet, lying between a stagnant marsh and a bleak moor, and with a constant stench from a ridge of putrefying seaweed. In actual fact, one mile along the coast from Eastbourne towards London would place

357

Sanditon at Langney Point, amongst the meadows and dykes of the Pevensey Levels—but the description later given of the village shows that Jane had a steeper coastline in mind, more resembling Ramsgate with its East Cliff and West Cliff developments each side of the old fishing settlement in the narrow valley between the cliffs.

The Sanditon estate has been owned by the Parker family for two or three generations before this present Mr Thomas Parker, and it provides a sufficiently large income for him not to need to engage in any profession. He is now aged thirty-five, married with four young children; his younger brothers and sisters, Diana, Susan, Sidney and Arthur, do not need any financial support from him as they are all comfortably off, and Sidney has his own collateral inheritance. As Charlotte meets these relations, we learn that Diana and Susan are small, thin hypochondriacs devoted to the enjoyment of ill health, who are doing their best to make their youngest brother, Arthur, flabby and bilious at the age of twenty-one, as bad as themselves. Sidney, who only makes a brief appearance very near the end of the fragment, is evidently the odd one out in this amiably foolish family, as he is 'very good-looking, with a decided air of Ease and Fashion, and a lively countenance'.

Until two years ago Mr Parker and his family lived in the original manor house of Sanditon, which lies in a sheltered dip within two miles of the sea—a moderate-sized house, well fenced and planted, and rich in the garden, orchard and meadows which are the best embellishments of such a dwelling—but they have now rented this old house to their chief tenant in the village, Farmer

Hillier, and live instead in their new house built on the top of the cliff. Past Sanditon Manor, at the foot of the hill, lie the church and the neat village of Sanditon, and Mr Parker is delighted to see that some of the cottages are smartening themselves up with white curtains and 'Lodgings to Let' notices, that William Heeley, the shoemaker, has got blue shoes and nankin boots in his shop-windows, that harp music can be heard through the upper window of the baker's shop, and that two females elegantly dressed in white are sitting with their books and camp stools on the little lawn in front of an old farmhouse. Another branch of the valley has a little stream winding down to the sea, where a small cluster of fishermen's houses can be seen in the distance.

As the Parkers' carriage drives up the hill towards the coast, they pass the lodge gates of Sanditon House, where old Lady Denham lives, the other chief landowner in the parish, and Mr Parker's collaborator in the speculation of developing the new resort. The roof of Sanditon House can be seen among the trees just before the carriage reaches the top of the hill and comes out on the open chalk downland, where the new development lies before Charlotte's eyes. On the highest spot is Mr Parker's own new Trafalgar House, completed in 1814—a light elegant building surrounded by a small lawn with a very young plantation around it, and about a hundred yards inland from the steep but not lofty cliff. It has low French windows to the drawing room, which overlooks the road and all the paths across the down; and Charlotte's bedroom has a Venetian window, which looks seawards over the roofs of the

Terrace, a short row of smart-looking houses close to the cliff edge. As the trees in the garden are still so small, Mr Parker fixes up a canvas awning instead to shield his children from the summer sun. Mr Parker is now rather sorry he named his house 'Trafalgar', because 'Waterloo' is currently more fashionable—and promises himself that next year he will build a 'Waterloo Crescent' to provide more lodging houses.

So far the rest of the development on the hill top consists of some separate larger buildings, such as Prospect House, Bellevue Cottage and Denham Place—which last contains at least two semi-detached houses. Lady Denham's nephew by her second marriage, Sir Edward, who lives further inland at Denham Park, has promised to build a *cottage orné* as his contribution to the improvement of Sanditon. The Terrace has eight houses, whose small, neat drawing rooms all overlook the sea, and No. 8 is the larger corner house with a balcony at first-floor level. The Terrace contains the best milliner's shop—displaying straw hats and lace—and Mrs Whitby's library, which also sells parasols, gloves, rings and brooches, and many useless and pretty souvenirs. The hotel with its billiard room is just past the end of the Terrace, and in front of all is a broad gravel walk with two green benches, which leads down to the beach and the bathing machines.

Charlotte presently meets the brisk, formidable and rather vulgar Lady Denham, who has climbed socially and gained riches from two childless marriages, and is now keeping a tight hold on her purse strings; this is greatly to the disappointment of young Sir Edward Denham, who cannot be as extravagant as he feels a baronet is entitled to be—he can only afford to drive a gig instead of a curricle—and of his discontented sister, Esther. By her first marriage Lady Denham has acquired the large and handsome Sanditon House, where she lives with a poor and beautiful young cousin, Clara Brereton, as her companion. When Charlotte and Mrs Parker walk up the long drive through the grounds to call at Sanditon House, Charlotte sees through the fence and trees that Clara and Sir Edward are having what is obviously a private conversation, out of sight of the house—and this is where the fragment ends.

*　　　*　　　*

Even in this short text there are further interesting social references to the post-war period. Now that French warships no longer posed a threat to transatlantic sea travel, the *nouveaux riches* plantation owners from the West Indies were able to come unhindered to England, with a view to buying their way into society. This is much to the annoyance of Lady Denham, who thinks that their free-spending will cause a rise in the cost of living at Sanditon if any of them visit the new resort. However, some of the visitors to Sanditon include Mrs Griffiths, the owner of a ladies' seminary at Camberwell near London, with three of her older pupils; 'of these three, and indeed of all, Miss Lambe was beyond comparison the most important and precious, as she always paid in proportion to her fortune. She was about 17, half mulatto, chilly and tender, had a maid of her own, was to have the best room in the lodgings, and was always of the first consequence in every plan of Mrs Griffiths.' As soon as Lady Denham hears all this, she is prompt to suggest that milk from her own two milch-asses will be just the thing to strengthen Miss Lambe. Lady Denham also owns a chamber-horse—which was the Regency equivalent of an exercise bicycle or similar fitness machine, being a wooden chair with a box seat containing concertina-like springs, upon which the user would bounce up and down as if trotting on a horse, in order to stimulate the system—and which she hopes to hire out to visiting invalids.

Several attempts have been made in recent years to complete the story, but none with any great success, as there is really no indication how Jane Austen intended to develop the plot. Charlotte Heywood is evidently the heroine, and Sidney Parker is introduced in terms which show him to be the hero; Sir Edward will be a foolish and probably incompetent sort of villain, who will undoubtedly fail to seduce the astute Clara Brereton; but what with the several visitors to Sanditon who have been introduced by name and are waiting in the background, as well as the Parker family themselves, there is such a large cast of characters to be manipulated that the possibilities remain endless.

EPILOGUE

Living in the south of England as she did, Jane Austen had no personal knowledge of the changes that the onset of the Industrial Revolution were already causing in the midland and northern counties, though she was of course aware that the Staffordshire potteries were turning out such high-quality ceramic goods as graced Northanger Abbey: 'The elegance of the breakfast set forced itself on Catherine's notice when they were seated at table.' Elizabeth Bennet and the Gardiners make a point of visiting Birmingham to admire the metalworking factories; and Manchester was already the centre of cotton production. If a shop described itself as being a 'Manchester Warehouse' or that it sold 'Manchester goods', this was the contemporary expression to signify that it stocked all kinds of cotton fabrics; the muslins that Harriet Smith chooses at Mrs Ford's shop in Highbury were by now made in Manchester rather than imported from India.

The growing network of inland canals meant that coal no longer had to be transported by sea from Newcastle to London, and it became more freely available as a domestic fuel. The fact that coal, when heated, would produce an inflammable gas, had been noticed earlier in the eighteenth century, and its first practical application for lighting was in a Birmingham factory in 1803, when the gas was produced on the premises. The first use of gas for street lighting was in London in 1807, but because of the initial expense of production and distribution it was not used for domestic lighting until many years later. Coal-gas was used to light Covent Garden Theatre in 1817, and the Prince Regent had it installed in his Brighton Pavilion the following year, though many people disliked its harsh greenish light because it was so unflattering to ladies' complexions in comparison with the softer and more shadowy light given by candles. In 1813 the first little steam locomotive, nicknamed Puffing Billy, was used to pull wagons at Wylam Colliery in Durham; a paddle-wheel steamboat first chugged up the Thames from London to Richmond in 1814, and by 1815 steamboats were on the open sea, making the journey from London to Margate on the north coast of Kent in twelve hours. A cross-Channel steamer service from Dover to Calais was in operation from 1821 onwards; and if Captain Wentworth returned to active service, he might well have found himself in command of steam rather than sail.

Following the end of the war in 1814 the English were again free to visit Europe after being twenty years cooped up at home, and a popular song of the time was called 'All the World's in Paris'. Frank Churchill is able to talk of going abroad to 'Swisserland', a statement he could not have made at any earlier period of his life; and in real life Jane Austen's brother Henry took two of their nephews to France in 1816 for a holiday tour. Also in 1816 the heiress to the English throne, the Princess Charlotte of Wales, made a love-match with a young German princeling, Leopold of Saxe-Cobourg; and as the Reverend Mr James Stanier Clarke pointed out to Jane Austen at the time, 'any

364

Historical Romance illustrative of the History of the august house of Cobourg, would just now be very interesting.' To the grief of the nation, Charlotte died in childbed on 6 November 1817 and the baby died with her, leaving George III without any legitimate grandchildren in the line of succession. It was not until 1819 that the Duke of Kent, fourth son of George III, and his self-important little Duchess, produced a small, plump, strong-willed baby who was christened Alexandrina Victoria, and who gave hope for the future of the Crown. George III himself had been living in obscurity at Windsor Castle for the last decade, and died peacefully at the end of January 1820; it was estimated that 30,000 people came to Windsor for the funeral a fortnight later, and a contemporary diarist wrote: '. . . and thus has sunk into an honoured grave the best man and the best King that ever adorned humanity and it is consoling that such a sovereign was followed to his last home by countless thousands of affectionate subjects drawn to the spot to pay a last tribute of respect to him who, for sixty long years, had been a father to his people.' In 1949, one of George III's direct descendants, Patricia, the daughter of Earl Mountbatten of Burma, married John, 7th Lord Brabourne, a direct descendant of the Reverend George Austen, a union of the two families in a romance that Jane, the creator of the most ordinary of everyday worlds, would never have dreamed of inventing.

After Jane's death, her sister, Cassandra, kept her surviving manuscripts and some of her letters. Not long before her own death in 1845 Cassandra divided them between her brothers and their families; over the ensuing years these documents have gradually come to light and been published, as interest in Jane Austen and her works has steadily increased. During the 1820s Jane's novels dropped out of popularity, as the craze for 'silver fork' novels arose instead; these were romances which held up for admiration the lives of the wealthy and fashionable, written by people who themselves lived in aristocratic circles, and who could therefore give recognizable portraits of the London hostesses, beauties, gamblers and rakes of the day.

However, those readers who had enjoyed Jane's works earlier in the century still remembered them with pleasure; Mary Russell Mitford, whose series of stories called *Our Village* had made her famous in the 1830s, towards the end of her life, in the 1850s, recalled her enthusiasm for Jane Austen's novels:

> A place full of associations is Bath. When we had fairly done with the real people, there were great fictions to fall back upon ... the heroes and heroines of Miss Austen, for example. . . . Her exquisite story of 'Persuasion' absolutely haunted me. Whenever it rained (and it did rain every day that I staid in Bath, except one), I thought of Anne Elliot meeting Captain Wentworth, when driven by a shower to take refuge in a shoe-shop . Whenever I got out of breath in climbing up-hill (which, considering that one dear friend lived in Lansdown Crescent, and another on Beechen Cliff, happened also pretty often),

I thought of that same charming Anne Elliot, and of that ascent from the lower town to the upper, during which all her tribulations ceased. And when at last, by dint of trotting up one street and down another, I incurred the unromantic calamity of a blister on the heel, even that grievance became classical by the recollection of the similar catastrophe, which, in consequence of her peregrinations with the Admiral, had befallen dear Mrs Croft. I doubt if any one has left such perfect impressions of character and place as Jane Austen.

FURTHER READING

Austen, Jane *Sense and Sensibility*; *Pride and Prejudice*; *Northanger Abbey*; *Mansfield Park*; *Emma*; *Persuasion*; *Minor Works* (which includes *The Watsons* and *Sanditon*); ed. R. W. Chapman, 6 volumes, Oxford University Press, Oxford, 1963 onwards; paperback editions in World's Classics, and in Penguin.

Jane Austen's Letters, ed. Deirdre Le Faye, Oxford University Press, Oxford, 1995 and paperback 1997

Batey, Mavis *Jane Austen and the English Landscape*, Barn Elms Publishing, London, 1996

Black, Maggie and Deirdre Le Faye *The Jane Austen Cookbook*, The British Museum, London, 1995

Byrde, Penelope *Jane Austen Fashion*, Excellent Press, Ludlow, 1999

Chancellor, E. Beresford *Life in Regency and Early Victorian Times*, B.T. Batsford, London, 1926

Collins, Irene *Jane Austen and the Clergy*, Hambledon Press, London, 1993

Darton, F. J. Harvey (ed.) *The Life and Times of Mrs Sherwood 1775–1851*, Wells Gardner Darton & Co., London, 1910

Devonshire, The Duchess of *Chatsworth: The House*, Frances Lincoln, London, 2002

Gotch, J. Alfred *The English Home from Charles I to George IV*, B.T.Batsford, London, 1919

Grant, Elizabeth (ed. Andrew Tod) *Memoirs of a Highland Lady*, Canongate Classics, Edinburgh, 1988

Hart, A. Tindal *The Eighteenth Century Country Parson*, Wilding & Son, Shrewsbury, 1955

Hett, Francis P. (ed.) *Memoirs of Susan Sibbald, 1783–1812*, John Lane, The Bodley Head, London, 1926

Hibbert, Christopher *George IV, Prince of Wales*, Longman, London, 1972 *George IV, Regent and King*, Allen Lane, Harmondsworth, 1975 *George III, a personal history*, Viking, Harmondsworth, 1998

Johnson, Joan (ed.) *The General, the travel memoirs of General Sir George Whitmore*, Alan Sutton Publishing, Gloucester, 1987

Kiste, John Van der *George III's Children*, Alan Sutton Publishing, Gloucester, 1992

Lane, Maggie *Jane Austen and Food*, Hambledon Press, London, 1995

Le Faye, Deirdre *Jane Austen, a Family Record*, The British Library, London, 1989

Writers' Lives: Jane Austen, The British Library, London, 1998

Murray, Venetia *High Society in the Regency Period*, Penguin, Harmondsworth, 1999

Piggott, Patrick *The Innocent Diversion: Music in the life and writings of Jane Austen*, Clover Hill Editions, London, 1979

Sackville-West, V. *Knole and the Sackvilles*, Ernest Benn, London, 1958

Scott, A.F. *Every One a Witness, the Georgian Age*, Martins Publishers, London, 1970

Selwyn, David *Jane Austen and Leisure*, Hambledon Press, London, 1999

Southam, B.C. *Jane Austen and the Navy*, Hambledon Press, London, 2000.

Summerson, Sir John *Georgian London*, Barrie

and Jenkins, London, new edition 1988

Tomalin, Claire *Jane Austen, a Life*, Viking, Harmondsworth, 1997

Tucker, George Holbert *A History of Jane Austen's Family*, Alan Sutton Publishing, Gloucester, 1998

Watson, Steven *The Reign of George III*, Clarendon Press, London, 1960

Whatman, Susanna (ed. Thomas Balston) *The Housekeeping Book of Susanna Whatman 1776–1800* ,Geoffrey Bles, London, 1956

Wild, Antony *The East India Company, trade and conquest from 1600*, Harper Collins, London, 1999

Williams, Clare (ed.) *Sophie in London, 1786*, Jonathan Cape, London, 1936

THE NOVELS:
DATES AND MAIN CHARACTERS

SENSE AND SENSIBILITY: first composed about 1795, as *Elinor and Marianne*; revised into *Sense and Sensibility* 1797–98; published 1811.
Colonel BRANDON, of Delaford, Dorset.
The DASHWOOD families, of Norland Park and Barton Cottage:
Mrs Dashwood and her daughters Elinor, Marianne, and Margaret; her stepson John Dashwood, his wife Fanny (*née* Ferrars) and son Henry.
The FERRARS family, of London: Mrs Ferrars and her sons Edward and Robert.
Mrs JENNINGS, of Berkeley Street, London.
Sir John MIDDLETON of Barton Park, Devon, his wife Mary (*née* Jennings) and their children.
Thomas PALMER, of Cleveland in Somerset, and his wife Charlotte (*née* Jennings).
The STEELE sisters, Nancy and Lucy, of Exeter.
John WILLOUGHBY, of Combe Magna, Somerset and London.

PRIDE AND PREJUDICE: first composed 1796–97, as *First Impressions*; revised about 1811–12 into *Pride and Prejudice*; published 1813.
The BENNET family, of Longbourn House, Hertfordshire:
Mr and Mrs Bennet, and their daughters Jane, Elizabeth, Mary, Kitty and Lydia.
Charles BINGLEY, of London; his sisters Miss Bingley and Mrs Hurst.

The Reverend William COLLINS, rector of Hunsford, Kent.

Fitzwilliam DARCY, of Pemberley, Derbyshire; his sister Georgiana.

Lady Catherine DE BOURGH, of Rosings Park, Kent.

Mr and Mrs GARDINER, of Gracechurch Street, London.

Sir William LUCAS and family, of Lucas Lodge, Hertfordshire.

Lieutenant George WICKHAM of the —shire Militia.

NORTHANGER ABBEY: first composed 1798–99, as *Susan*; revised 1803 and 1816; re-titled and published posthumously 1818.

Mr and Mrs ALLEN, of Fullerton, Wiltshire.

The Reverend Richard MORLAND and Mrs Morland, of Fullerton; their children James, Catherine and others.

Mrs THORPE, of Putney; her children John, Isabella and others.

General TILNEY, of Northanger Abbey, Gloucestershire; his children Captain Frederick, the Reverend Henry and Eleanor.

THE WATSONS: begun probably 1804, but never completed; fragment first published 1871.

Mr and Mrs EDWARDS and their daughter Mary, of Dorking, Surrey.

The Reverend Mr HOWARD, of Wickstead, Surrey.

Lord OSBORNE, of Osborne Castle, Surrey; his mother, the Dowager Lady Osborne, and sister.

Tom MUSGRAVE, friend of Lord Osborne.

The Reverend Mr WATSON, of Stanton, Surrey, and his children Robert, Elizabeth, Margaret, Penelope, Emma and Sam.

MANSFIELD PARK: composed 1811–13; published 1814.
Sir Thomas and Lady BERTRAM, of Mansfield Park, Northamptonshire; their children Tom, Edmund, Maria and Julia.
Henry CRAWFORD, of London and Everingham, Norfolk; his sister Mary; their uncle Admiral Crawford, of London.
The Reverend Dr GRANT, rector of Mansfield, and Mrs Grant.
Mrs NORRIS, sister of Lady Bertram.
Lieutenant PRICE of the Royal Marines, Portsmouth; his wife Fanny, sister of Lady Bertram; their children William, Fanny, Susan and others.
James RUSHWORTH of Sotherton Court, Northamptonshire, and his mother.
The Hon. John YATES, of London.

EMMA: composed 1814–15; published 1816.
Mrs and Miss BATES, of Highbury, Surrey.
Frank CHURCHILL, of Enscombe, Yorkshire.
The Reverend Philip ELTON and Mrs Elton, of Highbury.
Jane FAIRFAX, of London and Highbury.
Mrs GODDARD, schoolmistress in Highbury.
George KNIGHTLEY, of Donwell Abbey; his brother John, with wife Isabella (*née* Woodhouse) and five children.
The MARTIN family of Abbey Mill Farm, near Highbury: Mrs Martin, her son Robert and two

daughters.

Harriet SMITH, of Highbury.

Mr and Mrs WESTON, of Randalls, near Highbury.

Mr Henry WOODHOUSE, of Hartfield, Highbury, and his daughter Emma.

PERSUASION: composed 1815–16; published posthumously 1818.

Captain James BENWICK, R.N.

Mrs Penelope CLAY, of Crewkerne, Somerset.

Admiral CROFT, R.N., and Mrs Croft.

Sir Walter ELLIOT, Bt., of Kellynch Hall, Somerset; his daughters Elizabeth, Anne and Mary (Mrs Charles Musgrove junior).

William ELLIOT, of London, heir to Sir Walter.

Captain HARVILLE, R.N., and family, of Lyme Regis, Dorset.

The HAYTER family, of Winthrop, Somerset.

The MUSGROVE family, of Uppercross, Somerset: Mr and Mrs Charles Musgrove senior; Mr and Mrs Charles Musgrove junior and their two children; Louisa and Henrietta Musgrove, and others.

Lady RUSSELL, of Kellynch Lodge.

Mrs SMITH, of Bath.

Captain Frederick WENTWORTH, R.N.

SANDITON: begun 1817 and never completed; fragment first published 1925.

Clara BRERETON, of Sanditon, Sussex.

Lady DENHAM, of Sanditon; her nephew and niece, Sir Edward Denham and Esther Denham.

The HEYWOOD family, of Willingden, Sussex: Mr and Mrs Heywood and their daughter

Charlotte; thirteen other children.
The PARKER family, of Sanditon: Mr and Mrs
Thomas Parker, their young children; and Mr
Parker's brothers and sisters Sidney, Arthur, Diana
and Susan.

PHOTOGRAPHIC ACKNOWLEDGEMENTS

For permission to reproduce the images and for supplying photographs, the Publishers thank those listed below.

By permission of the British Library 198

Tim Clinch © Frances Lincoln Limited: 191, 192,193, 197.

Private Collections 194, 196, 197 (top and bottom)